The Wild Bunch

ALSO BY BILL MESCE
AND FROM MCFARLAND

*The Rules of Screenwriting and
Why You Should Break Them* (2017)

*Inside the Rise of HBO: A Personal History
of the Company That Transformed Television* (2015)

Overkill: The Rise and Fall of Thriller Cinema (2007)

The Wild Bunch
The American Classic That
Changed Westerns Forever

BILL MESCE, JR.

McFarland & Company, Inc., Publishers
Jefferson, North Carolina

ISBN (print) 978-1-4766-7746-0
ISBN (ebook) 978-1-4766-3800-3

Library of Congress and British Library
cataloguing data are available

© 2019 Bill Mesce, Jr.. All rights reserved

No part of this book may be reproduced or transmitted in any form or by any means, electronic or mechanical, including photocopying or recording, or by any information storage and retrieval system, without permission in writing from the publisher.

Front cover: Publicity photograph of the cast of the 1969 film *The Wild Bunch* (Warner Bros.–Seven Arts)

Printed in the United States of America

*McFarland & Company, Inc., Publishers
Box 611, Jefferson, North Carolina 28640
www.mcfarlandpub.com*

In memory of Newark's Elwood Theater
where my mom sent me almost every Saturday afternoon
which led to this.

Contents

Acknowledgments	ix
Introduction	1
One. A Perfect Storm—the 1960s	7
Two. Enter—and Exit—Sam Peckinpah	26
Three. A Giant Departs, an Opportunity Opens	39
Four. Hollywood's West	43
Five. Sires	55
Six. Peckinpah's Bunch	70
Seven. Mexico Lindo	90
Eight. Missing Pieces	98
Nine. *The Wild Bunch*	106
Ten. Undying Echoes and Dying Fires	116
Eleven. A Moment Come and Gone	131
Epilogue: Riding into the Light	145
Appendix A: *The Wild Bunch Production Credits*	153
Appendix B: *The Songs*	159
Appendix C: *A Collage of Reviews*	163
Appendix D: *Film Critic Stephen Whitty on* The Wild Bunch	167
Appendix E: *Reviewer and Pay-TV Film Programmer Youssef Kdiry—Meditations on* The Wild Bunch	169

Contents

Appendix F: Film Critic Brian Marks on The Wild Bunch—
Starting at the End   173

Appendix G: Author David L. Robbins on The Wild Bunch   175

Appendix H: The Stock Company   179

Appendix I: Sam Peckinpah Filmography   181

Bibliography   187

Index   195

Acknowledgments

For research assistance, the author wishes to thank Kathleen Bryant-Turitz, Bill Maass, and Maribel Mesce.

Photographs courtesy of Jerry Ohlinger's Movie Material Store, Inc., of New York City.

Special thanks to Bill Marlborough and the staff at JOMMS.

Another special thanks to Kimberly Verhines at Stephen F. Austin University Press for her assistance with some of the photographs in this book.

Unless otherwise noted, box office figures are from website Box Office Mojo.

Also thanks to these contributors:

Gerald Abrams: Emmy-nominated producer of over 70 films for TV including *Nuremberg* (2000) and *Houdini*, the top-rated cable miniseries of 2014.

Jeff Bewkes: Named CEO of Home Box Office in 1995, then elevated to CEO and Chairman of the Board of Time Warner (now WarnerMedia) in 2009, leaving after TW's successful merger with AT&T in 2018.

Abraham Gordon: Head of development for Spectacor Pictures in the mid–1990s.

Marshall Fine: Journalist, critic and author who has served as nationally syndicated film and TV critic and entertainment writer for Gannett News Service, and film and TV critic for *Star* magazine. His several books include *Bloody Sam: The Life and Films of Sam Peckinpah*.

Youssef Kdiry: After six years as a film programmer for pay-TV giant Home Box Office, Kdiry set up his own film review site, The MoonStar Film Odyssey.

Brian Marks: Film critic and arts journalist from the Midwest, now based in Los Angeles. His writing has been published in *The Los Angeles Times*, *The Village Voice*, *LA Weekly*, and *Sordid Cinema*.

Bill Persky: Five-time Emmy-winning writer/producer/director

Acknowledgments

whose credits include *The Dick Van Dyke Show*, *That Girl*, and *Kate & Allie*.

David L. Robbins: Bestselling author and playwright whose twelve novels include *War of the Rats*, *The End of War*, *The Low Bird*. He is currently a visiting professor teaching advanced creative writing in Commonwealth University's honors college.

Josh Sapan: CEO of AMC Networks.

Betty Jo Tucker: Betty Jo Tucker serves as editor/lead film critic for ReelTalk Movie Reviews and writes film commentary for the *Colorado Senior Beacon*. She also hosts *Movie Addict Headquarters* on BlogTalkRadio.

Stephen Whitty: Long-time journalist, critic and teacher, who also writes fiction and does consulting work for studios. He is the author of *The Alfred Hitchcock Encyclopedia*.

Introduction

"Since I cannot rouse heaven, I intend to raise hell."
—Josh (David Warner) in *The Ballad of Cable Hogue*

Fifty years.

The world can change in a half-century; not a little bit, but so much so that if someone from *then* could visit *now*, people of today would—to steal a line from *Planet of the Apes* (1968)—"think you were something that fell out of a tree" (Schaffner).

Fifty years ago the hippie movement was in full flower: ragged bell-bottom jeans, Army surplus jackets, peasant skirts and sandals, peace signs and love beads, long hair, acid, grass, magic mushrooms, free love, Woodstock. At the other end of the demographic scale, businessmen looked, well, the same way businessmen have always looked (and still do): narrow lapels, short hair, cuffed pants and brogans. Somewhere in between were the self-styled cool suburbanites in broad lapels, shag cuts, ankle boots, Peter Max ties, Nehru jackets, mini-midi-maxi skirts with go-go boots (Knauer, *America* 78–79). One emblematic story of the time from my mother: going to a party, being introduced to a newly-minted young priest who opened up his somber black jacket to reveal an explosively paisley lining.

Six years after The Beatles had opened the modern rock era in 1963 with bouncy but innocent tunes like "Love Me Do" and "Please Please Me," rock had grown more ambitious with The Who's rock opera *Tommy*, and darker and more carnal with Led Zeppelin's "Whole Lotta Love" (Knauer, *1968* 44). The top three TV series in 1961 had been *Wagon Train*, *Bonanza*, and *Gunsmoke*, but in 1969 it was the transgressive *Rowan & Martin's Laugh-In* with its rapid-fire humor confronting issues of race, politics, and sex, while *The Smothers Brothers Comedy Hour* had finally lost its long-running battle against CBS execs who cancelled the show for—in the network's eyes—going too far in its ruthless lampooning

Introduction

of government, religion, social conventions, and in its obvious anti-war sentiments (Brooks 1262; 1264; 949).

The war the Smother Brothers were so anti about was grinding on in Vietnam. Three years after U.S. Marines had landed on the beaches at Da Nang, Richard Nixon was elected president, in part for campaigning on getting America out of the war—and then in 1969 began withdrawing troops so gradually that nearly half of the nation's 58,000 war dead would be suffered in the four years *after* Nixon took office ("Vietnam War").

In one of the most-viewed events in television history, people around the world watched in amazement as Neil Armstrong stepped onto the surface of the moon, the first human being to walk on an alien landscape, a startling technological advance coming just eight years after Soviet astronaut Yuri Gagarin became the first man to travel into space (Barnouw 427).

The Cold War was still on, it was yet another summer of race riots in inner cities, and, antagonized by the war in Vietnam, the psychological gap between young and old had never been wider. America had witnessed, in the short span from 1963 to 1968, the assassinations of a young, inspiring president in John F. Kennedy, a champion of civil rights in Martin Luther King, and a presidential hopeful in Robert F. Kennedy—the nation's young hoped he could course-correct a country they saw as going horribly wrong (Knauer, *America* 80–81).

And on June 18, 1969, Sam Peckinpah's Western *The Wild Bunch* premiered in Los Angeles. Afterward, Peckinpah's career, the Western genre, and American movies would never be the same.

But then, neither would America.

* * *

Fifty years.

In an odd bit of synchronicity, that's about the same span, give or take, from the beginning of the classical Western period—1860—to the setting of *The Wild Bunch*, put by various sources as 1913–1914 (Wright 5). That period also covers most, if not all, in some cases, of the life span of the movie's main characters. The men of the Bunch would have seen a time when personal transportation was defined solely by the horse replaced by the first mass-produced automobiles and the early years of powered flight; muzzle-loading rifles and the first generation of cap-and-ball revolvers give way to pump-action shotguns, semi-automatic pistols, bolt-action rifles, and machine guns.

Introduction

The mayor of a settling-down frontier town in Burt Kennedy's *Support Your Local Sheriff!* (1969) gives a comic view of the transition:

> **MAYOR:** It's been a lot of fun around here up to now. I mean, everything all kind of wide-open and relaxed. Nobody looking down their noses at anybody who happened to shoot someone else. Nobody poking their noses into nobody else's business without them getting their big noses blasted off in the process. Ah, I guess now that we got law and order, churches will start moving in ... and then the women will start forming committees and having bazaars. And then they'll chase Madame Orr's girls out of town, or make them get married, or something even worse. But, what the hell ... the law's the law and we got to face up to it sometime [Kennedy].

In 1890, the U.S. Census declared the American frontier "closed," and the era of the Wild West ended with settlements turning into towns and cities, the vicious range wars of the cattle baron era over, Native American tribes confined to reservations, the continent bound together by telegraph and railroad ("Closing"). To the citizens of the early 20th century, the aging outlaws of the Wild Bunch would also have been akin to something that had fallen out of a tree, and just as unwelcome. By the beginning of the second decade of the 20th century, the Bunch were, as the film's promotional poster described them, men who were "out of step, out of place, and desperately out of time."

That's the difference fifty years can make.

One can make the case that even though Sam Peckinpah, who, at the time of *The Wild Bunch*'s release, was around the same age of many of the movie's characters—44—despite having made one of the signature movies of a certain era in American filmmaking, was also someone out of step, out of place, and running out of time.

* * *

Some years ago, when I was a contributing writer to the now defunct film and TV site *Sound on Sight*, I wrestled with the topic of "What Makes a Classic Movie Classic?" "What are the elements, the components ... that turn a movie from a fun day at the matinee into an evergreen still being saluted, still moving audiences decades later?" (228).

What is it that makes *The Maltese Falcon* (1941) a classic, but not *Across the Pacific* (1942), despite Warner Bros.' conscious attempt to replicate the success of the former by reuniting its director and principal cast (Huston 48)? What's the alchemic process which turns an indifferently treated property like *Casablanca* (1942)—manhandled

Introduction

by six writers, featuring a third-choice cast, and helmed by a house director—into an all-time cinematic classic (Dirks 1)?

More directly to the point: why are we still talking about *The Wild Bunch* fifty years later? Is it just a fondness for an oldie-but-goodie? Or is there something about the movie, which in many ways was so much a product of its time, that still speaks to us? Something universal, something eternal.

We don't still applaud a good production of Shakespeare's *Hamlet* because we particularly care about 13th-century Danish mores, or *Macbeth* for insight into 16th-century Scottish politics, or *Romeo and Juliet* for opening our eyes to family tribalism in 16th-century Italy. And there's a reason we remember Shakespeare above his peers like Francis Beaumont and John Fletcher. Shakespeare told us stories that, whatever they may have reflected about their time, also told us something for all time, and we remember his work above others because he told those stories as well as they could be told.

Sam Peckinpah directed more misses than hits, turned out more interesting-but-flawed works than solid, cohesive pieces. His work was often misunderstood in its own time. His needlessly combative attitude often clouded appraisal of his work, his penchant for self-destructive vices sometimes interfered with his artistry, and there's an argument to be made that from certain filmmaking perspectives, *The Wild Bunch* is not his best-made film.

But...

It is easily his best-remembered film, arguably his most fondly remembered (Patterson). For all its flaws—and the movie has them—no Peckinpah film better balances art with entertainment, timeliness with timelessness. Among his 14 directorial features, it is singular in its ability to touch something in the American soul, while still being—and never underestimate this value—his most fun movie to watch again and again.

Why are we talking about *The Wild Bunch* on its fiftieth birthday? Thirty-five years after the film's release, film critic Elvis Mitchell, looking at the persistent cultural resonance of the movie, described *The Wild Bunch* as "something that contains the weight and the cultural resonance of its time. It's supposed to be a statement, a signature" (Thurman, *Sam Peckinpah's*).

We are still talking about the film because every time we talk about it—in the way it energizes while paradoxically demythologizes the iconography of the American Old West; in the way each era since its

Introduction

original release seems to tragically find a point of connection both to its violence and its sense of a larger, national spiritual death—we find there is still something to say about this half-century-old bit of storytelling, and some statement it can still make to us.

The reason we're talking about Sam Peckinpah and *The Wild Bunch* fifty years later?

Because every time we watch it, we find a new reason to talk about them.

One

A Perfect Storm—the 1960s

> *"It's all an accident ... an accident of hands, mine, others ... all without mind ... one extreme to another ... and neither works ... nor will ever!"*
> —Steiner (James Coburn) in *Cross of Iron*

The Wild Bunch arose out of—to employ a now overused phrase—a "perfect storm" of circumstances, an intersection of evolving, accelerating dynamics: what was happening in American society at large in the 1960s, and a not-disconnected sea change in the movie industry. Taking Elvis Mitchell's idea of the movie as a "signature" of its time, in its cataclysmic violence, in its context of social upheaval and the passage of a generational mindset, in its moral ambivalence, *The Wild Bunch* was in many ways a mirror of its time, but with those reflected concepts passed through the prism of that uniquely American myth: the Old West.

"A time of tumult..."

In a retrospective of an era defined as beginning with the assassination of President John Kennedy in 1963 through the bringing down of Richard Nixon by the Watergate scandal in 1974, *Life* described the period as "a time of tumult" in which the nation experienced its greatest social upheaval since the Civil War. The igniter for much of that unrest was the war in Vietnam ("A Time" 187).

Over the course of just a few years, the war in far off Southeast Asia went from a back-page news item to one of the consuming tragedies of the age. When Kennedy had taken office in 1961, he had inherited a commitment started by the Eisenhower Administration which stood at just 900 American advisors assisting South Vietnamese forces in their fight against the communist Viet Cong. By the time of Kennedy's death, the U.S. commitment had risen to 16,000 advisors (Maclear 81). Nine months later, seeing that the South Vietnamese needed direct support or face defeat, Kennedy's successor, Lyndon Johnson, committed the United States to an active role, first with a rigorous air campaign, and then, in 1965, with the first ground troops: 3,500 Marines. By the time of Johnson's last year in office—1968—that initial combat contingent had swollen to 543,000 troops (85).

The eroding credibility of government assurances that the American effort in Vietnam was progressing favorably, even as troop levels continued to escalate, finally collapsed with the Tet Offensive of 1968; attacks mounted throughout South Vietnam by an enemy the American people had been consistently told was losing ground. Ultimately, the attacks may have netted the Viet Cong and North Vietnamese no military victories, but Tet demonstrated to the American public that the enemy was far from finished, and that Vietnam was a war with no end in sight (Dougan, *Nineteen* 67).

Only a few weeks after being sworn in as president in January of 1969, Richard Nixon, while appearing to honor his campaign pledge to get the United States out of Vietnam with an initial small withdrawal of troops, intensified the violence of the war with an aggressive bombing campaign which secretly expanded the war into neighboring Cambodia (Maclear 284–285). At that point, it was hard for the young generation tasked with fighting the war not to see Vietnam as an endless, pointless, Molochian nightmare slowly devouring the nation's young, conducted by one administration after another leading through deceit and secrecy (Dougan, *Nineteen* 67–68).

As the American commitment to the war escalated, anti-war demonstrations sprang up on college campuses across the country, ROTC buildings were torched, campuses shut down (Dougan, *A Nation* 100, 101). The war drove an ever-widening rift between young and old, particularly with blue-collar, working-class adults. It was a divide as much cultural as political—maybe even more so—with the so-called "Hard Hats," many of whom while agreeing with protesters that the United States needed to get out of Vietnam, still saw themselves as apart from young demonstrators whom they viewed as having "rejected the traditional American values" (157–158).

Social divisions went beyond the war and issues specific to the conflict, i.e., inequities in the draft system, government credibility, the escalating brutality of a war without front lines and where the enemy was

ONE. A Perfect Storm—the 1960s

not always in an identifiable uniform. The war seemed to spark, among the younger generation, a great re-examining of national myths: was America everything it had always espoused itself to be? Were we always the Good Guys? Were we always in the right (Conroy 305)? Anger over the war acted as an accelerant to other issues, some of which had been on the societal back-burner for years, others of which were already just a degree from boiling over (Dougan, *Nineteen* 91). It sometimes seemed as if every constituency with a grievance was out in the streets protesting.

Burning Cities, Burning Passions

One of the signatures of the 1960s as tragic and emblematic of the time as the expanding conflict in Vietnam was a jarring series of riots in the racially segregated ghettos of American cities. Significant progress had been made in the cause of Civil Rights by the early 1960s, but legislative accomplishment did not necessarily translate into social equality for African Americans. The war in Vietnam only aggravated racial tensions as financing the war effort drained money away from anti-poverty programs, and the military draft fell disproportionately heavily on poor blacks (Dougan, *A Nation* 108–109, 80).

The same frustration and rage which had fueled the Civil Rights marchers of the late 1950s and early 1960s finally transformed into violence in the summer of 1965 in Watts, a black ghetto in the heart of Los Angeles (Dougan, *A Nation* 64). For the remainder of the decade, each subsequent summer would see a number of American cities—Detroit, Newark, Chicago, Atlanta, to name just a few—experience similar paroxysms of violence and looting, all bred out of the despair and anger which was part and parcel of inner city living. By 1968, urban riots around the country had left 250 dead and 10,000 injured, and had gutted the commercial heart of stricken neighborhoods, some of which still have yet to completely recover (108).

Other constituencies—ignored, repressed, dispossessed, disenfranchised—also declared themselves, sometimes violently, in the 1960s. The month *The Wild Bunch* was released was the same month of the first Stonewall riots, a series of clashes sparked by the New York City Police Department's raid on the Stonewall Inn, a gay bar in lower Manhattan. Stonewall would, thereafter, become a rallying cry for the Gay Rights movement ("Stonewall").

The Wild Bunch

Later that same year, a group of Native Americans took over the deserted federal prison on Alcatraz Island to draw attention to the U.S. government's long history of mistreatment of and broken treaties with Native American tribes. The occupation would last 14 months until protesters were forcibly removed by authorities (Lapin).

Not every protest movement was marked by moments of violence, yet at least one represented no less a seismic shift in the national consciousness. That many American women were discontent with their second class social status was hardly news in the 1960s, but the women's movement, inspired by the writings of Betty Friedan and Gloria Steinem, among others, became more vocal and visible throughout the decade, and women, too, found reason to march in the streets (Steinem, 11).

For every group that went into the streets with a cause, another group came out to protest the protesters. When the long hairs marched against the war, the Hard Hats came out against them (Dougan, *A Nation* 157); when blacks marched for Civil Rights, as they did in Birmingham in 1963, police turned fire hoses and dogs loose on the marchers (Knauer, *Visions* 40–41); when women carried placards and called for social and professional parity, social conservatives like Marabel Morgan and Phyllis Schlafly pushed back with traditional views of the willingly subjugated American woman (Schnall 2).

Protests and counter-protests did not always end with competing placards and slogans. There were times when fists were thrown, bricks went through windows, somebody set a match to a building, sometimes to an entire neighborhood. In a sad parallel to the war in Southeast Asia, the divisions, the vitriol, the violence all seemed to escalate throughout the 1960s, reaching a fever pitch in the last years of the decade. *Smithsonian* would, in a recent look back, declare 1968 "The Year That Shattered America" (*Smithsonian*). And it was all captured on film and videotape for the evening news: rioting, street fights between Anti-This and Pro-That, and, of course, the war; the first American conflict its citizens could witness day-by-day in their own living-rooms (Maclear 221).

Perhaps the event which best encapsulated the moral chaos and flashpoint violence at its peak was the 1968 Democratic Convention in Chicago. Inside the convention, a divided Democratic party argued heatedly over everything from party policy on Vietnam to allegations of racially discriminating delegate seating (Knauer, *1968* 89). Outside, approximately 5,000 protesters representing a host of issues, from the

ONE. A Perfect Storm—the 1960s

During the heyday of Old Hollywood, the studios maintained massive salaried pools of creative personnel and craftsmen allowing them to pump out a steady stream of entertaining product of relatively consistent quality. In the 1930s, Warner Bros., for example, specialized in urban crime dramas regularly tapping their platoon of criminal archetypes to star, i.e., James Cagney, Humphrey Bogart, Edward G. Robinson, John Garfield, George Raft. Typical—and arguably best—of the lot is *Angels with Dirty Faces* (1938) starring Cagney (in prison garb) escorted to the electric chair by regular co-star Pat O'Brien (in clerical wardrobe). The factory-like workings of Old Hollywood production are evident in Cagney's career at Warners where, as his popularity increased, the studio ran him through an incredible fourteen productions in one two-year period (Baxter 110).

flippant to the heartfelt, faced off against a force of 24,000 police, National Guardsmen, and Army troops (84). Taunts escalated into street violence, and unrestrained billy club-wielding police waded into the protesters in what a later report described as a "police riot" (86–88).

Richard Schultz, who prosecuted some of the Chicago protesters the following year—the year *The Wild Bunch* was released—would later try to describe the mood of the established authorities at the time: "What's hard to remember today is that we took the threat of overthrowing the government seriously—this was a credible threat.

These people had come to Chicago hoping to ignite a revolution in the streets.... They were tapping into a very real division in the United States" (Knauer, *1968* 86).

To Mr. Schultz's point, it was hard for the average American, tuning into the network news every evening and seeing scenes of National Guardsmen patrolling burning inner cities, campus revolts, protesters in the streets representing a dizzying array of causes and issues clashing with police and/or other protesters, all against the backdrop of a war in which, by 1969, most of the country had lost faith, and not feel the national social fabric was being pulled apart. After a 1968 filled with "ghastly events: assassinations, black riots, student protests, rising crime," *Time* described the condition of the collective American psyche at the beginning of the last year of the decade, as "verging on a national nervous breakdown ... why has the can-do country become a country that can't?" (Knauer, *1969* 5).

Synchronously, the American motion picture industry was going through its own cultural upheaval; violence-free, but no less revolutionary an overturn of its own status quo. The movie studios, which had long ago been dubbed The Dream Factory for their ability to pump out a steady stream of diversion and fantasy, was, during the 1960s, becoming overtaken by a different mindset; that the way to connect with the new generation of young moviegoers of the day was not to manufacture dreams, but to somehow reflect the national nightmare those young people felt they were living through (Greenberg 19).

"The furious springtime of world cinema"

Old Hollywood—the Hollywood which had brought American moviegoers the likes of *The Wizard of Oz* (1939), *Casablanca* (1942), *Gone with the Wind* (1939), Bogie, The Duke, Clark "The King" Gable, Fred Astaire-Ginger Rogers and Busby Berkeley musicals, Bette Davis and Joan Crawford chewing through scenery like hungry hamsters, machine gun-paced screwball comedies like *His Girl Friday* (1940), the Universal monster stable, i.e., Frankenstein, Dracula, the Wolf Man, etc.—had been in slow-motion collapse since the end of World War II. The men who had built Old Hollywood—studio moguls like MGM's Louis Mayer, Columbia's Harry Cohn, the brothers Warner at their eponymous studio, Darryl Zanuck at 20th Century-Fox—were now

ONE. A Perfect Storm—the 1960s

presiding over its decline, and, besieged on a number of fronts, seemed incapable of doing anything to even slow the descent.

* * *

After its chaotic early years in which myriad small production companies sprang up and just as quickly disappeared through failure or merger, the movie industry gelled, in the 1920s, into a business dominated by seven major studios; brand names still existing today—Columbia (now part of Sony), Universal (NBC Universal), Warner Bros. (part of

As Old Hollywood began to crumble and a new generation of moviegoers began to nudge mainstream filmmaking in non-traditional directions, the young audience wanted to see their world reflected on-screen. In the early 1960s, with Cold War tensions at their height, a number of films confronted the then-perceived real possibility of nuclear devastation, including the darkly comic *Dr. Strangelove or: How I Learned to Stop Worrying and Love the Bomb* (1964), directed by Stanley Kubrick and starring Peter Sellers (pictured here in the title role).

WarnerMedia which is a division of AT&T), Metro-Goldwyn-Mayer and United Artists (MGM acquired UA in 1981), 20th Century-Fox (at this writing an acquisition target of The Walt Disney Company), and RKO (after a series of ownership changes, now a minor distributor which rarely produces). Below them were a number of smaller companies and independent producers, but these seven, for all intents and purposes, came to define what we think of as Golden Age Hollywood (Balio 213).

Most of these studios either owned large theater chains or, more often, were owned by theater organizations forming what we would, today, describe as "vertically integrated" entertainment companies (Bach 32). The studios turned out a steady stream of movies for their affiliated theaters which, in turn, provided a guaranteed exhibition platform for even the weakest studio title (Webb 5).

Dream Factory was not just a fanciful sobriquet. The studio system was both cost- and time-efficient. With vast on-hand resources—back lots which could provide settings from the Old West to Medieval Europe, and an on-tap army of salaried creative talent and craftsmen—the studios were able to operate like true factories pumping out a feature every week or so in assembly line fashion along with shorts, cartoons, and newsreels (Webb 5). The ability to turn out an unceasing river of visual entertainment year after year, supported by equally energetic publicity and marketing machines, made movies the dominant pop culture vehicle of the period (Evans 17).

But by the end of World War II, the gears of that prolific, smooth-running machine began to wobble and grind. Hollywood found itself besieged on multiple fronts, and was losing the fight on each of them.

There had been an antitrust suit from the Department of Justice grinding its way through the courts since 1938 to separate the studios from their theater chains (Borneman 332). In 1948, the Supreme Court finally decided against the studios, and over the next several years, one movie company after another split from its exhibition arm (Balio 317). This not only deprived the studios of the cash flow from their once-affiliated theaters, but they also lost their guaranteed exhibition platform; thereafter, every movie had to compete with every other contemporaneous release for screens (318).

Even before the major studios had lost their theater chains, they were losing their audience. Weekly attendance had peaked during the war years at 84 million, an astronomical number considering the U.S. population was just a little over 132 million and millions of men

ONE. A Perfect Storm—the 1960s

were overseas in military service (Finler, *Hollywood* 288; "A Look" 3). But attendance had begun to slip in 1945, the last year of the war, to 82 million. Thereafter, slippage turned into an increasingly precipitous slide, dropping to 55 million by 1950. With the exception of rare upticks, it was a fall-off which wouldn't bottom out until 1971 at 16 million (Finler, *Hollywood* 288).

That collapse in audience was accelerated by the growing popularity of television which, for the first time, brought mass visual entertainment into the home. The year the Supreme Court had decided the Justice Department's antitrust suit against the studios, only 350,000 American households owned a TV (Simon 32). But just two years later, that number exploded to almost four million, and by 1960 to over 45 million; 87 percent of U.S. homes. By the end of the next decade, just about anyone who could afford a TV set had at least one in their house (Finler, *Hollywood* 289).

The more TVs that came into use, the more people opted to stay home over going out to the movies. While today we tend to characterize the era of Old Hollywood by the classics still revered today, every movie wasn't a *Casablanca*, and most of what the studios had churned out in their Dream Factory heyday was filler; passable entertainment that only had to divert an audience for a week or two before the next studio release came along (Bach 5). By the mid–1950s, people could see that same kind of B-caliber fluff on their living room television: cop and crime stories, private eye tales, Westerns (Sklar 300). In an on-target diagnosis of the situation, producer Sam Goldwyn declared, "It is a certainty that people will be unwilling to pay to see poor pictures when they can stay home and see something which is at least no worse" (Webb 10).

A key strategic weakness of the studios at the time was that the men running some of the movie companies post-World War II were the same men who had been running—and in some cases had founded—the major companies as long as two decades (or more) before. They had become disconnected from their audience, growing older as their audience had grown younger (Biskind 20). By the end of the 1950s, teenagers "were fast becoming the largest population group in the U.S., and they controlled billions of dollars ... in disposable cash" (Hirshey 44). Age, however, was not the only difference between studio chieftain and ticket-buyer.

The moguls still identified with the movie audience of the 1920s-1930s: generally mass audiences of working and immigrant classes (Sklar

The Wild Bunch

ONE. A Perfect Storm—the 1960s

271). But after World War II, the nation's box office was increasingly driven by ticket-buyers 21 and under, and they were a generation the aging moguls neither recognized nor understood (Carey 281).

The great old studio chiefs had built their industry during a time when a substantial percentage of young people didn't finish high school, and many were supporting a family before they'd even made it out of their teens. It had been a time of biplanes and Model T cars, of jazz and flappers. But the post–World War II years saw a young generation better-educated, comparatively affluent, living in an era of mass-produced suburbs, jet planes, rock 'n' roll, the first steps in space exploration, and the threat of nuclear war (Freeth 110).

By the 1960s, their movie empires in collapse, the moguls who had made Hollywood into *Hollywood* were all either dead, retired, or had been pushed out from or sidelined within their studios. In their place came a new generation of production executives: people like Paramount's Robert Evans, Warner Bros.' John Calley, Fox's Richard Zanuck. This new breed was considerably younger than their predecessors, and in synch with the 1960s cohort of young moviegoers—a cohort which itself was as radically different from their 1950s counterparts as the 1950s youngsters had been from pre–World War II ticket-buyers.

To craft the kind of film entertainment which would engage this upcoming generation of movie consumers, the new production execs opened their doors to an infusion of bold, daring, boundary-pushing filmmakers. Some were directors who'd already been hovering around the edges of the industry for years, but now, with access to the major studios, finally delivered their breakout films and did some of the most notable work of their careers: among them directors like Robert Aldrich (*The Dirty Dozen* [1967]), Don Siegel (*Dirty Harry* [1971]), and Stanley Kubrick (*Dr. Strangelove or: How I Learned to Stop Worrying and Love the Bomb* [1964]). Others were directors who'd already made a name for themselves overseas in their native countries and were now invited to bring their distinctive European flair to American films: John

Opposite top: **A younger generation questioning the values of their parents' generation sees disaffection reflected in one of the milestone movies of the tumultuous 1960s: *The Graduate* (1967), starring Katharine Ross and Dustin Hoffman.**
  Bottom: **That same year saw a quite different manifestation of youthful discontent as the ultimate 1960s rebels were transplanted to the 1930s in *Bonnie and Clyde* (1967), starring Faye Dunaway and Warren Beatty in the title roles. The movie also took screen violence to a new, controversial level.**

The Wild Bunch

Boorman (*Point Blank* [1967]) and John Schlesinger (*Midnight Cowboy* [1969]) from England; Roman Polansky (*Rosemary's Baby* [1968]) from Poland; Michaelangelo D'Antonioni (*Zabriskie Point* [1970]) from Italy, et al. Then there were the "movie brats" who were coming out of the filmmaking programs blossoming around the country, and particularly the programs at NYU and USC, names still legendary today: Francis Ford Coppola, George Lucas, Martin Scorsese, Brian DePalma, Steven Spielberg (Biskind 15–16).

There was also a substantial crop of directors who had served something of a *de facto* directing apprenticeship working in the young TV medium, i.e., Sydney Pollack (*They Shoot Horses, Don't They?* [1969]), Franklin J. Schaffner (*Planet of the Apes*), Sidney Lumet (*Fail-Safe* [1964]), Robert Altman (*M*A*S*H* [1970]), John Frankenheimer (*The Manchurian Candidate* [1962]), William Friedkin (*The French Connection* [1971]), Arthur Penn (*Bonnie and Clyde* [1967]). Among them, possibly

Outside the restraints of the Hollywood mainstream, reflecting both the moral chaos of the Vietnam era as well as the display on living room TVs of street protests, burning cities, and war footage on the evening news, screen violence pushed to new extremes in movies like George Romero's *Night of the Living Dead* (1968).

ONE. A Perfect Storm—the 1960s

"the most important of all American directors to have graduated in TV," was Sam Peckinpah (Wicking 103).

The new production execs eagerly looking for films which could connect with the young audience of the 1960s granted this bumper crop of directorial talent an unprecedented amount of creative freedom. Said Paul Schrader, a one-time film critic who also wound up behind the camera during the period, "the door was wide open and you could just waltz in and have these meetings and propose whatever. There was nothing that was too outrageous" (Biskind 22).

Consequently, the cultural revolution and generational disaffection which had been spilling into the streets throughout the 1960s now began to show up on movie screens (Knauer, *1968* 76).

* * *

Increasingly through the 1960s and well into the 1970s, movies had become—to put it simply—*cool*; a sort of pop culture "secular religion" (Biskind 17). Wrote film critic Susan Sontag of the period: "It was at this specific moment in the 100-year history of cinema that going to movies, thinking about movies, talking about movies became a passion among university students and other young people. You fell in love not just with actors but with cinema itself" (Biskind 17). "In colleges, people studied film history and foreign films," film critic David Thomson wrote of the era, "In book stores, film was a new section" (90).

The young moviegoers of the 1960s hungered for and were given movies reflecting the issues of their day: the threat of nuclear annihilation (*Dr. Strangelove, Fail-Safe, The Bedford Incident* [1965], *Planet of the Apes*); race (*A Raisin in the Sun* [1961], *To Kill a Mockingbird* [1962], *Pressure Point* [1962], *Black Like Me* [1964], *A Patch of Blue* [1965], *Guess Who's Coming to Dinner?* [1967], *In the Heat of the Night* [1967]); the Holocaust and anti-Semitism (*Exodus* [1960], *Judgment at Nuremberg* [1961], *Lisa* [1962], *The Pawnbroker* [1964], *Ship of Fools* [1965], *The 25th Hour* [1967]); distrust of the government and the self-destructive side of Cold War paranoia (*The Manchurian Candidate, Seven Days in May* [1964], *The President's Analyst* [1967]); Vietnam-inspired digs at military adventurism (*The Sand Pebbles* [1966], *The Charge of the Light Brigade* [1968], *Burn* [1969]); and the generational/cultural rift and disaffection which seemed central to the angry temper of the age (*Wild Seed* [1965], *The Graduate* [1968], *Wild in the Streets* [1968], *Medium Cool* [1969], *WUSA* [1970], *Joe* [1970], *Zabriskie Point, RPM* [1970]).

The Wild Bunch

Beyond such literal reflections, in a rebellious time it was natural for young moviegoers to gravitate toward movies celebrating rebels and the actors who regularly played them; characters who "rejected the traditional American values" and lived outside the mainstream status quo. These were drop-outs and social outcasts, oddballs and rebels, con men and crooks, outlaws and those who just seemed like outlaws (Thomson 45). Think of Paul Newman's gallery of outsiders: the demimonde-dwelling pool shark of *The Hustler* (1961), the free-spirited petty vandal of *Cool Hand Luke* (1966), the cynical private eye with a battered nobility in *Harper* (1966). Or "King of Cool" Steve McQueen's equally if-they-give-you-lined-paper-write-the-other-way rebels: the cocky POW breakout artist of *The Great Escape* (1963), the high-stakes backroom poker player of *The Cincinnati Kid* (1965), the bored millionaire executing a perfect bank robbery to challenge "the system" in *The Thomas Crown Affair* (1968), the GQ-styled rule-bending/breaking cop in *Bullitt* (1968). And along with them throw in the itinerant con man of *The Flim Flam Man* (1967); the master bank robber of *Dead Heat on a Merry-Go-Round* (1966); the bumbling wannabe criminal of *Take the Money and Run* (1969); the 42nd Street denizens of *Midnight Cowboy* (1969); the repressed prep schoolers who take up arms against their repressors in *If...* (1968); the military misfits of *The Dirty Dozen;* the conniving scam artists of *The Producers* (1967); the punch-throwing poet of *A Fine Madness* (1966); the moderately insane, boozy, oversexed medics of *M*A*S*H;* the social drop-outs of *A Thousand Clowns* (1965), *Five Easy Pieces* (1970) and *Alice's Restaurant* (1970); the reclusive oddball trying to build mechanical wings to fly like a bird in *Brewster McCloud* (1970); cool-as-cool-can-be superspy James Bond; bubbly anarchists The Beatles in *A Hard Day's Night* (1964). These and others constituted a generation of resonant movies in which traditional concepts of right and wrong, Good Guys and Bad Guys, even the distinctions between them, were cast aside creating a "world [in] films ... as complex and as frightening as anything you'd come into the theater to escape from" (Thomson 44).

Probably the movies which best defined the generational mindset are *The Graduate, Easy Rider* (1969), and *Bonnie and Clyde* (Sklar 301): *The Graduate* for its portrait of a young generation alienated from its parents' "culture of affluence and consumerism"—the 1950s ideal of success as 1960s nightmare (Knauer, *1968* 76; Baxter 235); *Easy Rider* which cast its drifting, dope-peddling bikers as counter-culture heroes

One. A Perfect Storm—the 1960s

"perfectly [capturing] the late '60s zeitgeist, in which society is a monster and only those who defy its laws are pure of heart" (Knauer, *1969* 65).

As for *Bonnie and Clyde*...

* * *

Like *Easy Rider*, *Bonnie and Clyde* positioned its outlaws—the notorious Depression-era bank robbers—not as the thieves and murderers they were in real life, but as "saints for a disenchanted age.... Unable to find anything worthy of emulation in a society devoid of social purpose" (Baxter 236). The movie "legitimized violence against the establishment, the same violence that seethed in the hearts and minds of hundreds of thousands of frustrated opponents of the Vietnam War" (Biskind 49).

The movie also escalated an increasingly heated debate over violence in movies and, to a larger point, the profound changes which had occurred in just a few years in mainstream movie content. In 1962, for example, *Cape Fear* featured Robert Mitchum as a convicted rapist now released and on a revenge quest against Gregory Peck—whose testimony had led to his conviction—and Peck's family, the ultimate goal of which is to rape Peck's middle school-aged daughter. Over the course of the movie, Mitchum tells a story of raping his ex-wife after his release, and the movie suggests Mitchum's possibly violently assaulting another woman and Peck's wife (presumably—the depiction for both attacks is a bit vague). But not once in the movie is the word "rape" ever uttered (Server, 359). Less than 10 years later, Sam Peckinpah's *Straw Dogs* (1971) was *showing* multiple rapes on-screen. In the years between, mainstream movies had pushed back the restraint on sexual content in movies like *Blowup* (1966), *Reflections in a Golden Eye* (1967), *Midnight Cowboy*, *The Graduate*, *The Fox* (1967), *The Killing of Sister George* (1968), *The Detective* (1968), *The Sergeant* (1968), and *Women in Love* (1969).

On-screen violence progressed even more rapidly than sexual content in movies like *The Dirty Dozen, Point Blank, Bullitt*, reaching a certain fever pitch with the slow motion death ballet climaxing *Bonnie and Clyde* as the titular couple are felled in an ambush by a hail of machine gun bullets, and then going still further with the graphic horror of *Night of the Living Dead* (1968). While some damned such depictions as purely exploitative, answering the challenge of declining audiences through titillation and visceral thrills, *Living Dead* director/co-writer George Romero justified pushing the limits of on-screen violence with his sense that by the late 1960s, moviegoers had become so numbed by the violence dished up on a daily basis on the nightly news, that excess was necessary to get any kind of shock from them (Schickel 8; Emery). Said *Bonnie and Clyde* director Arthur Penn in a retrospective article about *The Wild Bunch*, "You had to be an ostrich with a neck two miles long buried in the sand not to see we were living in a violent time" (Greenburg 19).

Filmmakers of the time were as adventurous in *how* they told their stories as much as in the stories they told. Think of the flash cut flashbacks of *The Pawnbroker* (1964), the multiple split screens of *The Thomas Crown Affair*, the marriage of absurdist black humor with wartime horror in *Catch-22* (1970), *Dr. Strangelove* and *The Producers* making a joke out of, respectively, nuclear war and Adolf Hitler, the is-it-real-or-a-dying-man's-hallucination surreality of *Point Blank*, the non-linear non-narrative cinematic poetry of *2001: A Space Odyssey* (1968), and, of course, the slow-motion finale of *Bonnie and Clyde*.

This was, in short, incontestably one of the most creative periods in American commercial filmmaking (Knauer, *1969* 65). The circumstances were unique in the history of the industry, unprecedented, and never since repeated—a new breed of production execs willing to take outrageous risks to get the young audience in theaters; a new breed of filmmakers often not much older than their audience eager to push the boundaries on content and style; a new breed of audience, cinema savvy and up to the challenge of innovative ways to tell stories that reflected/connected with their worldview of troubled, chaotic times. Declared the French film journal *Cahiers du Cinéma*, it was "the furious springtime of world cinema" (Fine 120).

* * *

Young ticket-buyers may have wanted movies more connected to their reality, more in touch with their passions, and visually influenced by the more stylistically-daring films being made by European directors like Roman Polanski, Federico Fellini, Ingmar Bergman, Michaelangelo Antonioni, et al., yet there was also something paradoxical in their film tastes, something akin to but not quite nostalgia (Biskind 21, 45). Even as the young generation of the 1960s rejected so much of the cultural and social status quo they were inheriting, they found in the Old Hollywood black-and-white classics they'd grown up watching on TV an iconography which curiously resonated with their sense of disaffection.

One. A Perfect Storm—the 1960s

Walk through the college dorms of the 1960s-1970s and it wasn't unusual to see dorm room walls adorned with movie posters saluting not the cinema of the present but of the past. In that time of tumult and social revolution, of disaffection and disillusionment, young people found connection with the anti-authority anarchy of the Marx Brothers and the Three Stooges, the sarcastic misanthropy of W.C. Fields, the defiance of King Kong astride the top of the Empire State Building. There was a particular affinity for the mix of cynicism and battered idealism Humphrey Bogart inculcated in movies like *Casablanca* and *The Maltese Falcon* (1941) (Bogdonavich 221). Wrote critic Gerald Weales of Bogart's persistent popularity and resonance almost a decade after his 1957 death, "his world-weary Galahad will continue to speak to young men who want to do the right thing in the wrong tone of voice" (168).

Unsurprisingly, then, some of the most popular movies of the era blended strands of the new and relevant with the traditional and classical (Sklar 301). It was infinitely more entertaining (and, one could argue, still is) to deal with racism in the form of a cop thriller (*In the Heat of the Night*), corporate dehumanization in a hard-boiled crime thriller (*Point Blank*), the same sense of youthful disaffection of *The Graduate* in a fast-paced shoot-'em-up like *Bonnie and Clyde,* or middle class malaise in a paranoid thriller (*Seconds* [1966]).

In a sweet bit of irony for that revolutionary time, no genre proved as hearty and plastic a vehicle for the cinema of New Hollywood than Hollywood's oldest: the Western.

* * *

Movie storytelling as we know it—something more than a filmed skit or vignette—began with a Western: Edwin S. Porter's 12-minute *The Great Train Robbery* (1903), making the Western arguably the movies' first genre (Parkinson 11). For decades thereafter, the Western would be a reliably popular part of Hollywood's output. But as happened with other genres, come the 1960s, the Western was subject to deconstruction and reconstruction, revisionism and re-envisioning. Toward the end of the decade and into the early 1970s, this oldest of Hollywood storytelling forms demonstrated an unequaled capacity for being stretched into an infinite variety of shapes, a pliability Sam Peckinpah recognized. "The Western," he once observed, "is a universal frame within which it is possible to talk about today" (Ferrara).

The Wild Bunch

Perhaps it was the nature of the Old West itself—a vast, open expanse with isolated settlements where law and social order had a bare toehold, if that—which allowed for a pliability other genres couldn't match. On that social blank slate, filmmakers could address issues from the topical and relevant to the universal and existential. The possibilities offered by the Western at a time of great social re-examination and upheaval explain a massive surge in the form from the late 1960s into the early 1970s unmatched before or since (Parkinson 89; Hackett).

The range of what Westerns could do seemed limitless. There were traditional Old Hollywood-style action/adventures including those starring that most classic of Western icons, John Wayne (*The War Wagon* [1967], *The Sons of Katie Elder* [1965], *El Dorado* [1967]), and those driven more by psychology than gunplay (*Invitation to a Gunfighter* [1964]), more by personal drama than action (*The Outrage* [1964], a Western revamping of Akira Kurosawa's *Rashomon* [1950]). There were contemporary Westerns (*Hud* [1963], *Lonely Are the Brave* [1962], *The Misfits* [1961]), those rooted firmly in the history of the Old West (*How the West Was Won* [1964]), those which revisited in revisionist fashion the legends we thought we knew (*Hour of the Gun* [1967], *Little Big Man* [1970]), and those which put too-familiar genre tropes through comedic deconstruction (*Support Your Local Sheriff!*).

There were Westerns which dealt forthrightly with the abominable way Native Americans had been treated (*Hombre* [1967], *Little Big Man*) and continued to be treated (*Flap* [1970]), with racism (*The Scalphunters* [1968]), women's equality (*The Ballad of Josie* [1967]), and those which acted as social parables (*Welcome to Hard Times* [1967]).

Even the general sense of disillusionment and cynicism young people felt in a country which seemed to be abandoning its best principles could show up in a Western like *The Professionals* (1966) thanks to writer/director Richard Brooks' subtly melancholic screenplay. Four mercenaries take a job riding into a Mexico racked by civil war to save the kidnapped wife of a Texas millionaire. Two of them had been *simpaticos* who had once fought with the rebels but had left the cause, disenchanted. Says one: "When the shooting stops, and the dead are buried, and the politicians take over, it all adds up to one thing: a lost cause." And at another point, with the moral muddiness of the Mexican Revolution reflecting the 1960s' own moral chaos, it was said, "Maybe there's only one revolution, since the beginning, the good guys against the bad guys. Question is, who are the good guys?" (Brooks, *Professionals*).

ONE. A Perfect Storm—the 1960s

It was in the midst of this Western surge Sam Peckinpah would find his breakout success as a feature director, but that should've been no surprise. Years before *The Wild Bunch*, he had already demonstrated a mastery of the genre. To the casual observer, the only surprise might've been that his breakthrough to the big screen had taken so long.

But to study Peckinpah's career closely, without the circumstances specific to that time that breakthrough might not have happened at all. *The Wild Bunch* was, in fact, his ticket back from professional exile.

Two

Enter—and Exit— Sam Peckinpah

> *"Nobody loses all the time."*
> —Bennie (Warren Oates) in *Bring Me the Head of Alfredo Garcia*

Sam Peckinpah's career began in earnest in 1955 when director Don Siegel (*Invasion of the Body Snatchers* [1956]), for whom Peckinpah had been an assistant on several films, recommended him for a writing assignment on a new prime time Western series, *Gunsmoke*. The future filmmaker showed an immediate affinity for the genre, and would spend the next several years pumping out a steady stream of scripts for Western series like *Trackdown, Tales of Wells Fargo, Have Gun—Will Travel*, and others, finally getting his first opportunity to step behind the camera with an episode of *Broken Arrow* (Simmons, "Sam Peckinpah's" 1–2).

Peckinpah's flare for Westerns was natural. His upbringing had been a Hemingwayesque one of manly-men-doing-manly-things. He'd been born in Fresno, California, in 1925, a time and a place which, like many other interior pockets of the state, hadn't yet completely shaken off its wild and wooly past (Gentry 60–61). "A lot of the old-timers dated back to when the place had been the domain of hunters and trappers, Indians, gold miners," Peckinpah would remember in a 1972 interview (W. Murray 72). Growing up, Peckinpah hunted and camped in the Sierra Nevada foothills around Fresno, spent time on a family ranch, all the time steeped in tales of his pioneering ancestors (Patterson). As he grew older, diversions came to include more manly-men-acting-badly pastimes like boozing, whoring, and scrapping, but all of his experiences, savory and otherwise, fed an eye, an ear, an overall *feel* for Western authenticity which would texture his best work (Fine 21–22; Finler, *The Directors* 224).

Two. Enter—and Exit—Sam Peckinpah

Particularly through the early part of Peckinpah's career, he would strip-mine his memories for names, places, situations, even lines of dialogue to incorporate into his TV and film projects. Much about his young days on the family ranch went into *The Rifleman* and *The Westerner*, two TV series he helped launch, and in an oft-repeated story about Peckinpah, one of the episodes from *The Westerner*—"Jeff"—had come from "a 75-year-old Nevada prostitute who told me the story of her first love for $3.00 and a four-bit bottle of beer" (Simmons, "Sam Peckinpah's" 2–3; Wicking 102). One of the most memorable lines of dialogue in the Peckinpah canon was a direct lift from his father and given to the character of Gil Westrum (Joel McCrae) in *Ride the High Country*, effectively a self-eulogy about a hoped-for sum of a life: "All I want is to enter my house justified" (Fine 70).

It also happened to be the perfect time for someone with Peckinpah's particular talent for Westerns. By the mid–1950s, TV was transitioning away from being a niche medium serving the small upscale audience which could afford expensive sets to a mass audience platform. Consequently, the live TV dramas telecast from New York which had been the signature format during the medium's early years increasingly gave way to filmed series out of Hollywood, and Westerns were particularly popular (Sander

Sam Peckinpah on the set of *Cross of Iron* (1977).

Peckinpah gains his first real foothold in the industry in 1955 when his mentor, director Don Siegel, helps him get work as a writer on one of the first, and considered one of the best, of a swelling number of TV Westerns, *Gunsmoke*. Peckinpah will write 10 episodes for the frontier drama before moving on to write for a variety of Western series, perfecting his writing and, in time, directorial skills during his time working for the small screen. Left to right: series star James Arness, regular cast members Amanda Blake, Milburn Stone, Dennis Weaver.

Two. Enter—and Exit—Sam Peckinpah

79; Barnouw 214). The year Peckinpah took on his first directing assignment, no less than thirty Western series were dominating prime time on all three major broadcast networks (Barnouw 214).

In 1958, already with a fair body of work under his belt as a writer as well as his first directing credit, Peckinpah experienced a major career break with *The Rifleman*. Peckinpah developed the concept about a single father, played by Chuck Connors, raising a son on a ranch in 1880s New Mexico, with Jules Levy of the production company Levy-Gardner-Laven. The show aired as a pilot on the Western anthology series *Dick Powell's*

Peckinpah has a major career breakthrough in 1958 when he helps create the successful TV series *The Rifleman*, starring Chuck Connors (pictured here), although he quit the series early in his first major battle with producers over the creative direction of the show. These kinds of conflicts with executive offices would, sadly, become a signature of Peckinpah's career.

Zane Grey Theater that spring, and by the following fall, was in series production (Simmons, "Sam Peckinpah's" 2–3). But only a few episodes into the first season, Peckinpah quit the series convinced the producers had taken his concept and "perverted it into pap" (4).

Peckinpah's willingness to go to war with producers and executives would become as much a trademark of his work as his Western authenticity, and, sadly, came to him just as naturally.

Today we would use the word "dysfunctional" to describe the Peckinpah household. His mother, Fern, was a manipulative hypochondriac who psychologically emasculated her husband, at one point exiling him to a cabin on the family property (Fine 58). She was also snobbishly dismissive of the rustic side of the family of which her son was enamored, and eventually sold off the family ranch, something for which Peckinpah never forgave her (Fine 15; Patterson). Eventually, Fern Peckinpah would end her days in a nursing home a diagnosed schizophrenic (Fine 362). As for his father, Dave, a typically "gentle man," he could turn violent when disciplining the Peckinpah brood (19). The psychological scars of that upbringing would forever remain with Peckinpah, and for the rest of his life his relationships with women, friends, and authority figures would be marked by volatility and an almost instinctive rebelliousness, often aggravated by his drinking and, later, drug use. Said one lifelong friend, "[Sam] torpedoed everybody who ever did anything with him. Why do you fuck with loyalty? He always did it" (328–329).

Despite Peckinpah's carping about *The Rifleman*, the series was nonetheless a popular success, and success is a currency in Hollywood which buys both tolerance and opportunity. Dick Powell, the man behind *Zane Grey Theater*, commissioned another pilot from Peckinpah for the anthology which aired in 1959, and would be spun off into the series *The Westerner* with Brian Keith starring as an Old West drifter (Wicking 103–104). This time, Peckinpah was not a gun-for-hire writer or director on a series, but its producer with full creative control (Simmons, "Sam Peckinpah's" 5). Emblematic of Peckinpah's best work, the resulting series seamlessly interwove "the Old West of legend and an exploration of the reality behind that legend" (Wicking 104). Despite universal praise, the show never found an audience and was cancelled at the end of its fall season. Still, *The Westerner* would open the door to Peckinpah's first big screen assignment.

Like a number of TV's behind-the-camera talents (Lumet, Franken-

Two. Enter—and Exit—Sam Peckinpah

heimer, Penn, et al.), Peckinpah had always been on the lookout for an opportunity to graduate to the big screen. In 1957, he'd been offered the job of adapting Charles Neider's novel *The Authentic Death of Hendry Jones*, a fictionalized take on the Pat Garrett/Billy the Kid story. By the time the material passed through several hands in development (including an uncredited Rod Serling) and wound up as Marlon Brando's quirky directorial one-shot, *One-Eyed Jacks* (1961), Peckinpah's original material was unrecognizable (Seydor, *Peckinpah* 183).

Before Levy-Gardner-Laven began working with Peckinpah on *The Rifleman*, they also tried him on a big screen project, an adaptation of Hoffman Birney's novel *The Dice of God*, a fictionalized take on the events leading up to and including Custer's Last Stand, but the film would not make it to the screen until well into the 1960s (Fine 42–43).

Peckinpah's work on his self-created, critically-lauded series *The Westerner* leads to his debut as a feature director on *The Deadly Companions* (1961). Effectively executed but hardly buzz-worthy, the film further entrenched a career-long pattern of Peckinpah getting into a war with the executives behind the film. Shown here are Brian Keith, star of Peckinpah's *The Westerner* who recommended him for the job on *Companions*, and Maureen O'Hara.

It would, ironically, be his failed series *The Westerner* which finally brought Peckinpah the call for his first theatrical feature. When *Westerner* star Brian Keith was cast opposite Maureen O'Hara in the big screen oater *The Deadly Companions*, he recommended his old series boss for the director's job (Finler, *The Directors* 224).

Keith played a guilt-ridden bank robber agreeing to escort dance hall hostess O'Hara across the Western wastes with the body of her son, killed by a stray bullet of Keith's, to bury him beside his father's grave. *Companions* was an ideal vehicle to serve as Peckinpah's theatrical apprenticeship: small in scale, a drama-driven piece, more akin in many ways to his TV work than the large-canvas pieces coming later in his career.

It was, however, a troubled shoot from the outset with Peckinpah almost immediately going to war with producer Charles FitzSimons, who was both a partner to the project's writer, A. S. Fleischman, and brother to O'Hara. Peckinpah hated the script; FitzSimons felt married to his partner's screenplay and hated the gritty images Peckinpah wanted to integrate into the story. Peckinpah chafed at the tight shooting schedule and budget; FitzSimons hovered over Peckinpah to keep him on time and within budget (Fine 60–61). FitzSimons hated Peckinpah's director's cut of the film; Peckinpah despised FitzSimons re-cut (62–63).

Still, it was a respectable if not particularly buzzy feature debut. Though *The Deadly Companions* flopped at the box office, it did demonstrate Peckinpah could handle feature work, and earned the fledgling movie director some positive reviews though it did so without bringing people banging on his door with more big screen jobs. (Fine 63). It's some indicator of how off-the-radar *Companions* was and always would be that when *Village Voice* film critic and *Cahiers du Cinéma in English* editor-in-chief Andrew Sarris compiled his landmark directory of filmmakers in 1968—*The American Cinema: Directors and Directions 1929–1968*—beyond listing *Companions* as the first of the director's feature credits, not a single word would be spent on the film in the entry on Sam Peckinpah (Sarris, *The American* 219).

Unsurprisingly, then, it was not *The Deadly Companions* which brought Peckinpah his second feature gig, but rather the continuing resonance of *The Westerner* which made producer Richard Lyons tap him to direct for MGM what would become one of the defining films of the director's career: *Ride the High Country* (aka *Guns in the Afternoon*) (1962) (Simmons, "Sam Peckinpah's" 8).

Two. Enter—and Exit—Sam Peckinpah

Joel McCrea (left) and Randolph Scott in *Ride the High Country* (1962), the film which established Peckinpah as a big screen director of worth. Peckinpah smartly cast two actors with a history in Westerns and in the twilight of their careers; elements subtly reinforcing the sentiment of a movie about men who have outlived their time.

High Country's story of two aging former lawmen trying to find ways to survive in a West which no longer needs them is something of a gentler, more romantic treatment of the same driving theme—men outliving their time—which would emerge more emphatically in *The Wild Bunch*. Even the dynamic between the two lead characters, Gil Westrum (Randolph Scott) and Steve Judd (Joel McCrae), presages the one between former riding partners Pike Bishop (William Holden) and Deke Thornton (Robert Ryan) in *Bunch*; in each case there being one who pragmatically compromises himself, while the other chooses to go down remaining true to his nature (although, curiously, in *High Country*, the compromiser goes bad while in *Bunch* the compromiser sides with the law). *High Country* even climaxes, as does *Bunch*, with its outnumbered heroes walking into a seemingly suicidal face-off with the bad guys (although Scott's character survives). Peckinpah would return to these elements, amplify them and send them down more morally ambiguous paths in *The Wild Bunch*, but the DNA of that latter film can be traced directly to *Ride the High Country*.

In casting two actors well past their peak marquee years in McCrae and Scott—a tactic he would also repeat in *The Wild Bunch*—Peckinpah was able to give *Ride the High Country* a subtle, subtextural melancholy, showing an awareness he knew his audience shared; of the "myths [McCrae and Scott] inculcated" as part of a Hollywood which was fading away much like the Old West of Gil Westrum and Steve Judd (Sarris, *The American* 219).

Ride the High Country went off in a (rare for Peckinpah) smooth shoot, and he delivered a film unanimously hailed at home and abroad as an instant Western classic (Everson 225). This time around, the war between Peckinpah and the studio executives Hollywooders often disparagingly refer to as "The Suits" didn't ignite until *after* the film was delivered.

When the finished *High Country* was screened for Joseph Vogel, head of Loew's Inc., MGM's parent, Vogel, who hated the film, was convinced the studio had a loser on its hands. He ordered the film "dumped"—buried on the bottom half of double bills (Fine 74). Oscar-winning screenwriter William Goldman (*Butch Cassidy and the Sundance Kid*) tells the story of tracking down one of MGM's marketing people to find out why such a universally praised film had been handled so badly; had *High Country* previewed poorly? The MGM man replied that, on the contrary, the response cards filled out by preview audiences had been stellar. But "we didn't believe those preview cards" (Goldman 70).

After the director's go-around with Charles FitzSimons on *The Deadly Companions* and seeing the mess Marlon Brando had made of *The Authentic Death of Hendry Jones* with *One-Eyed Jacks*, the virtual assassination of *Ride the High Country* by Joseph Vogel only further entrenched Peckinpah's hatred for those who controlled the destiny of his work. In time, those feelings would escalate into outright, booze-fueled paranoia (Fine 100).

Ride the High Country performed well overseas, and it did have its fans at home, one of them being producer Jerry Bresler who reached out to Peckinpah with a project offering the possibility of being the director's breakout film: *Major Dundee* (1964) (Seydor, *Peckinpah* 70, Fine 84). It was a grand-scale, big-budget story of a maverick Union cavalry officer during the Civil War (Charlton Heston), punitively assigned to

Two. Enter—and Exit—Sam Peckinpah

command of a POW camp in New Mexico, who tries to redeem his career by leading a motley collection of Union soldiers, Confederate prisoners, and civilian odds-and-ends on an epic chase into Mexico after an Apache raider.

But the project was damned even before filming began. Despite months of work, Peckinpah was never able to lick serious problems in the screenplay, and on the eve of the start of production, he was told more than two weeks had been cut from the shooting schedule and the budget chopped by one-third (Heston 249; Seydor, *Peckinpah* 49). In an almost predictable dynamic, the more Bresler and execs at Columbia pressed Peckinpah on speed and costs, the more Peckinpah's screw-you attitude kicked in (Fine, 91). As filming ran behind and over-budget, only the intercession of Heston kept Columbia from firing Peckinpah (Heston 252–253). Columbia and Bresler got their revenge after Peckinpah

Left to right, a mostly hidden Michael Anderson, Richard Harris, and Charlton Heston in *Major Dundee* (1965). The popular notion is of *Dundee* as victim of studio mangling, and it is, but Peckinpah also may have been in over his head on the epic-scaled action adventure.

delivered his director's cut by severely re-editing the film. Between the budget cuts and Columbia's re-cutting, "fifty-five minutes of material that Peckinpah considered essential were removed or never included in the first place" (Seydor, *Peckinpah* 52). Unsurprisingly, then, Peckinpah's hoped-for breakout film flopped with both critics and the public (Fine 99).

Peckinpah did himself little good coming off such a high-visibility failure by going to war with yet another boss, this time Martin Ransohoff, producer on his next project, *The Cincinnati Kid* (1965). The project would've been a marked change from the Western genre with which Peckinpah was already closely identified; a Depression era drama about high-stakes poker players starring Steve McQueen and Edward G. Robinson. There hardly seemed a choice—from casting to Peckinpah's decision to shoot the film in black and white to his whole gritty take on the story—on which he and his producer didn't disagree (Farber 7). Four days into shooting, objecting to what he felt would be, in the mid–1960s, box office-killing nudity as well as a riot scene not in the screenplay, Ransohoff called a halt to shooting and fired Peckinpah (Terrill 113–114) (Norman Jewison would replace Peckinpah).

* * *

In Robert Rossen's pool room classic *The Hustler*, busted-out pool shark Fast Eddie Felson (Paul Newman) defends his play in a marathon match lost to pool hall ace Minnesota Fats (Jackie Gleason) to hustler manager Bert Gordon (George C. Scott) by talking up how well he'd played against Fats ... until he lost. Rebuts Gordon: "This game isn't like football. Nobody pays you for yardage. When you hustle you keep score real simple. The end of the game, you count up your money. That's how you find out who's best. That's the *only* way" (Rossen).

Hollywood has always run on a similar metric. Rave reviews are fine ... as long as they put money in the box office till. Studio execs doing the calculus on Sam Peckinpah after his firing from *The Cincinnati Kid* would have been confronted with nothing but negative numbers. Of his four directing jobs, he'd been fired from one and almost fired from a second. He'd given headaches to producers and/or studio execs on all of them. And when it came time to tally up the number that mattered more than all others, he was three for three, failing to deliver a single U.S. box office success.

After *The Cincinnati Kid*, Sam Peckinpah found himself branded

Two. Enter—and Exit—Sam Peckinpah

with that most toxic of industry labels: "difficult." Translation: He wasn't worth the ulcers he'd cause in people who might hire him (Fine 104).

Peckinpah's name didn't completely disappear from the big screen, although now it would only be for a writer's credit. *The Dice of God*, which he'd adapted for Levy-Gardner-Laven back in the late 1950s, finally made it to the screen retitled *The Glory Guys* (1965). In a bit of synchronicity, it was released the same year as his own cavalry pic, *Major Dundee*.

The movie is of some value to deep-diving students of Peckinpah's work as one can see some story elements in the older material resurfacing in *Dundee*. But other than as a Peckinpah curio, the most generous judgment one can make of the film is that it's a moderately diverting if formulaic Cavalry vs. The Indians flick with a few interesting touches.

Not even that much could be said of *Villa Rides!* (1968), virtually a re-hash of the 1956 Robert Mitchum starrer *Bandido!*, down to casting Mitchum in a similar part as an American gun runner trying to exploit the Mexican Revolution only to end up siding with the rebels under the command of Pancho Villa (Yul Brynner). Despite some big-action sequences, the film comes off generic, flavorless. Even Robert Towne, who was brought in to massively rewrite Peckinpah's script after Brynner had Peckinpah axed from the project, would later admit *Villa Rides!* was only made on something of an in-for-a-penny-in-for-a-pound basis because of the expensive pay-or-play deals Paramount had in place with Mitchum and Brynner (pay-or-play: both stars would get their fat fees whether the movie was made or not). "What happens," Towne said, "is you pay a lot of people a lot of money to make a movie that *nobody* particularly wants to make" (Fine 111; Brady 387). As another Peckinpah curio, the movie is, perhaps, mildly interesting as the Mexican Revolution setting would become an integral part of *The Wild Bunch*.

With neither film lighting up either critics or the box office, neither offered much of an argument for bringing Peckinpah back from his *de facto* banishment from big screen directing. The only work open to him was back where his career had begun: in television.

After both *The Deadly Companions* and *Ride the High Country*, Peckinpah had returned to TV, but the circumstances now were different. He'd been slowly working his way up the feature ladder during those earlier returns. Now, he was in exile, and television the Elba from which he hoped to mount his professional resurrection.

In 1966, Peckinpah was approached by producer Daniel Melnick for a television adaptation of Katherine Ann Porter's novella *Noon Wine*, a turn-of-the-century drama set in farm country about jealousy, murder, and guilt. After a year and a half without work and tacitly blacklisted from features, Peckinpah knew how high the stakes were with *Noon Wine*. He pushed his cast and crew with his own perfectionist drive (Fine 108–109). The end result was a highly praised work which earned Peckinpah a Writer's Guild nomination for Best Television Screenplay Adaptation, and from the Director's Guild for Best Television Directing (Simmons, "Sam Peckinpah's" 13).

The attention for *Noon Wine* brought Peckinpah back from career death. "Sam was a hero again," Melnick would recall years later (Fine 110). Another TV project came his way, *Villa Rides!* sold, his name started getting bandied about for features, and in 1967, Kenneth Hyman, newly-installed production chief at Warner Bros.-Seven Arts, showed Peckinpah a one-page treatment for something called *The Wild Bunch* (Simmons, "Sam Peckinpah's" 13–14, Fine 113).

Sam Peckinpah was, again, the right man in the right place at the right time.

Three

A Giant Departs, an Opportunity Opens

"I was robbed and left to die without a drop. Well, do I look dead? No, sir! Climbed up on my hind feet and walked straight to water."
—Cable (Jason Robards) in
The Ballad of Cable Hogue

By 1967, Jack Warner was the last of a breed of giants.

Almost a half-century before, in 1919, after nibbling around the edges of the fledgling movie industry for years, the brothers Harry, Albert, Sam, and youngest Jack Warner (an Anglicized version of their Polish given name, Wonskolaser) opened their first small studio in Hollywood (they would not officially become Warner Bros. Inc. until 1923) (Finler, *The Hollywood* 228). Jack had seen the company through its struggling early years when the only thing keeping it afloat was its one star—a clever German shepherd named Rin-Tin-Tin (Gaita). He had been there when the company—in "a daring, last-ditch gamble to stay in business"—had launched the industry into the sound era with *The Jazz Singer* (1927) (Jennings 36). And he had seen the namesake studio grow from desperate junior player into a powerhouse boasting a star roster including some of the most iconic names in Hollywood lore: James Cagney, Errol Flynn, Doris Day, Edward G. Robinson, Bette Davis, Joan Crawford, and, of course, Humphrey Bogart.

Jack had helped the company survive the 1950s Hollywood decline by pushing the company heavily into TV production, one of the first major studios to do so, and dabbling with 3-D (Finler, *The Hollywood* 231). In a bit of shareholder chicanery, he'd outmaneuvered his two surviving brothers, Harry and Albert (Sam had died in 1927), ousting them from the company they'd created (Gaita).

He'd not only outlasted his brothers (Harry would die in 1958;

Sam in 1967), but all the rest of the fraternity of Hollywood's founding fathers: Paramount's Adolph Zukor, 20th Century-Fox's Darryl Zanuck, Columbia's Harry Cohn, MGM's Louis Mayer, Universal's Carl Laemmle ... all gone. Warner was the last of them still in power ... and some felt a bit of a dinosaur (Gaita).

He was 75 and appeared to be losing his touch. The measure of once-a-titan Jack Warner—as well as a gauge of how Old Hollywood was giving way to New Hollywood—can be measured by two of the studio's 1967 releases: *Camelot* and *Bonnie and Clyde*.

The film adaptation of the Broadway musical *Camelot* had been a pet project of Warner's, possibly an attempt to re-capture the glory of another adaptation of a big stage musical, the studio's 1964 *My Fair Lady*, which had won Warner his third Best Picture Oscar (Biskind 24; Finler, *The Hollywood* 241). But the once autocratic Warner failed to get *Camelot* director Joshua Logan to cast more commercial names, and, like *My Fair Lady*, while *Camelot* was one of the studio's top earners of the 1960s, the box office couldn't offset the movie's exorbitant cost (Gaita; Finler, *The Hollywood* 240, 241).

Bonnie and Clyde, on the other hand, was a project Warner hated from the moment it was brought to him by the project's star and producer, Warren Beatty. In his account of the massive changes in the industry during the late 1960s-early 1970s, *Easy Riders, Raging Bulls: How the Sex-Drugs-and-Rock-'n'-Roll Generation Saved Hollywood*, Peter Biskind tells a story—which he acknowledges Beatty denies—that Beatty only got Warner to greenlight the project by falling to the floor and grabbing Warner around the knees promising to kiss the studio chief's shoes ... and by offering to bring the movie in for a paltry $1.6 million (24). Warner didn't like the project any better when Beatty screened it for him before its release (35). Warner's judgment notwithstanding, *Bonnie and Clyde* went on to become the studio's top earning film of the 1960s as well as earn 10 Oscar nominations (budget v. rentals: *Bonnie and Clyde*—$1.6 million v. $22 million; *Camelot*—$15 million v. $12.3 million [Finler, *The Hollywood* 240)]).

It was a growing feeling in the industry—and Jack Warner apparently agreed—that it was time to get out. That spring, Warner sold the company to Canadian-based Seven Arts Productions, a company with which Warner Bros. had had a relationship since 1960 when the studio had sold Seven Arts television rights to part of its film library (Biskind 35; Hoyt 241).

THREE. A Giant Departs, an Opportunity Opens

Headed by Eliot Hyman, one of the company's founders, Seven Arts not only distributed old film and TV shows, but produced films for other companies, among them John Huston's quirky contemporary Western *The Misfits*, John Frankenheimer's pungent political thriller *Seven Days in May*, Stanley Kubrick's controversial adaptation of Vladimir Nabokov's scandalous novel *Lolita* (1962), and the smash hits *West Side Story* (1961) and *The Dirty Dozen*.

Hyman's 38-year-old son Kenneth, who had several producer's credits under his belt by the time of the Warner acquisition, was tasked with heading up production for the now re-christened Warner Bros.-Seven Arts (Hoyt 191). Typically when new management takes control of a studio, they weed out unproductive old talent relationships while reinforcing the profitable ones, but they also look to develop new relationships and new projects; the kind that will establish both their industry credibility and their brand. As was happening throughout the circle of major studios also undergoing a change in management at the time from the old to the new, Hyman set out to attract filmmakers by offering them the kind of creative control the Hollywood old guard would never have allowed.

Hyman and Peckinpah had met the year before at Cannes where Peckinpah had looked Hyman up after a screening of Seven Arts' World War II drama *The Hill* (1965) on which Hyman had been a producer. Hyman, in turn, took a look at *Ride the High Country* and was as impressed with Peckinpah's work as Peckinpah had been with Hyman's (Fine 112).

They bonded over their respective service in the Marines, and Hyman was not one to be intimidated by Peckinpah's radioactive reputation (Fine 113). He had worked with directors before who may not have had the same ostracizing reputation as a—to be blunt—pain in the ass Peckinpah had, but who certainly had reputations as Hollywood mavericks, like John Huston, Stanley Kubrick, and Robert Aldrich, the latter with whom Seven Arts would make three films including two produced by Hyman: *Whatever Happened to Baby Jane?* (1962) and *The Dirty Dozen*. Hyman signed Peckinpah for two films: *The Wild Bunch* and another Western, *The Ballad of Cable Hogue* (1970) (Biskind 36).

Considering how completely the filmmaker had been shut out of feature directing since being fired off *The Cincinnati Kid*, it's entirely possible that had not Seven Arts come into the picture, no major studio would, again, have let Sam Peckinpah through its gates. This was, for

Peckinpah, an extravagant alignment of favorable circumstances, something akin to a lottery win: a new regime at a major studio looking to build its talent roster by offering then-unprecedented creative latitude; a new, young production exec, a Hollywood outsider unimpressed by the community's bad-mouthing of Peckinpah, and unafraid of either hard-headed filmmakers or provocative material.

    Filling out what was already a winning hand, Hyman was playing to Peckinpah's strong suit by offering him Westerns. It was another lovely bit of synchronicity as the Western genre was about to have its moment just as Sam Peckinpah was about to have his.

Four

Hollywood's West

> "But they're all following you."
> "No, they ain't. I'm just in front of them."
> —Melissa (Ali MacGraw) and Rubber Duck
> (Kris Kristofferson) in *Convoy*

The Wild Bunch did not constitute an overturn of the Western genre although at the time, to many, it appeared that way. But broken down into its basal elements, one surprisingly finds the film was neither wholly new nor unique even in its time. *The Wild Bunch* represented less a break with Western genre traditions than a 0–120 acceleration in an already ongoing evolution in a number of the genre's DNA strands.

That Was the West That Was

From the remove of 21st-century America, it can be difficult to keep in mind that the Old West wasn't always old. In fact, during the early days of the motion picture business, the Old West was still the Wild West; a living—if somewhat fading—part of the country even as movies and literature were transforming it into the stuff of legend (Everson 14; D. Murray).

Although the U.S. Census had declared the frontier closed in 1890, in the early years of the 20th century, the United States still wasn't finished becoming the United States. The continental United States of that time only consisted of 45 states (Oklahoma wouldn't achieve statehood until 1907; New Mexico and Arizona in 1912, just a year or two before *The Wild Bunch* takes place). The Ford Motor Company may have begun mass producing Model T automobiles a few years before the events of *The Wild Bunch*, but much of the country looked much as it had during the last decades of the 19th century with the horse still dominating transportation and field work (the equine population wouldn't peak until 1915 at 21 million—approximately one for every five citizens), and most of the U.S. population living a rural life ("Ford Motor"; Sapan 33, 32).

At the time Edwin S. Porter had his celluloid cowboys pretending the New Jersey woods were the Wild West in *The Great Train Robbery* in 1903, many of the most iconic incidents of the historical West were still within living memory (Parkinson 11, 12). The Battle of the Little Big Horn aka Custer's Last Stand had taken place just 27 years before, in 1876, the same year Wild Bill Hickock was gunned down in a Deadwood saloon. Wyatt Earp, his brothers, and Doc Holliday had faced off with the Clanton Gang at Tombstone's O.K. Corral only a few years later, in 1881 (Earp himself wouldn't die until 1929 in Los Angeles). The year the Earps and Clantons blasted away at each other in Tombstone was the same year Billy the Kid was shot down in New Mexico by Pat Garrett who was, himself, shot to death 27 years later in 1908. Jesse James was killed in his Missouri home in 1882 by Robert Ford, who, in turn, was shotgunned to death in a saloon ten years later, the same year the Dalton Gang infamously tried to rob two banks in Coffeyville, Kansas, setting the town's main street ablaze with gunfire. The bloody Johnson County War—a years-long range war between cattle barons and small landowners—had only come to an end the following year, in 1893. And just two years before Porter filmed the first true Western movie, the real Butch Cassidy and the Sundance Kid, together with schoolteacher Etta Place, lit out for South America to escape the law, while Hole-in-the-Wall—the one-time hideout for Cassidy's gang as well as other outlaw outfits—remained a Bad Man's lair as late as 1910 (Parkinson 11).

Even during those days when the Wild West was still wild, there were those transforming living history into legend, memory into myth. Long before Edwin Porter's cameras rolled—or even existed—dime novelists like Ned Buntline, more serious literary figures like Owen Wister (*The Virginian*), and traveling Wild West shows were bringing a portrait of the West—albeit a highly melodramatic, sometimes outrageously hyperbolic one—to the more settled parts of the country, in the process translating historical reality into American myth (Parks 14). The iconography and tropes created by the Buntlines and Wisters and showmen like Buffalo Bill Cody were already entrenched by the turn of the century: "the lawmen, the outlaws, the honorable and the

Four. Hollywood's West

tarnished ladies, the railroad, the town" (Parks 104). The West itself would be forever defined as "a virgin world suspended out of time and history, awaiting the inevitable intrusion of civilization" (Folsom 58). These would become and remain the pillars of the Western tale, on both the page and the screen, for decades to come.

The Western early on established itself as a mainstay of the movie companies, offering—with the barest modicum of historical accuracy—a platform for any number of scenarios: man vs. nature, law vs. outlaws, cattle barons vs. settlers, cavalry vs. Indians, settlers vs. Indians, railroad builders vs. Indians, and so on (Wright 5). Many, if not most, of the offerings of the 1920s-early 1930s were low-budget "B" productions, ranging from the stunt-filled action fests of Tom Mix to, in the sound era, the singing cowboy flicks of Gene Autry and Roy Rogers (Parkinson 36). But if, like its literary predecessor, the Western had more than its share of Ned Buntlines, so, too, did it have its Owen Wisters: filmmakers who saw the Western as a platform for legitimate drama. None mined the dramatic lyricism and visual poetry of the Western as deeply, nor defined the serious Western as clearly, as John Ford (165). Ford would, until the end of his life, be the gold standard in the Western genre, from silent era epics like *The Iron Horse* (1923), to *Stagecoach* (1939), which proved to be the breakout feature for John Wayne, to his post-World War II classics like *My Darling Clementine* (1946), *She Wore a Yellow Ribbon* (1949), and what many critics consider his masterwork, *The Searchers* (1956) (Finler, *Directors* 44).

But if there's a caveat to Ford, it's this: he was an Easterner with no personal acquaintance with the West, Old or new (Parkinson 164). He filmed the West not as it was, but as he sentimentally imagined it to be (166). His storytelling code was articulated by one of the characters in his late-career Western, *The Man Who Shot Liberty Valance* (1962): "This is the West, sir. When the legend becomes fact, print the legend" (Ford).

This was an aesthetic not exclusive to Ford, but up through the 1930s it was the near-universal ethos of the movie Western. While it was a conceptual view that never went away, it would make room for another mindset, and the demarcation point between the traditional legendary vision of the Old West and a new view was World War II.

Approximately one in eight Americans saw military service by the end of the war in 1945, and of those, over 1.1 million (about one in every 127 Americans) were killed or wounded. The horrors of the war had been unprecedented: the Blitz, the firebombing of cities, the nuclear vaporization of Hiroshima and Nagasaki, the predations of the Japanese in their conquered territories, and, of course, the Holocaust. Estimates of the war's total dead range anywhere from 50 million to over 70 million, killed in combat, by disease and starvation, by mass murder. Most of the deaths were civilian ("WWII").

This greatest of all human tragedies certainly offered enough in the way of fodder for a national emotional trauma, but then came the added turmoil of the postwar years; the great global conflict may have ended with the defeat of Axis evil, but it brought no universal peace. Nearly as soon as the one great evil was laid to rest, a hundred smaller ones sprang up.

There was the Cold War, with the democratic West facing off with the communist East, tensions which grew higher when the contest broke out into open warfare in Korea in 1950, and grew still more fearful as both sides began to build up their nuclear arsenals and devise weapons systems to carry them across what had once been the safe barriers of oceans (Manning 10, 12; Fehrenbach 703; Halberstam 25–26). Violence and bloody revolt plagued the once-great European colonial empires now weakened by the war, as one territory after another fought to tear itself toward independence (O'Brien 250–251, 256–257).

The sense of great victory that had come with the end of World War II was, then, replaced with unease, cynicism, frustration, paranoia, and the clear real-world evidence that not every story would have a happy ending ... or even a hero. Out of this sentiment arose the genre postwar French critics would dub *film noir* (Sklar 253).

The signature *noir* film was the urban thriller, shot in cigarette smoke-laced shadows, set among a city's demimonde, populated with *femme fatales* and protagonists of dubious morality clad in trench coats and broad-brimmed fedoras walking down rain-slicked streets at night (Server 78). That may have been the archetypal *look* of *noir*, but that *sensibility*—that good didn't always win, that in some scenarios there might not even be any good to be had—seeped out of *noir*'s cityscapes and across the genre spectrum. There were *noir*ish horror movies (*The Body Snatcher* [1945]), *noir*ish war films (*Attack!* [1956]), *noir*ish sci fiers (*Invasion of the Body Snatchers*), even *noir*ish comedies (*The Big Steal* [1949]) and melodramas (*Mildred Pierce* [1945]). And, as you might have guessed by now, Westerns were hardly immune from the *noir* mindset. Think of William Wellman's broody *The Ox-Bow Incident* (1943); the

FOUR. Hollywood's West

psychological duel between captive Bad Guy and fraying Good Guy in Delmer Daves' *3:10 to Yuma* (1957); the brutal little Westerns director Budd Boetticher made with Randolph Scott like *The Tall T* (1957); Anthony Mann's psychologically overheated tales of the West, often starring James Stewart, like *The Man from Laramie* (1955); *Pursued* (1947) and *Blood on the Moon* (1948), both starring Robert Mitchum—a virtual *noir* icon at the time—which even echoed the shadowy look of urban *noirs* (Server 116).

While the *noir*ish Westerns offered one kind of de-romanticized West, another strain of anti-myth was appearing: movies looking to present some level of honesty about what the Old West had really been like; an ethos nicely outlined by a rich rancher in Richard Brooks' *Bite the Bullet* (1975) in a rebuff to a Fordian enrapturization of the West by an English visitor: "I don't see what's so inspiring about a flash flood or a blizzard, or a landslide or a sandstorm or a dust storm or any sudden disaster, personal or financial. Today the desert will broil you royal, tomorrow the mountain will freeze you stiff. That's your West: violent, treacherous. Every prairie dog hole is a gold mine, every molehill is a mountain, every creek is a river, and everybody you meet is a liar" (Brooks, *Bite*). And when another character chimes in with a quote from Owen Wister's *The Virginian*— "When you call me that, smile, stranger"—the rancher grins and responds, "Ah, Owen Wister! Another liar!!" (Brooks, *Bite*).

One of the best early Western makers in this vein was Delmer Daves who, like Peckinpah, was descended from pioneer stock and who had, himself, been raised in the West. One of Daves' best works is his harsh, deliberately demythologizing rendering of that Western staple, the cattle drive, in the appropriately named *Cowboy* (1958). Adapted from a memoir by Frank Harris, *Cowboy* captures the harsh realities of the cattle trail: the callous indifference to death, the miserable conditions, the capriciousness of disaster. The movie's most incisive moment comes as tenderfoot Jack Lemmon wrongly thinks he's shucked his rookie's naiveté, mistaking his near-cruelty for the brutal pragmatism of the trail veterans: "you'll never learn," veteran trail boss Glenn Ford tells him. "You haven't gotten tougher. You've gotten miserable" (Daves).*

---

*In many ways, *Cowboy* is a precursor to *The Westerner* episode "Line Camp," written and directed for Peckinpah's series by Tom Gries. Gries would later develop the material into the 1967 feature *Will Penny* which, like *Cowboy*, was praised for the deglamorizing authenticity of its portrait of the life of a cowhand. Some have said *Will Penny* may be the best Sam Peckinpah movie Peckinpah never made.

But whether it was Fordian legend-making, or a dose of reality mixed with some *noir*ish moral ambiguity, an increasingly recurring theme in the postwar Western was the passing of the West itself; a passing more often symbolic than literal in its import (Hackett).

There Were Giants in Those Days

In *Inherit the Wind*, the 1955 stage fictionalization of the infamous Scopes "Monkey Trial" of the 1920s, Henry Drummond, a lawyer defending a young teacher charged with teaching evolutionary theory in his classroom, explains the cost of progress: "Sometimes I think there's a man who sits behind a counter and says, 'All right, you can have a telephone but you'll have to give up privacy, the charm of distance. Madam, you may vote; but at a price; you lose the right to retreat behind a powder-puff or a petticoat. Mister, you may conquer the air; but the birds will lose their wonder, and the clouds will smell of gasoline'" (Lawrence 46).

By the years after World War II, the Wild West had obviously receded into history; it was truly an era over and gone. This became a theme which began to bubble up repeatedly in the movie Western, even in the still-romanticized picture of the West John Ford would keep offering into the 1960s. Perhaps—and this is purely supposition—it was a theme which had little to do with the historical Old West and more to do with the passing of something of more contemporary relevance.

Again, this is supposition, but it would be hard to have lived through the global trauma of World War II and not think the nation had made some passage into a new form of being, breaking with a past that was simpler in every way: technologically, socially, morally. The country had gone into the war with an army still equipped with bolt-action rifles and had come out armed with atomic weapons. The war had begun with Good Guys and Bad Guys clearly defined, but within a few years of the end of the war, the United States was allied with recent enemies against recent allies turned enemies. In the same way the *noir*-tinged Western reflected postwar confusion and fears, so, too, perhaps it was also catching that sense of an era—one of moral clarity and simplicity—had passed.

One of the mainstays of the Western myth, going back to its literary days, had been the idea of the wilderness giving way to settlement; that aforementioned idea of "a virgin world … awaiting the inevitable intrusion

Four. Hollywood's West

of civilization." From the Western's early days, the technological taming of the West—the hardware which would bind the country together across the western expanse—was viewed as a positive in movies like *The Iron Horse, Wells Fargo* (1937), *Western Union* (1941), *The Pony Express* (1953). Lawmen cleaning up the raucous towns of the frontier was another facet of Wild West-taming; doing in the Bad Guys, replacing the law of the gun with social and moral order, i.e., *Dodge City* (1939), *My Darling Clementine* (1946), *Gunfight at the O.K. Corral* (1957), *Warlock* (1959), *The Man Who Shot Liberty Valance*, etc. The cattle barons who ran the West like their own private fiefdoms, the only law being their armies of gun hands, now gave way to the settlers and farmers and small ranchers—community-builders—in the likes of *Shane* (1953), *Man Without a Star* (1955), *Forty Guns* (1957), *The Big Country* (1958), and, again, *Liberty Valance*. It was the role of civilization to take the wild out of the Wild West.

But during the postwar period, the idea seeped into the Western—Henry Drummond's "man who sits behind a counter"—that this civilizing of the West came with a cost. The most obvious price was paid by the people who'd been living in the West before the coming of white civilization. Consequently, a more sympathetic picture of the plight of Native Americans regularly began to appear in movies like *Broken Arrow* (1950), *Apache* (1954), the 1960 remake of 1931's *Cimarron*, and the epic-sized *How the West Was Won* and *Cheyenne Autumn* (1964).

The victimization of the American Indian was an obvious, historical fact. The postwar Western, however, had something else on its collective mind. The genre began to show a sense that some of the costs of progress were less obvious, less tangible, and less historical; that something was being lost *today*, and that something was, well, let's use the word *spiritual*.

Along with all that postwar *noir*y cynicism and disappointment came another reason for unease; America had gone ... *corporate*. With the United States having the only intact economy in the industrialized world after the war, the subsequent years were a time of unprecedented national affluence, and with all that money-making came the growth of the modern-day corporation. It was the era of the "company man," the dutiful, white collar type now populating the swelling suburbs (Halberstam x). But with corporatization came a fear of depersonalization, of material wealth suffocating moral health, of a reduction in the value of the individual to a temporary and ultimately disposable corporate asset (526). This was, after all, the era of Arthur Miller's stage play *Death of a Salesman*, Sloan Wilson's novel *The Man in the Gray Flannel Suit* (later adapted into a 1956 movie), Rod Serling's TV drama *Patterns* (also adapted into a movie in 1956), and films like *The Hucksters* (1947), *Executive Suite* (1954), *Woman's World* (1954), all of which argued there was something soul-crushing about corporate America. Some filmmakers saw, in the idea of the Death of the West, a way to reflect this Death of the American Soul.

In 1950's *The Gunfighter*, Gregory Peck is an aging gunman who returns to his hometown to visit his ex-wife and finds the town, like other towns, closed to him; in the 1953 Western classic *Shane*, another gunfighter senses his days, too, are coming to an end. These are not cases of gunmen being chased out by town-taming lawmen, but of men—and here is the melancholy Death-of-the-West element to both movies—coming to the realization that the West has no room for them anymore.

If the passing of gunmen is a dubious loss, other less arguable costs of progress were showing up in the Western as well, for whatever in the way of progress civilization was bringing to the West, so, too, did it also bring all of its foibles. In another Western classic from the 1950s, *High Noon* (1952), townspeople refuse to support their marshal in a face-off with a band of vindictive Bad Guys rather than possibly damage the town's image with even a momentary reversion to its shoot-'em-up past. Over the course of the grand scale *Cimarron*, a community grows from frontier settlement to city, and in the process, steamrolls over the local Native Americans, develops a snobby social hierarchy, and eventually has little need of the free spirits who first pioneered the territory. In another king-sized piece, the aptly titled *The Big Country*, a self-styled, self-appointed ranching aristocracy tries to bully a lower-class ranch family in a competition for domination that's as much about cultural snobbery as it is about ranching and water rights.

That the genre had more on its mind than the historical West is evident in similar themes showing themselves in Westerns set in the modern day. In *Giant* (1956) and *Hud* (1963), the Noble Cattleman is being eclipsed by the Soulless Oilman; *The Misfits* (1961) and *Lonely Are the Brave* (1962) are modern day eulogies to characters essentially depicted as The Last Cowboys.

Collectively, the message was "The West is dying, and with it a kind of America; a place egalitarian, valuing the individual, that in its vastness allowed a free pursuit of one's destiny, even if it was as humble as seeing

Four. Hollywood's West

what was over the next hill." The concept of this national spiritual death became only more emphatic and painfully crystalline when played against the backdrop of the social and moral chaos of the 1960s.

In the earlier postwar years, that sense of spiritual damage and loss came out of a vague unease about the social and cultural direction of the country, along with the paranoias which went with the geo-political realignments and threats of the time. But in the 1960s, with the country mired in what came to be seen as an unwinnable and pointless war, and with the open hostility between the young and not-so-young, between white and black, even between men and empowered women, and with a corrosion of faith in the national leadership, there was no longer anything vague about the feeling. Whether gently chiding the arguable benefits of civilization (i.e., present day society) with wry humor in *Butch Cassidy and The Sundance Kid* (1969), or delivering the message with an upraised middle finger in the most contemporary of contemporary Westerns—*Easy Rider*—the message was clear: America had lost its way, the only heroes were the outlaws who didn't toe the societal line, and whose inevitable doom was as predestined as that of the dinosaurs (Knauer, *1969* 64–65).

South of the Border, Down Mexico Way

After a robbery goes bad, the Wild Bunch head for Mexico. Pausing on the northern bank of the Rio Grande—the border between Texas and Mexico—one of the Bunch, Mexican-born Angel (Jaime Sanchez), looks longingly across the river at his homeland. *"Ahhh, Mexico lindo."*

To which one of the Bunch responds, saying, "It just looks like more Texas to me."

And, in a sense, so it is.

Nearly in parallel to the rise of Death of the West themes came this idea of Mexico as an extension of the West; not the dying West, but south of the border the Old West, the Wild West, still lived.

There was a certain historical validity to the idea. For much of the 19th and early 20th century, Mexico was a country plagued almost incessantly by inner turmoil: breaking away from Spain, the war over the independence of Texas, invasion by the French during the time of the American Civil War (the setting of Peckinpah's *Major Dundee*), the oppressive 35 years of the *Porfiriato* under Porfirio Diaz, then the seemingly endless Mexican Revolution of 1910–1920. Unsurprisingly, then, that the vast and under-populated north country of Mexico took on, in the American Western, the character of a place barely settled, rarely policed, often lawless. Narrator/balladeer Roger Miller caught the flavor of the Western's view of Mexico in the comedy Western *Waterhole #3* (1967): "Ol' Mexico is just ahead, so gambler move along. There ain't nobody there to care if you done right or wrong" (Grusin).

In the movie Western of the postwar years, Mexico would be a safe haven for Bad Guys (*The Left-Handed Gun* [1958], *The Ride Back* [1957], *The Bravados* [1958], *The Wonderful Country* [1959], *Major Dundee*, *Waterhole #3*, *Hour of the Gun*, and *Butch Cassidy and the Sundance Kid* which took the concept even further, the titular duo not stopping on their run south until they reach Bolivia); a retreat for renegades to hole up and reconstitute (*The Comancheros* [1961], *Rio Conchos* [1964], *The Undefeated* [1969]); a place whose internal chaos left it ripe for exploitation by mercenaries and adventurers (*Vera Cruz* [1954], *Bandido!*, *The Magnificent Seven* [1960], *The Professionals*, *Villa Rides!*). Western movie Mexico became something of an outlaw/gunman heaven ... or, as circumstances dictated, hell.

* * *

You can see these themes come to maturation and integration in John Sturges' *The Magnificent Seven*, with its screenplay by William Roberts and an uncredited Walter Newman.* One could even make a case that *even* is more of a precursor to *The Wild Bunch* than Peckinaph's own oft-cited *Ride the High Country*, with *The Magnificent Seven* and *The Wild Bunch* displaying all the same elements within plots of roughly the same general configuration: Death of the West; men having outlived their time; the anti-hero as hero; Mexico as the last redoubt of the Wild

---

*There has long been discussion about which writer deserves the most credit for what's on the screen in *The Magnificent Seven*, adapted from Akira Kurosawa's *Seven Samurai* (1954). Walter Newman had been hired to draft a screenplay after a version by Walter Bernstein had been scrapped (Heaton). When shooting began in Mexico, a writer was needed on-set to make changes. Newman, then preoccupied with the birth of his first child, declined to make the trip (Froug 73–74). William Roberts was then hired to do the on-location rewrites. Arbitration over screenplay credits went to the Writer's Guild of America which decided that Newman and Roberts should be credited as co-writers. Newman, feeling he deserved sole screenplay credit as—in his opinion—Roberts' contributions were minimal, so strongly objected to that decision that he took his name off the film. However, according to Lou Morheim, associate producer on the film and who seems to have been the person who first acquired the remake rights to the Kurosawa film, most of the finished film comes from Newman's screenplay (Heaton).

Four. Hollywood's West

West; the civilizing of the West being as oppressive as it is progressive; and with each film reflecting something of its time. Taking the argument one step further, *The Wild Bunch* can be viewed as *The Magnificent Seven* with all the nobility beaten out of it by the moral horror show that was the 1960s (Hackett).

The dying West is set up in the opening scene of *The Magnificent Seven*, when Mexican bandit leader Calvera (Eli Wallach) leads his band of forty thieves into the small village he has repeatedly subjected to his raids for food and sundries. Calvera vents his frustration to the villagers over his changing fortunes: "The days of good hunting are over. Once there were horses, cattle, gold, fruit from the trees…. No more! Now I must hunt with a price on my head, *rurales* at my heels." Later it's revealed Calvera isn't just worried about raiding for food for the coming winter as he claims, but that his bandit army hasn't eaten for days. As bad as Calvera's situation is, it's worse north of the border for those who live by the gun.

Several of the villagers trek across the border to Texas to buy guns to fend off the next Calvera raid. They find a border town frozen by a dispute over a burial. A sympathetic traveling salesman has put up the money to inter a man he'd seen lying dead and ignored in the street for hours, but the town mortician has told him the funeral is off. Some of the townspeople object to the burial because the dead man was an Indian. "How long's this been going on?" the incredulous salesman asks. Answers the mortician: "Since the town got civilized."

Two drifting, out-of-work gunfighters—Chris (Yul Brynner) and Vin (Steve McQueen)—take on the job of shepherding the hearse to the cemetery for no reason other than the thrill. In the conversation between the two, we quickly get a picture of a West where their kind of work is drying up: "People all settled down-like," says Vin. "Same all over," agrees Chris. And as for this particular town? The only opportunities are, according to Vin, "grocery clerk, bouncer in one of those bars…."

When the villagers approach Chris about helping them buy guns, he tells them to hire men instead: "These days men are cheaper than guns." How cheap? Chris approaches Vin about taking the villagers up on their offer of a paltry $20 for four-six weeks' work. Vin shakes his head. "Why that's ridiculous…. That wouldn't even pay for my bullets." But when having to choose between the villagers' offer and a job as a "crackerjack grocery clerk" offering, says one of the villagers, "good, steady work," Vin opts for the ride to Mexico.

Even more pathetic is the situation of O'Riley (Charles Bronson), a gunman reduced to chopping wood for his breakfast. Approached by Chris and Vin, the two recount O'Riley's past gunfighting gigs and the hefty fees that went with them.

"You cost a lot," comments Vin.

"That's right," O'Riley says defiantly, "I cost a lot."

Chris makes the offer, O'Riley angrily turns his back on them, but before they ride off, "Twenty dollars? Right now, that's a lot."

Kicking off the movie's last act, and not unlike Peckinpah's Bunch, given a choice between riding off or facing impossible odds in a suicidal face-off with the Bad Guys, the Seven opt for the face-off (although unlike the Bunch, several will survive) (Sturges, *Magnificent*).

The Seven are gunman who can't—or won't—change, just as the Bunch are outlaws who despite knowing they have to "[think] past our guns," can't. At one point in *The Wild Bunch*, leader of the Bunch Pike (William Holden) talks about making one last good score and then "backing off," to which his friend Dutch (Ernest Borgnine) snaps, "Back off to *what*?" Pike has no answer. Similarly, at one point in *The Magnificent Seven*, Vin muses about his hope of possibly settling down in the village after the fighting is over. Yet, after the climactic last battle, Vin rides out of town along with Chris. The Bunch, the Seven: they are what they are—unchanging, unchangeable (Sturges, *Magnificent*).

The Magnificent Seven came out in 1960, and, reflected in the Seven's mission of protecting the villagers—however mercenary it began—according to cultural historian Richard Slotkin, is "the paternalism, pride, personal motivations and alienation that mirrored subsequent military involvement in Vietnam" (Hackett). But *The Wild Bunch*, coming after a decade of social upheaval, violence, and the sinking realization that the country was stuck in a war gone bad, was really a "brutal sendup of *The Magnificent Seven*" (Hackett).

The Magnificent Seven, says director John Carpenter, marks "the beginning of the end of the great American Westerns," meaning the traditional, classical, Fordian Western (Heaton). If one buys into Carpenter's idea that *Seven* was, indeed, the beginning of the end for the genre, *The Wild Bunch* has to be considered the great American Western's cataclysmic eulogy.

Five

Sires

"If you're lookin' for hard-ridin,' Injun-fightin,' whiskey-drinkin' mulepackers, then, by God, you've got one!"
—Wiley (Slim Pickens) in *Major Dundee*

Writes Malcolm Gladwell in his bestselling analysis of successful achievers, *Outliers: The Story of Success*: "It makes a difference where and when we grew up. The culture we belong to and the legacies passed down by our forebears shape the patterns of our achievement.... It's not enough to ask what successful people are like.... It is only by asking where they are *from* that we can unravel the logic behind who succeeds and who doesn't" (19).

Made famous in the same book is the 10,000-Hour Rule. Gladwell quotes neurologist Daniel Levitin: "The emerging picture from (studies of expertise) is that ten thousand hours of practice is required to achieve the level of mastery associated with being a world-class expert—in anything" (40).

Those points in mind, Sam Peckinpah's route to *The Wild Bunch*, overlaid on the postwar development of the Western, may or may not have involved 10,000 hours of practice, but they do offer a near-perfect Gladwellian marriage of placement and timing.

Recall that Peckinpah gained his foothold in the film industry through television, coming to the relatively new medium at a time when the popularity of the TV Western was surging; a genre for which, by virtue of his family history and upbringing, Peckinpah was a natural match.

During the seven years in which Peckinpah served what was, in effect, an apprenticeship in TV, developing first his writing, then later, his directing and producing skills, the big screen Western was going through a pivotal evolutionary period, growing beyond the action/adventure formula which had sustained it for decades to include stories dramatically and morally more complex, exploring darker, increasingly morally ambivalent realms. In a bit of sad synchronicity, because of Peckinpah's dysfunctional upbringing, Peckinpah's background also gave him the creative tools for these emerging forms of the Western feature. Between the memories of bygone days shared with him by Fresno's old-timers and his mother's selling off of the family ranch, Peckinpah understood the sense of loss, of an era's end; the feeling that would underpin the growing number of Death of the West films, and that would haunt so many of his characters and anchor so many of his own films.

The Deadly Companions, with its compact story and simple logistics, provided an ideal transition for Peckinpah to graduate from the small to the big screen. With that experience under his belt, he elevated with *Ride the High Country*; still a small-scale story, but one in which he could more fully test the range of his dramatic palette. But, as gratifying and respected as *High Country* is, it still retains a classical Fordian romanticism, standing as a cross between Peckinpah's go-to melancholy and confrontational realism, and Fordian sentimentality.

For all its flaws, *Major Dundee* is the clearest early expression of a true Peckinpah voice. Its protagonists—the arrogant, self-destructive, pig-headed Dundee, and the equally self-destructive "would-be cavalier" that is his Confederate opposite number—are the quintessential postwar antiheroes, true reflections of the moral confusion and misguided military adventurism that was beginning to engulf the 1960s, closer in nature to the doomed dinosaurs of *The Wild Bunch* than the noble ex-lawmen of *Ride the High Country*. Still, Peckinpah hadn't quite yet grown past the genre's stale traditions, i.e., the, momentum-killing, digressive, and purely obligatory love interest which derails the middle act of the story and from which the last act of the movie must stagger back.

Yet, even as a failure, *Major Dundee*—part of Gladwell's 10,000 hours—pushed Peckinpah's filmmaking evolution forward if, in no other way, in how it confronted him with his then limitations. Besides the above-mentioned storytelling flaw, the film's large-scale logistics were beyond him. Even one of his loyalists—frequent collaborator Jim Silke— would later confess to Peckinpah biographer Marshall Fine, "*Dundee* was a mess. He was lost on *Dundee*" (Fine 91).

And there were still key visual tools over which Peckinpah had yet to develop a command, most clearly evident in some of *Dundee*'s major action sequences. Although the film's climactic battle between Dundee's ragtag command and French cavalry is appropriately both savage and

Five. Sires

thrilling, two other key action scenes are, considering Peckinpah's later reputation as a director of violent action, astoundingly bland: a nighttime ambush of Dundee's troop during a river crossing which cripples his command; and what should be the cathartic turnabout when Dundee sets his own ambush for the Apache raider he and his men have been chasing around Mexico for months, seeming almost perfunctory in its execution (Gaydos S-22).

Peckinpah's subsequent exile from feature directing also served him well. It gave him time to gestate; to reflect on his missteps, to store up ideas and visual concepts (Fine 106, 111). The years he'd spent developing *Villa Rides!* provided him with a storehouse of material on the Mexican Revolution, a key element of *The Wild Bunch* (113). By the time Sam Peckinpah was offered *Bunch*, it was the perfect intersection of his own matured artistic development, and the evolving Western film.

The years away from features did something else for Sam Peckinpah. They made him hungry.

* * *

The Wild Bunch is so closely associated with Sam Peckinpah—probably the film most immediately associated with his name—that it's ironic the filmmaker had nothing to do with the original inception of the story (Patterson). But this was not unusual for Peckinpah.

One of the paradoxes of Peckinpah's career is that despite years of pumping out original scripts for television, he never directed an original feature script of his own. In fact, the only Peckinpah original material to make it to the big screen was *The Glory Guys* and whatever was left of his vastly rewritten screenplays for *One-Eyed Jacks* and *Villa Rides!* Rather, Peckinpah would take over an existing piece of material, or work in a collaborative process with a writer, sometimes credited, sometimes not (Fine 127). Peckinpah acted, then, more the doting adoptive father in his feature work than a birth parent.

It was not always a process that worked. When it did, it could turn out a gem like *Ride the High Country*. When it went off the rails, it led to disaster. On *Pat Garrett & Billy the Kid* (1973), screenwriter Rudy Wurlitzer became so fed up with Peckinpah's incessant and eventually daily calls for changes that, at one point, he complained to the press, "There's *no* script left" (Seydor, *Peckinpah* 190).

In the case of *The Wild Bunch*, the birth dad was Roy N. Sickner who conceived of the story of over-the-hill Western outlaws out for one last

The Wild Bunch

big score as a vehicle for his friend, actor Lee Marvin. Sickner, however, was no writer. In fact, his shared story credit for *The Wild Bunch* would be the only writing credit in his 16-year career in film and TV. By trade, Sickner was a stunt man and occasional bit-part actor and second unit director (he'd actually been part of the stunt crew on *Major Dundee*). Perhaps his most notable on-screen accomplishment was serving as the original Marlborough Man in TV commercials for the cigarette. He was also a hellraiser whose conduct put even Peckinpah's alcohol-fueled outrages to shame. (Sickner's conduct was so over the top that, while working on *Bunch*, Mexican authorities eventually escorted him out of the country and banned him from returning) (Ferrara).

Sickner, who happened to be a friend of Peckinpah's, reached out to Walon Green whom he'd met while doing stunt work on the World War II thriller *Saboteur: Code Name Morituri* (1965), on which Green was a dialogue director (Fine 123; Ferrara). Green himself was hardly a writing heavyweight, having, at the time, never written a produced dramatic work. His total filmography at that point in his career consisted of writing, producing, and directing a handful of one-hour TV nature documentaries, most for a series of specials for *National Geographic.*

Green fleshed out Sickner's story and married it with a long-percolating idea of his own about the horrible way American railroads had treated people as they began to spread through the West (Fine, 122). Green hammered out a screenplay, the spine of which was, said Green, to produce "a Western that was as mean and ugly and brutal as the times, and the only nobility in men was their dedication to each other." Some of Green's influences—and they're clear in the finished film—were historian Barbara Tuchman's book *The Zimmerman Telegram* about Imperial Germany's attempts to create friction between Mexico and the United States during World War I, as well as accounts of the real Wild Bunch, Butch Cassidy's Hole-in-the-Wall Gang.* Green, who'd lived and worked in Mexico for a time, also had great affection for the country. "*The Wild Bunch*," he would later recall, "was partly written as my love letter to Mexico" (Ferrara).

With his penchant for Western authenticity as well as for outsiders and losers, it's easy to see how Peckinpah immediately connected with Green's concept (Seydor, "*The Wild Bunch*"). After Ken Hyman brought

---

*Butch Cassidy's gang was often referred to in the press as "The Wild Bunch." Ironically, *The Wild Bunch* was released just four months before 20th Century–Fox released *Butch Cassidy and the Sundance Kid* (Snider).

FIVE. Sires

Peckinpah onto the project, the director, working with one of his go-to collaborators, Jim Silke, spent six months building on Green's material which was heavy on action but light on character and story, expanding it through rewrites, "layering the characters with backstories, deep-rooted motivations, and a sense of Shakespearian tragedy" (Fine 123; Ferrara; Eggert). Peckinpah also had his storehouse of research he'd done on the Mexican Revolution for *Villa Rides!* to draw on. His contributions were substantial enough that even Green agrees Peckinpah well-earned his co-writer credit (although it took WGA arbitration to decide whose name would come first, and also that Peckinpah did not rate the story credit he claimed, that credit going only to Sickner and Green) (Fine 127, 128).

For all the months of work Sickner and Green and Peckinpah put into the screenplay, it bears keeping in mind that for some filmmakers—and Peckinpah was one of them—a completed screenplay is not necessarily a completed screen story. For some moviemakers, the writing is never finished.

* * *

The function of a screenplay varies from director to director. It can provide a blueprint, or a framework, or only a point of departure, depending on the creative process of the filmmaker (Giannetti 313).

Alfred Hitchcock, for example, was a legendarily meticulous filmmaker (Giannetti 323–325). He always worked from a "locked" screenplay which might even include specific requirements for the story from Hitchcock in terms of wanting a particular setting or action for which he'd envisioned one of his memorable set-pieces (like the chase across the face of Mt. Rushmore in *North by Northwest* [1959]).* (Knudsen, "The Bizarre"). He would then map the film out shot by shot in storyboards to the point where he would sometimes joke he wasn't needed on the set; the crew only had to follow his storyboards (Higham 98; Giannetti 41–43).

One hundred and eighty degrees in the other direction was a filmmaker like Stanley Kubrick. Using his work on *The Shining* (1980) as an example, Kubrick not only ran through a number of screenplay drafts,

---

*A "locked" script isn't carved in stone. It's the version that goes out to production departments and the cast, but revisions can always be added. They will, however, be color-coded to differentiate them from the original pages. There are also any number of films—some quite successful—which went into production without a finished script such as *Casablanca*. It is, however, not anyone's idea of the best way to go into making a feature film.

59

but continued to rework the material all the way through shooting, and then even during the editing process (Knudsen, "How Kubrick").

Peckinpah didn't storyboard, he didn't work from a shot list. In fact, he didn't do much pre-planning at all for particular scenes. According to Gordon Dawson, one of his regular assistants, "You'd be lucky if you knew the day before" what Peckinpah would be shooting (Fine 135). For Peckinpah, the script was no more or less than a guide (88).

He was regularly—and often to the dismay of his crew—improvisational, taking inspiration in the moment. Despite the logistical headaches

Peckinpah's work style was the antithesis of a meticulous preparer like Alfred Hitchcock. Hitchcock didn't deviate from a script once it was "locked," and storyboarded every shot to the point it was joked a crew could shoot one of his films by following the storyboards without ever the director having to be on the set. Peckinpah, on the other hand, sometimes didn't know how he'd shoot a scene until he showed up on the location for filming. Pictured here, a scene from one of Hitchcock's self-admitted favorites, *Shadow of a Doubt* (1943). Left to right: Charles Bates, Henry Travers, Edna May Wonacott, Teresa Wright, Joseph Cotten.

FIVE. Sires

that went with these episodes, in the case of *The Wild Bunch*, they also provided the film with three of its most memorable moments, none of which were in the script (Seydor, "*The Wild Bunch*").

The War of the Ants and Scorpions

The Wild Bunch was already in pre-production, a stage by which a screenplay is, ideally, locked, when Emilio Fernandez, who'd been cast as the corrupt Mexican general Mapache, "remarked [to Peckinpah] that [the story's] characters reminded him of his childhood experiences torturing scorpions on an ant hill" (Eggert). Peckinpah immediately saw the visual and metaphorical potential and included the scene of children pitting an army of ants against struggling scorpions in a walled-in arena made of small sticks.

The ants swarming around the scorpions not only presaged the soon-to-come shoot-out in the main streets of a Texas town where a robbery attempt by the Bunch goes wrong, but even more so the horrific carnage of the movie's finale. The scene also carries a larger, metaphorical weight, ending as it does with the children engulfing all the combatants with burning straw. Like the Bunch, and Mapache, and his equally corrupt army, and the bounty-hunting posse, it doesn't matter who wins; progress, such as it is, will bury them all.

Riding into History ... or Whatever

After the Texas robbery goes bad, the Bunch are on the run. They cross into Mexico and rest in Angel's village, a place already pillaged by Mapache. The Bunch join in with the villagers in a fiesta, and then it's time for them to leave.

The villagers line the road out of town, waving goodbye to the Bunch as they pass. Peckinpah added bits to the scene "one by one until, for him, it was complete": a woman handing Dutch (Ernest Borgnine) a flower, another gifting Lyle Gorch (Warren Oates) with a sombrero, and so on, until a simple ride out of town became a "majestic departure" (Eggert).

Some of the Bunch's passage is shot in slow motion, sunlight coming through the canopy of trees in a gauzy, soft whiteness, campfire smoke drifting through the image, all combining to give the scene a dreamy, ethereal quality. On the soundtrack, several voices are joined in singing the Mexican folk song "La Golondrina." The song is not delivered by a chorus of angelic voices as John Ford was wont to do, but the raw, unvarnished voices and twanging guitar which could very well be these villagers singing to a cheap, maybe even homemade guitar, an authenticity which gives the dreaminess a paradoxical sincerity. The scene ends with a shot of the Bunch literally riding "into the light," a shot Peckinpah repeats at the end of the closing credits.

At that moment during the village interlude, Peckinpah felt the story had reached a turning point. The village passage humanizes these men we've only thus far seen as killers and robbers prone to squabbling among themselves. As Peckinpah himself explained, "If you can ride out with them there and feel it, you can die with them and feel it" (Seydor, "*The Wild Bunch*"). And the exit from the village is, indeed, a turning point. Once the Bunch leave on their way to Agua Verde and Mapache's headquarters, their doom is foreordained.

The passage into the gauzy light, especially in its re-appearance at the end of the film, can be viewed as the Bunch's passing into history, into legend, into eternity, into…? It is an image poetic enough to work as any or all such interpretations and becomes the perfect closing punctuation mark for the film. The Bunch are no more … but will be remembered forever.

For all its import and its flawless integration into the dramatic flow of the story, the exit from the village was one of Peckinpah's on-the-spot inspirations, a scene not in the screenplay, and shot in less than a day (Seydor, "*The Wild Bunch*").

The Gunman's Walk

The long walk to a showdown is as much a Western staple as, well, as the showdown. Yet, the Gunman's Walk in *The Wild Bunch* is particularly memorable, even though it's simply one hundred seconds of four men walking down a dirt street.

And yet, it's not so simple.

The Bunch—Pike (William Holden), and Lyle and Tector Gorch (Ben Johnson)—on the run from the American posse, and humiliated at letting Mapache take and torture one of their own—Angel—rather than take on the general and his 200 men, have retreated to a squalid little whorehouse. Outside the house, Dutch sits sulking.

Five. Sires

Pike reaches a decision. He leaves his whore and turns to Lyle and Tector who are haggling price with their own prostitute, and in one of those moments fans have since and will forever quote, rumbles, "Let's go."

The Gorches look to each other, then Lyle turns back to Pike: "Why not?"

They step outside, out of the gloom of the whorehouse into the bright sun. A look and an exchanged smile between Pike and Dutch, and Dutch is on his feet. They go to their horses for their guns and…

And that's where the screenplay cuts to the hacienda courtyard where Mapache is engaged in a bacchanal. The transition from whorehouse to courtyard is just three lines in the screenplay. But it was during shooting when Peckinpah got his inspiration: "I want to do a walk thing" (Seydor, "*The Wild Bunch*").

Peckinpah wants that moment, that build, that anticipation, because this is not the typical Gunman's Walk to a showdown. There's no way to reasonably interpret the whorehouse scene as other than that the Bunch have collectively made the decision that this will be the end of their story. This is what distinguishes Peckinpah's "walk thing" from the long parade of ritualistic showdown walks which had come in countless Westerns in all the years before. In every other Gunman's Walk, it was always understood one side would walk away victorious, and the other as trade for the local mortician. Peckinpah's Bunch knows their time is over; that, in fact, it may be long past. All they can do is pick their end. This isn't about winning; this is about leaving.

The Wild Bunch's "walk thing" gives the audience time to let that soak in, and to feel the same escalating excitement the Bunch feel walking toward the courtyard, well aware of and looking forward to the hell they're about to let loose.

A simple action, a dense texture, and thought up on the fly by a filmmaker standing in the middle of his location thinking, "I want to do a walk thing."

Unindicted Co-Conspirator

When Ken Hyman tapped Phil Feldman to be producer of *The Wild Bunch*, although Feldman had been in the movie business for almost twenty years, he'd had little production experience. A one-time entertainment lawyer, he'd been a business manager for Seven Arts and had only gained his first—and until *The Wild Bunch*, only—producer's credit when he persuaded the company to back the low-budget *You're a Big Boy Now* (1966) with a young, still-up-and-coming Francis Ford Coppola at the helm.* ("Phil Feldman"; Stafford)

Feldman's relationship with Peckinpah would later disintegrate over cuts made in release prints of *The Wild Bunch*, but up until then, Peckinpah felt he had a creative collaborator in his producer. In a 1969 *Film Quarterly Review*, the director, still in a honeymoon period with Hyman and Feldman, described the working dynamic between the three of them: "[Kenneth Hyman and Phil Feldman are] enormously creative people, and I feel we work together very well. I respect them, and they respect me. They let me do my thing ... and whenever they can, they highlight it, and give me all the help that I could possibly need. They're *damn* good, they're tough, they've got good ideas. And I either have to get a better one, or I use theirs. You don't mind working with people like that, it's a delight (Farber 6).

"If it wasn't for Phil Feldman," Peckinpah regular cast member L.Q. Jones would later say, "I don't think Sam would have made anything of consequence" (Fine 125). Feldman offered advice on characters and dialogue, worked with Peckinpah on casting, and even helped the director improve the integration of the ants vs. scorpion scene into the movie's opening. It was also Feldman's suggestion to, in the closing scenes of the movie, kill off the surviving bounty hunters as they're heading back to Texas off-screen rather than with a planned action sequence. Peckinpah thought this was such a spot-on call that he later sent Feldman a thank-you note, telling the producer he'd been "absolutely correct" (Ferrara).

Perhaps most importantly, Feldman acted as a buffer between his director and Warner Bros.–Seven Arts execs—the kind of people with whom Peckinpah almost instinctively went to war—particularly when the production began to run over budget. Said Peckinpah collaborator Gordon Dawson, "[Phil Feldman] was really a champion for Sam as long as he lasted" (Fine 125).

---

*While Peckinpah's relationship with Feldman soured over the deletions made to Peckinpah's cut of *The Wild Bunch*, Peckinpah's hostility toward his producer was hardly universal. Francis Coppola was so grateful for Feldman's getting him the gig directing *You're a Big Boy Now* that Feldman was one of two producers Coppola thanked by casting them as senators on the committee grilling Michael Corleone (Al Pacino) on the Mafia in *The Godfather: Part II* (1974). The other producer was Roger Corman, who'd given a young Coppola some of his first professional screenwriting and directing jobs.

FIVE. Sires

It Ain't the Motion, It's the Meat

Peckinpah once said, "I want to be able to make Westerns like Kurosawa makes Westerns" (Ferrera). In the case of *The Wild Bunch*, instead, the filmmaker made a Western—epic-sized, episodic, with an ensemble cast—built like a Tolstoy novel.

While there have been books about screenwriting kicking around since 1913, the dam on how-to's on writing movies seemed to break with the publication of Syd Field's *Screenplay: The Foundations of Screenwriting* in 1982, and Robert McKee's STORY seminars which McKee began offering in 1983 and turned into the screenwriting bible *Story: Substance, Structure, Style and the Principles of Screenwriting* in 1997 (*"How to..."*). Since then, hundreds—if not thousands—of books, seminars, instructional videos, workshops, and institutional courses have followed, many, if not most, taking the stance that there are rules or some kind of template, formula (or formulae), recipe, system, etc., to write an effective screenplay. The lingo of all of these instructional platforms has seeped into production company development personnel many of whom have also read the books, or gone to the seminars, etc. It's not unusual for script development sessions to include talk about story beats, character arcs, three-act structure, decisions on "whose story is this?" when the first-to-second act turn needs to take place, how every scene needs to push the narrative forward, and so on.

The Wild Bunch predates that kind of creative standardization, and in this, what the movie shares with so many of the iconic titles of its time— and what makes those iconic movies so damned iconic—is that it doesn't play by any rules other than its own. Sam Peckinpah and Walon Green constructed a story which opens up not along prescribed beats, but in an organic, almost—by today's standards—lackadaisical rhythm. There are a number of scenes today's development execs, with an eye on a young audience which can seem afflicted with a generational case of ADD, would consider unnecessary, digressive wastes. From its construction to its characters to the very nature of its story, *The Wild Bunch* does not chase after an audience, it offers viewers no appeasement. In many ways, it outright *challenges* an audience to connect with it. It could be argued that the movie—again, like most of the memorable movies of its day—is a major, even epic commercial release with the heart of an independent film. Most of what is so *right* about *The Wild Bunch* is what it does "wrong."

There's no greater support for that view than the film's first 50 minutes most of which, by most of the templates and formulae marketed by the how-to's of today, would never have made it into the screenplay's final draft let alone be put on film.

Before we take a close look at those 50 minutes, let's refresh ourselves on the difference between *plot* and *story*. Even though the words are often used interchangeably, in storytelling craft, they actually mean two different things. Plot is *what happens*; the sequence of events and actions we see on the screen. Someone knocks on the door, opens the door, goes into a room—that's plot. Story is what we *don't* see. It's the answer to the question not of what happens, but what's it about? Or to get a little arty about it, what does it all *mean*? What is the significance of our character going into that room? Does it mean he's going forward with some inner decision about his life? Going backward? Facing/avoiding his deepest fears? Plot is the skin; story is the meat underneath (Mesce, "The World's" 352).

The film opens with the Bunch's attempt to rob a railroad office, the robbery turns into an ambush, there's a huge shootout in the main street of the town, some of the Bunch are killed, some escape. Sometime after, the posse which mounted the ambush, led by Deke Thornton (Robert Ryan), who once rode with Pike, leader of the Bunch, start out after the gang, Thornton having made a deal with the railroad to bring in Bunch leader Pike Bishop to avoid a prison stretch of his own.

The Bunch rendezvous on the other side of the Mexican border with another member of the gang, Freddie Sykes (Edmond O'Brien), who has been waiting for them with a change of horses. The Bunch squabble over how to share up the take from the robbery, but it turns out there's nothing to share: the supposed coin stolen from the railroad turns out to be nothing but bags of metal washers: a decoy. Their tempers frayed by the dupe, they squabble again.

That night, Pike and Dutch muse over their next move, and the next day, the Bunch begin drifting south. There's a misstep on the way as they're crossing the desert dunes resulting in most of the gang becoming unhorsed, and the Bunch turn on each other yet again. Thornton's posse, meanwhile, stops at the border river and turns back, trying to anticipate the Bunch's next move. The Bunch take a respite in Angel's village where Angel learns his girlfriend has run off with the corrupt general Mapache. There's a fiesta, and then later, the Bunch leave, heading for Agua Verde, the town where Mapache and his troops are quartered.

FIVE. Sires

In terms of plot "beats," scenes that move the narrative forward, conventional three-act structuring in which the first act is supposed to set the film's plot, there's not a lot to those first 50 minutes after the robbery shoot-out. It would be a stretch to even define that first section of the film as a true Act I. A case can be made that *The Wild Bunch* doesn't really get into forward gear until the Bunch meet up with Mapache and strike a deal for the proverbial Last Big Job. But before that...?

There's no real narrative engine. Yes, the Bunch are being pursued by Thornton's posse, but there doesn't appear to be any great urgency on the part of the Bunch, particularly once they cross into Mexico. There are no *must*s, no *has-to-happen*s, no imperatives. There are, in fact, no major plot points at all pushing the movie forward. The Bunch escape from the robbery, drift south not having anything more than a vague idea of a next move, take a breather at Angel's village, and eventually—over one-third into the movie—wind up in Agua Verde. The first 50 minutes has so little connection to the more driving plot which kicks in once the Bunch meet with Mapache that it stands as less a first act than a prologue.

It's also worth noting that almost an hour in and we know surprisingly little about the characters. We learn that Thornton and Pike and Sykes all rode together at one time, that Bishop escaped a whorehouse ambush which nabbed Thornton, but there are no expository scenes with a major revelation which "explain" any of the major characters or the relationships between them, no attempts to soften them beyond what we've seen or rationalize their behavior. They're not the symbolic free spirits of *Easy Rider*, not the misunderstood young-in-loves of *Bonnie and Clyde*. They are what they are: desperate, aging, down-on-their-luck outlaws, prone to arguing among themselves almost to the point where guns come out, and—as they proved during the opening shootout—ruthless, using civilians as shields and decoys, killing without remorse. And when it seems we are about to perhaps get one revelatory little speech—the night after the shootout, when Pike muses with Dutch about making one last score so he can "back off"—Dutch calls him out with, "Back off to *what*?" and it's clear these men don't even have the dimension of dreams. They are outlaws without much to look back on and nothing to look forward to.

One could argue that in terms of conventional narrative construction, much of that first 50 minutes—including the seven-minutes set in Angel's village—could be cut, or at least seriously truncated, without losing any narrative cohesion. But then it wouldn't be *The Wild Bunch*, because if that first section is short on plot, it is packed to the brim with *story*.

Peckinpah had a penchant for disingenuously presenting himself as a simple soul just trying to make a living; a "whore," he once said, trying to "slip in a few comments on the side" (Champlin, "A Maverick's"; Berman 1-B). *The Wild Bunch* he one time described with outrageous understatement as "a simple story…. *The Wild Bunch* is simply what happens when killers go to Mexico" (Seydor, "*The Wild Bunch*"). But there is nothing simple about what Peckinpah puts into place beyond what we see on the screen.

It is probably more appropriate to think of *The Wild Bunch* less in terms of theatrical acts than as an epic novel whose episodes occasionally move the plot forward, but which just as often are about creating a rich, enveloping universe. According to the film's soundtrack composer, Jerry Fielding, *The Wild Bunch* was "a love affair on Sam's part with the ambience of the time and the place, the real estate. *That* was what that picture was about. It was not about gunshots and open wounds and children getting shot and blowing to shreds" (Seydor, "*The Wild Bunch*").

In Peckinpah's own words: "It's a very uncompromising film. The language, the action, the details, the lives of these people are as I imagine they were. We tried to recreate an environment, an era" (Seydor, "*The Wild Bunch*").

Those first 50 minutes bring home—in action, dialogue, and a developing sensibility of—men who have outlived their time. "We've got to start thinking beyond our guns," Pike says after the botched robbery. "Those days are closing fast." But, indeed, they've already closed.

In these brutal, ruthless men, we also see the difference between them and the posse of carrion birds led by Thornton, and the frighteningly amoral 20th century in the body of Harrigan (Albert Dekker), Thornton's railroad handler. Under pressure, there is a cool professionalism in the Bunch we see in no one else around them; not the posse, not Mapache's mob/army, not Harrigan. The Bunch may squabble and fight, they may even be facing off with each other as they reach for their guns, but it takes only Pike's "I either lead this bunch or I end it right now" to bring the gang back in line.

There is, in fact, for this motley little group of survivors of the close of the 19th century, no worse punishment then to be iced out of the circle of—to use a cliché—real men. After the fall in the dunes when the Bunch, again, begin to turn on each other, it's up to Pike, again, to

Five. Sires

remind them of the code differentiating them from nearly everybody else we see in their universe: "When you side with a man, you stay with him! And if you can't do that, you're like some animal, you're finished! *We're* finished! *All* of us!" Later, in Angel's village, when Angel threatens to become obsessed with the loss of his girl, Pike warns him: "Either you learn to live with it, or we'll leave you here." And, apparently, that's threat enough as Angel responds, "I go with you, *Jefe*."

For all their flaws and frankly frightening capabilities, there's a dignity to the Bunch, even a nobility apparent nowhere else in the universe Peckinpah and Green created. Says Thornton later in the movie, fed up with the "egg-sucking, chicken-stealing gutter trash" who comprise his posse, "We're after *men*, and I wish to God I was with them."

When Warner Bros.-Seven Arts had first become interested in the project, they saw in Walon Green's original script and Roy Sickner's idea of the film as a vehicle for Lee Marvin the kind of Marvin-starring actioner like *The Professionals* and *The Dirty Dozen*. Reworked by Sam Peckinpah, *The Wild Bunch* was not, as he too glibly said, the simple story of killers going to Mexico, but the story of men, a certain breed of men, a world of them, crushed under the weight of a new age that had no place for them.

Six

Peckinpah's Bunch

> *"You thieves, renegades, deserters, you gentlemen of the South. I want some volunteers.... I need horse soldiers—men who can ride, men who can shoot.*
> *In return, I promise you nothing ... saddle sores, short rations, maybe a bullet in your belly ... and free air to breathe, fair share of tobacco, quarter pay ... and my good will..."*
> —Dundee (Charlton Heston) in *Major Dundee*

Until a director says, "Roll 'em!" a screenplay is just words on a page. It is only at the director's command that the words become a movie. British director Alexander Mackendrick, famed for his work on the Ealing Studio comedies of the 1950s as well as the acrid urban drama *Sweet Smell of Success* (1957), would diagram out the function of a film's director for the students at the California Institute of the Arts (Mackendrick was the founding dean) as "a huge spider web of people" with the director at its center (Buford 43). With a screenplay in hand, Sam Peckinpah and Phil Feldman now had to build *The Wild Bunch*'s creative web.

Peckinpah *had* to know what the professional stakes were for him with *The Wild Bunch*. It was not only his ticket back from big screen oblivion, but with his 0-for-3 box office record and toxic reputation, it could very well be his last and only shot at a return.

The Eye in the Hole

At the time Peckinpah turned to cinematographer Lucien Ballard to shoot *The Wild Bunch*, Ballard was already well on his way to being ranked as one of Hollywood's all-time cinematographic greats. By then, his career was into its fourth decade, and included work ranging from

Six. Peckinpah's Bunch

comedy shorts with The Three Stooges and Charlie Chase to the films of Josef von Sternberg and a young Stanley Kubrick, as well as an Oscar nomination for his black & white work on *The Caretakers* (1963) (Gomery).

The two men already had a productive working relationship in place. Years earlier, Peckinpah had tapped Ballard to shoot several episodes of *The Westerner*, and went back to him for *Ride the High Country*, a film Ballard dressed in elegiac autumnal colors appropriate for a story about men past their prime; a look he would return to but on a much larger canvas in *True Grit*, released the same year as *The Wild Bunch* (Collins). He had demonstrated an affinity for the wide screen making his a perfect eye for Westerns; stories set against the dwarfing majesty of the plains and mountains of the West which, in itself, became something of an explanation for the tough-hided characters of *Nevada Smith* (1966), *Hour of the Gun*, *Will Penny*, and, of course, *Ride the High Country*. Throughout his career, Ballard believed in utilizing the entire wide screen frame, resisting the growing trend in the 1960s-70s of centering action in the frame to accommodate a film's eventual sale to television where TV's squarish proscenium could cut off as much as one-third of a wide screen image (Hopwood, "Lucien"). An archetypal Ballardesque image from *The Wild Bunch*: Deke Thornton leading his posse across the scrubland at a gallop toward the camera, the image compressed by a long lens into iconography, the horsemen riding side by side in a wall-to-wall image of pounding hooves, men tall in their saddles, clouds of dust rising behind them.

Think of what Ballard did with the Gunman's Walk in *The Wild Bunch*, and compare it to a somewhat similar sequence he shot for John Sturges' *Hour of the Gun* released just two years before.

Hour of the Gun opens with the three Earp brothers and Doc Holliday on a Gunman's Walk to the OK Corral. Not to take anything away from the sequence (which is less than half the length of *The Wild Bunch*'s "walk thing"), but it is the familiar, ritualistic Gunman's Walk; stoic lawmen moving along deserted streets to a showdown. Ballard shoots most of the walk in a single shot, the camera off to one side profiling the foursome at an angle.

The Gunman's Walk in *The Wild Bunch* is covered by several shots, but the "anchoring" image—the shot Peckinpah keeps cutting back to—is a face-on shot of the foursome, the camera set far back shooting through a long lens. Instead of a walk down empty streets, as happened with the departure from Angel's village Peckinpah and his crew layered in a variety of elements to fill the frame and give it texture: drunken soldiers warbling their way through "El Corrido de Santa Amalia," other troopers milling about, soldiers and civilians on the sidelines curious/puzzled over the *gringos* marching determinedly toward Mapache's hacienda. The shallow plain of focus resulting from the long lens compression gives the Bunch a certain solidity the Mexican soldiers drifting in and out of the frame in front and behind them don't have. The soldiers don't have the substance—the *steel*—these four men cutting through them do.

There's the visual discipline of the opening. Ballard has the Bunch enter the Texas town of Starbuck moving left to right, and in every shot of the opening they continue to move left to right; a "psychologically natural" movement which tends to put the viewer at ease (Giannetti 96). It is only after the Bunch, now in the railroad office, have discovered that an ambush is waiting for them out on the street and plan on using a parade of temperance marchers to cover their escape that Ballard changes movement direction; when the parade reaches the railroad office, it makes a sharp turn going from left to right to a subtly unsettling right to left (97). When Pike shoves a railroad employee out into the street to draw the posse's fire, Ballard films the parade marchers waist high moving through the frame right to left while two of the members of the band turn to look over their shoulders (left to right) at the sound of the railroad employee crashing through a porch railing; a jumble of directions psychologically ratcheting up tension just before the Bunch open fire.

Besides his great eye, in Ballard Peckinpah knew he had a sharp problem-solver. On *Ride the High Country*, Ballard had come up with a close-up of Joel McCrea so well composed it drew the attention of film critic Leonard Maltin. But, according to Ballard, the shot may have been less about creative iconography then "because we couldn't show the water towers ... at the Metro lot" (Fine 73).

Peckinpah worked out with Ballard the color palette he wanted for *The Wild Bunch*. "Sam and I ran everything we could find on Mexico around 1913," Ballard later recalled (Fine 124). Most of the film is shot in "dusty reds and golds and browns"; a landscape beaten tired and dry by the sun, by a revolution without end, and stripped clean of anything of value by professional pillagers like Mapache (Ebert). In marked contrast, the refreshing interlude at Angel's village is shot amidst rich,

Six. Peckinpah's Bunch

dark greenery—an island of vitality in a sea of sparse scrub and dust—and the Bunch's exit as a transition from the aliveness of green into a gauzy, ethereal light. And then there is the whorehouse scene just before the Gunman's Walk; draped in dark, morose shadows, William Holden's "Let's go" close-up nearly a repeat of the half-light/half-black close-up which climaxes the opening credit sequence—"If they move, kill 'em"—each man's face in the whorehouse scene broken up by light and dark, only to become whole when they pass outside into the bright, unifying light of the sun.

Peckinpah also had a collaborator in Ballard, someone with whom there could be a give-and-go of creative ideas to bring an unplanned, deeper texture to a scene. In his biography of Peckinpah, *Bloody Sam*, Marshall Fine gives the example of the scene where the Bunch are sitting with Mapache and his German advisors planning the Bunch's raid on a U.S. Army train and its cargo of guns. Ballard suggested punching up the scene he feared might be visually dull by shooting it at night. Peckinpah came back with filling the set with candles and running the funeral procession of Angel's girlfriend (Angel had killed her that afternoon) through the middle of the scene (136). The collaboration of the two men turned a perfunctory expository conversation into a near-Fellini-esque grotesque.

Of course the most critical role Ballard played was in working with Peckinpah on how to shoot what were then groundbreaking action sequences.

Like everyone else in Hollywood, Peckinpah had been impressed with what director Arthur Penn had done with the slow-motion machine gun ambush at the finale of *Bonnie and Clyde*. Penn had used four cameras running at different speeds to capture the then stunning images, cutting between slow and regular motion to capture what the director described as "the spastic lyricism" of the fugitive couple's death throes. If that was the new bar for screen violence, then Peckinpah had it in mind to top it: "We're going to bury *Bonnie and Clyde*" (Greenberg 26). This wasn't just a morbid competitiveness on Peckinpah's part. Peckinpah, with his usual disingenuousness, may have said, "I wasn't trying to make an epic…. I was trying to make a few comments on violence and the people who live by violence," but, as usual, he had more on his mind (Ferrara).

During Peckinpah's time in the Marines, while he never saw combat, he had been stationed in China during a time of violent unrest between the Communist forces under Mao Tse-Tung and the ruling nationalists under Chiang Kai-shek. During his service in China, Peckinpah found himself riding on a troop train which came under Communist fire. In *Bloody Sam*, Marshall Fine says Peckinpah would change his version of the incident many times, but it seems clear the young Marine saw *something* of the horror of the moment of violent death; the way it bent and distorted time, turning it into "one of the longest split seconds of my life" (Fine 23). But how to convey that?

Both Penn and Peckinpah had studied Akira Kurosawa's use of slow motion in *Seven Samurai*, Kurosawa using the device to "dignify and solemnize" a swordsman's death, giving it the same kind of macabre ballet-like grace Penn had used for his climax of *Bonnie and Clyde* (Giannetti 128–129; Greenberg 26). Walon Green was also a fan of Kurosawa's film and had written the use of slow motion for the action sequences into his draft, expecting, however, they would be ignored (Fine 144–145).

By the time Peckinpah was shooting *The Wild Bunch*, a number of American films had experimented with slow motion violence: Don Siegel's crime thriller *The Killers* (1964), John Derek's World War II flick *Once Before I Die* (1965), John Boorman's *Point Blank*, and, of course, *Bonnie and Clyde*.* George Roy Hill, who was shooting *Butch Cassidy and the Sundance Kid* at roughly the same time Peckinpah was working on *The Wild Bunch*, when filming a pivotal scene where Butch (Paul Newman) has to kill for the first time, feared that even by 1969, it had "become a cliché to shoot death in that manner" which, if Peckinpah shared the same concern, only raised the bar higher on how to get the impact of violence he wanted (Crawford).

At least in part, Peckinpah's approach was inspired by the way NFL Films did its football coverage, using multiple cameras running at different speeds to break down the chaos on the field into individualized moments of sometimes surprising grace (Roessing 72). The approach he worked out with Ballard, then, was to film a specific piece of action with as many as six cameras all running at different speeds: 24, 30, 48, 60, 90, and 120 frames-per-second (Eggert).

This would obviously produce massive amounts of footage. Sculpting

---

*The Killers, directed by Peckinpah's early mentor Don Siegel, was made for television, but the violence—which included two assassins emptying their pistols into John Cassavetes in slow motion—was deemed too violent for TV and was released as a theatrical instead (Baxter 229).

Six. Peckinpah's Bunch

all that footage into something which would have the effect Peckinpah wanted required yet another collaborator.

The Cutter

While at the time of *The Wild Bunch* Lucien Ballard's career was reaching its peak, Lou Lombardo's career as an editor had barely begun.

Lombardo had been slowly working his way through the industry since the early 1950s when he'd been a cameraman for Robert Altman when Altman was making industrial films in Kansas City. After moving to Los Angeles, Lombardo served as a cameraman for Republic Pictures, then decided to switch career paths to editing and served an eight-year editing apprenticeship at Revue Studios doing uncredited work. By then a working TV director, Altman came back to Lombardo to tap him to edit a TV pilot for him, and that work led to gigs on several low-budget films (*The Incredible Sex Revolution* [1965]; *The Name of the Game Is Kill!* [1968]) and on the short-lived TV series *The Felony Squad*. It was a sequence he'd cut for an episode of the latter which landed him the job on *The Wild Bunch* (LoBrutto 125–126).

Lombardo had been working as an assistant cameraman for Peckinpah on *Noon Wine* and the two struck up a relationship. Lombardo had expressed an interest in cutting features (Fine 124–125). When Peckinpah got the job on *The Wild Bunch*, he remembered Lombardo and asked him for a sample of material he'd edited. Lombardo sent Peckinpah a sequence from *The Felony Squad* episode "My Mommy Got Lost," in which Joe Don Baker goes down in a shoot-out with police. According to Lombardo: "I had to manufacture slow motion, because they didn't shoot slow motion in television.... I printed every frame three times and created slow motion. I intercut [Baker] being shot, falling, this guy shooting, that guy running, Baker falling. Sam and Phil Feldman ... said, 'You've got the job ... we'll use that kind of thing'" (LoBrutto 127).

Lombardo's cameraman days held him in good stead in cutting the film's stunning action sequences as he would actually be behind the camera on the film's second unit. Lombardo would shoot his footage with it already in mind how he would cut it. "I sketched it out and then Sam ... told me how to paint it," making this—as it was with Lucien Ballard—another give-and-go collaboration (Fine 145).

The Wild Bunch

Lombardo's TV background also served the editor well. The speed required to cut a weekly TV series was what Lombardo, editing even as Peckinpah was filming, needed to keep up with the skeins of footage the director was producing with his multiple camera set-ups (Fine 139). A representative example of how the skills of this triumvirate came together so seamlessly in *The Wild Bunch* occurs during the opening shoot-out. All of the movie's major action sequences have an elegant architecture to them; moments of chaos which build to peaks where the action becomes dominated by a certain single action which monopolizes the scene for a few seconds, and then back to the chaos. Put another way, the action scenes are not minutes of wall-to-wall gunplay, but built with rises and falls, each rise higher than the one before.

One of the most memorable of those peak moments occurs in the opening shootout about 2:54 after William Holden shoves a railroad employee into the street. The sequence runs:

> Long shot of two small children huddled together watching the battle in the street;
> Medium shot of Thornton taking a shot from a rooftop;
> Tracking shot of one of the Bunch being hit, falling from his horse and being dragged for a distance;
> Close-up on the two children;
> Two shots of Dutch galloping down the street and scooping up the money-stuffed saddlebags dropped by the wounded man;
> Repeat close-up on the two children, beginning a zoom in to a closer shot;
> Full body shot of one of the rooftop posse (Strother Martin) taking a shot;
> Slow motion long shot of the horse dragging the wounded member of the Bunch being hit and going down;
> Repeat close-up on the two children;
> From the same angle as the horse going down, still in slow motion, a zoom in as the wounded man is getting to his feet;
> Repeat close-up of the children;
> Same slow motion angle of wounded man still getting to his feet;
> Close-up on Strother Martin taking another shot;
> Slow motion shot of the wounded Bunch member being hit;
> Cut to a different angle of the same bullet strike but in regular motion, capturing his violent spinning under the impact;
> Repeat close-up of the two children;
> Struck man still twirling in slow motion;
> Close-up of a second posse member (L.Q. Jones) taking a shot;
> Bunch member takes this second hit in regular motion;
> Long shot, man falls in slow motion;
> Repeat close-up of children, one finally turns away from the violence in the street;
> Return to slow motion shot of falling man finally hitting the ground.

The sequence involves 15 different camera set-ups, 21 cuts with a number of shots running less than a second and none longer than 2.9 seconds, a mix of regular and slow motion, all within the span of just 23 seconds (the longest single sequence in the shootout). It's a brilliantly shot and edited moment bringing what is already a brutally violent scene to an aesthetic and visceral crescendo.

There was still another key member of the creative team who anchored, for the ear, what Peckinpah, Ballard, and Lombardo were doing for the eye.

Comeback Twins

When Sam Peckinpah reached out to Jerry Fielding to do the music for his hoped-for comeback picture, Fielding was on a bit of a comeback trail himself.

Fielding had been quite the tyro in his early days, doing the arrangements for theatrical pit bands when he was still a teenager in the 1930s, and by the 1940s, he was arranging for major swing stars like Tommy Dorsey and Kay Kyser (Ankeny). In the late 1940s, he made the move to television as band leader for a summer replacement show hosted by Jack Paar. A friend's recommendation got him the job doing the music for a children's album featuring Groucho Marx, which led to Marx hiring him to head up the band for Marx's hit game show, *You Bet Your Life*. Next to working for Tommy Dorsey, doing game show fanfares was comparatively easy work, but being associated with a TV hit significantly raised his industry profile, and by the early 1950s, Fielding's career was "roaring" with the composer/conductor juggling five radio shows and TV work (Marx 48, 84).

Highly politically and socially aware, Fielding was, by his own description, a "loudmouthed crusader," and during the height of the McCarthy era's anti-Communist hysteria, this put him on the wrong side of the House Un-American Activities Committee. He consequently lost his broadcast gigs, though he still kept busy for the rest of the decade recording and as music director for Las Vegas shows. Still, it did seem, at the time, that Fielding's Hollywood career was over (Ankeny).

On something of a blacklist-busting streak, director Otto Preminger, who had hired blacklisted writer Dalton Trumbo for his grand-scale

Exodus, at Trumbo's urging brought Fielding on to score his equally grand D.C. political drama, *Advise and Consent* (1962), Fielding's first feature score. That was all it took to make Fielding Hollywood hirable again (Ankeny).*

Well, sort of.

Fielding worked steadily after *Advise and Consent*, but only in television, handling music chores on a dizzying variety of TV shows, among them private eyes series' *77 Sunset Strip* and *Mannix*, sitcoms *McHale's Navy* and *Hogan's Heroes*, Western drama *Shane*, adventure series *Tarzan*, espionage series *Mission: Impossible*, and classic sci fier *Star Trek*. It was while toiling away in TV that Fielding crossed paths with Peckinpah when the director hired him to do the music for *Noon Wine*. Despite both men being equally hard-headed and argumentative, the two became friends, and when it came time to hire a composer for *The Wild Bunch*, Peckinpah turned to Fielding. Phil Feldman wanted a then young and up-and-coming Lalo Schifrin who had recently scored Warner Bros.-Seven Arts' *Cool Hand Luke* (1967), for which he'd been nominated for an Oscar, and *Bullitt*. But Peckinpah lobbied for and won the job for Fielding, even though it would be only the composer's second major film score (Fine 146).

While the Peckinpah/Fielding relationship could often be combative, as with Peckinpah's collaborations with Lucien Ballard and Lou Lombardo, the director and the composer, however testily, brought out the best in each other (146).

For *The Wild Bunch*, "Fielding spent time in Mexico, soaking up the salient flavors of the land and its people" (Quantrill). The movie's score is laced throughout with a feel for the country, whether it's in the flavoring of Fielding's orchestrations, as in a scene where the Gorch brothers are cavorting with a trio of whores in Mapache's wine cellar, or more directly in Fielding's use of era-appropriate Mexican folk tunes, like the corrido "La Adelita" which Angel sings to some children at the Bunch's camp after the robbery gone wrong in Starbuck, or more memorably, the farewell song "La Golondrina," which marks the Bunch's exit from

---

*The claim for who "broke" the Hollywood blacklist has long been a muddied one between Kirk Douglas, who'd hired Dalton Trumbo for *Spartacus* (1960), and Otto Preminger who'd used Trumbo on *Exodus*. According to Trumbo's family, the chronology runs something like this: In defiance of the blacklist, Preminger publicly announces he's hiring Trumbo for *Exodus* before Douglas makes it public he'll be using Trumbo on *Spartacus*, but *Spartacus* gives Trumbo his first on-screen writing credit since being blacklisted by being released in October of 1960, with *Exodus* following in December (Trumbo).

Six. Peckinpah's Bunch

Angel's village, and which Fielding brings back as an orchestral during the closing credits (Takis).

Fielding offers a rainbow of other musical colors as well: the "rinky dink" sound underscoring the whorehouse flashback showing Thornton's capture while Pike escapes; the full-out excitement of the Bunch's attack on an Army train and their escape from Thornton's posse; the dirge-like track which follows Pike, after the Bunch's horses have tumbled down a dune and Pike has had to squelch yet another almost-split in the group, as he manages to remount his horse despite having lost a stirrup, and rides off slope-shouldered and fatigued over the desert dunes (Takis).

In a uniformly excellent score, there are still moments that stand out: "I felt the task of the score to this movie was at the beginning," Jerry Fielding once told an interviewer (Takis). Visually, the opening of the movie is innocuous; a squad of soldiers ride into the Texas town of Starbuck. Anchoring the opening music is an insistent drum beat; "it's in 11/8 time and has one beat missing from the sort of march tempo the audience thinks it's hearing." The slightly off-rhythm rhythm creates a tension, an uneasiness under innocent visuals (Quantrill). Fielding takes the tension up still another notch during the opening credits which involve periodically freezing the image into a harsh black and white chiaroscuro to background the credits. One of the freezes takes place as the Bunch are passing a temperance meeting, stopping the action in the middle of a sentence by the town's mayor (Dub Taylor) who's leading the gathering. The image freezes and Fielding's strings hold a drawn-out note, just as frozen as the picture on the screen ... and then eases off when the action resumes. Fielding finally breaks his uneven rhythm when the Bunch enter the railroad office, start corralling employees and customers, the music transforming into "a wild orchestral trill and a hatchet-like descending tritone." A pause, close-up of William Holden—"If they move, kill 'em!"—and then "a solitary E-minor chord (with added second) splashes against Sam Peckinpah's director credit" (Takis).

Later in the opening scene, as the Bunch prepare to make their escape, waiting for the temperance marchers to pass their way and provide cover, the marchers sing the hymn "Shall We Gather at the River" along with their small marching band while Fielding—in a move of exquisitely precise subtlety—introduces against it a low ominous thrum, at first barely audible, almost sensed rather than heard. The band and singers draw closer, growing in volume, and so does Fielding's low, steady thrum, over which Peckinpah than lays an accelerating heartbeat. It is a powerful meshing of soundtrack, editing, camerawork.

Fielding later brings back that 11/8 rhythm during the Gunman's Walk, at first subservient to the drunken Mapache soldiers warbling their way through "El Corrido de Santa Amalia," then growing in volume as the Bunch draw closer to the hacienda square where a sodden Mapache is presiding over the torture of Angel, then eventually dominating the soldiers' singing, finally completely replacing it by the time the Bunch reach the square.

And then there is perhaps one of the loveliest moments in the score. The final shootout is over, Thornton and his bounty hunters arrive at the body-strewn square. Thornton sees the body of his old friend on the hacienda porch, and before the bounty hunters, who are already stripping the dead for booty, see him, Thornton goes to Pike and retrieves Pike's revolver; the one gun he never drew during the final shootout. Lucien Ballard gives us a close-up of the undrawn pistol, over Fielding's strings an accordion quietly draws out themes of memory, nostalgia, loss, then the strings take over, lilting, as Thornton retrieves the pistol to keep it from the posse.

Fielding's thinking behind that gentle, melancholic moment and how he reflected it in his scoring: "Sam's message in that picture, while it was very strongly the depiction of the horrors as they really were … there was a much more important … priority as far as he was concerned, as far as *I* was concerned which had to do with the relationship between two men, which was actually a right-down love affair, not a dirty one but a real one" (Seydor, "*The Wild Bunch*").

The Bunch

Roy Sickner had conceived of *The Wild Bunch* as a vehicle for his friend Lee Marvin. With Marvin on a hot streak of tough-guy roles since winning a Supporting Actor Oscar for the comedy Western *Cat Ballou* (1965), that's what appealed to Ken Hyman about the project as well. Whatever vision Marvin may have had of the project, it was eclipsed by what was then considered a monstrously fat $1 million offer to star in the Western musical *Paint Your Wagon* (1969); a

Six. Peckinpah's Bunch

testament to his soaring bankability.* With Marvin off to croon in the film adaptation of the Lerner and Loewe musical, Peckinpah and Feldman then looked at James Stewart, Peckinpah's *Major Dundee* star Charlton Heston, Gregory Peck, Sterling Hayden, Richard Boone, and Robert Mitchum before landing William Holden (Fine 124; "*The Wild Bunch:* Trivia"). Remembering the caustic, cynical, yet engaging characters Holden had played in movies like *The Bridge on the River Kwai* (1957) and *Stalag 17* (1953), Peckinpah judged Holden as actually a better choice than Marvin to make a statement as Bunch leader Pike Bishop (Ferrara).

At the peak of his career in the 1950s, Holden had been that priceless Hollywood commodity; sexy, handsome, and talented. Not for nothing were the publicity materials for his 1955 hit *Picnic* built around his bare torso, and not for nothing had he won the Academy Award for Best Actor for *Stalag 17*; he was, as they like to say in the business, the complete package. But by the mid–1960s, the glamour roles were no longer coming his way. Not only was he hitting middle age, but years of heavy drinking had taken a toll and he looked older than the fifty years he was carrying by the time Peckinpah cast him. On *Ride the High Country*, Peckinpah had used actors who carried with them echoes of their earlier career. Similarly, Holden—like Pike Bishop—authentically carried with him the air of someone who knew their peak years were behind them (Eggert).

Peckinpah/Holden was not always a smooth working relationship. Holden couldn't abide the demeaning tirades the director often inflicted on non-star actors and crew members. More than once, Holden threatened to walk off the picture if Peckinpah didn't rein in his darker impulses (Fine 131, 134).

They also quarreled over an aspect of the Bishop character. Peckinpah wanted Holden to wear a mustache which looked not unlike Peckinpah's own. Holden, never having done a movie with facial hair, responded with "Like hell I will!" but, in time, Peckinpah finally wore the actor down (Weddle 45–46).

The Peckinpah-esque mustache was not the only Peckinpah trait Holden acquired. During the shoot, as Holden began to divine what

---

*Lee Marvin would've been better served taking *The Wild Bunch*'s smaller paycheck. Although *Paint Your Wagon*, released the same year as *Bunch*, was a major earner, budget overruns and marketing costs offset the box office, and reviews—which targeted what an ill-fit Marvin and co-star Clint Eastwood made as singing leads—were universally bad.

Robert Ryan (left), with William Holden, on location on one of those lucky days when Peckinpah didn't have Ryan idling about unused but in costume.

his director wanted from him, the director's daughter, Sharon, noticed Holden was even picking up some of the physicality of her father. Peckinpah, one of Hollywood's legendary mavericks, saw himself, at least to some degree, reflected in outlaw Pike Bishop ... and Holden evidently saw it, too (Eggert; Seydor, "*The Wild Bunch*"). Editor Lou Lombardo would later say of Holden's performance, "He was playing Sam. He was running the Bunch like Sam ran the crew" (Fine 132).

* * *

As the old friend arm-twisted into hunting down the man he used to side with, Peckinpah looked first at *Major Dundee* co-star Richard Harris, then offered it to Brian Keith who had starred in Peckinpah's TV series *The Westerner* as well as his first feature, *The Deadly Companions*, but Keith declined. Other actors considered for the role: Henry Fonda, Glenn Ford, Van Heflin, Arthur Kennedy, and Ben Johnson (who would

Six. Peckinpah's Bunch

eventually land the role of Tector Gorch). Peckinpah settled on Robert Ryan after seeing his performance in *The Dirty Dozen* ("*The Wild Bunch:* Trivia"). Although never a star of the magnitude of Holden, Ryan had been a workhorse for the RKO studio in the late 1940s–1950s, bouncing between leads and co-starring roles, but by the mid–1950s, his career seemed to have hit a wall and thereafter he was mainly playing supporting roles specializing in an "aura of doomed regret" (Burr). Like Holden, Ryan had aged prematurely (he would die of lung cancer at age 63 only three years after the release of *The Wild Bunch*) giving him just the right shade of soul-sickness and world-weariness befitting a man who hates himself as much as he hates the railroad executive who has suborned him—the very definition of "doomed regret."*

There were times when Peckinpah rubbed Ryan the wrong way, too. Because of Peckinpah's improvisational method of shooting, Ryan was often idled, standing by in costume but never knowing when—or if—he was going to be used. When Peckinpah forbade Ryan from leaving the set for several days to work on Robert Kennedy's presidential campaign and then didn't use him, Ryan—a former collegiate boxer—threatened to "knock your teeth in" if Peckinpah ever spoke to him outside of filming (Fine 131).

Peckinpah, who could be petty and vindictive—and pettily vindictive—got his revenge on Ryan for what he felt was the actor's constant grousing. During the opening credits, most of the other principal actors got their freeze frame credits either along with their own close-ups, or close-ups of the children gathered around the scorpions/ants battle. But for Ryan's credit, Peckinpah laid it over a freeze frame of the asses of several horses ("*The Wild Bunch:* Trivia").

* * *

For the part of Dutch Engstrom, Pike Bishop's second-in-command—a part originally conceived as that of a younger man—Peckinpah first looked at Charles Bronson, Jim Brown, Alex Cord, Robert Culp, Sammy Davis, Jr., Richard Jaeckel, Steve McQueen, and George Peppard before

---

*Not to take anything away from Robert Ryan's excellent performance as Thornton, but one wonders what additional texture might've been added to the Bishop/Thornton arc if one of Peckinpah's earlier considerations—Glenn Ford—had been cast in the role. Ford and William Holden had met in the 1940s when Columbia chief Harry Cohn put both actors under contract with the idea of playing them off against each other. The two frustrated Cohn's designs by becoming close friends and remained so until Holden's death in 1981 ("Glenn Ford").

Ernest Borgnine indulging the attention of a young fan during the filming of *The Wild Bunch*.

casting then 52-year-old Ernest Borgnine ("*The Wild Bunch:* Trivia"; Axmaker). Never a star but an industry stalwart, by the time of *The Wild Bunch* Borgnine had spent nearly 20 years effortlessly gliding between the big and small screen, supporting and lead parts, his roles ranging from hissable villains to the slapstick comedy of his hit TV series *McHale's Navy*, to winning a Best Actor Oscar for the film adaptation of Paddy Chayefsky's TV romantic drama *Marty* (1955). Peckinpah had initially been reluctant to cast Borgnine, afraid that echoes of the silliness of *McHale's Navy* would undercut the actor's credibility as rough/tough Dutch, but evidently after seeing him in *The Dirty Dozen*, he thought the actor could pull off the part ("*The Wild Bunch:* Trivia"). It would be that combination of what Borgnine had brought to his more villainous portrayals (think of the sadistic bully of *Bad Day at Black Rock* [1955]) and an innate likability which males the character work as Pike's loyal #2 (Eggert).

Six. Peckinpah's Bunch

Peckinpah managed to get on Borgnine's bad side as well when he refused to do anything about the choking dust kicked up on the roads leading to the film location about which Borgnine regularly complained. One day, Borgnine had his car wait by the side of the road until Peckinpah drove by, and when Peckinpah stopped to ask what was going on, Borgnine told the director to have the road watered "or I'm going to beat the shit out of you" (Fine 131). Peckinpah could not have had any doubts that the burly actor was tough enough to follow through on the threat; Borgnine limped through most of the *Bunch* shoot in a walking cast having broken his foot on his previous film, *The Split* (1968) (Snider).

* * *

Having considered Walter Brennan, Andy Clyde, Lee J. Cobb, William Demarest, Paul Fix, and his *Noon Wine* star Jason Robards for the role of old Freddie Sykes, a character who had ridden with Pike Bishop and Deke Thornton during headier days, Peckinpah finally went with Edmond O'Brien ("*The Wild Bunch:* Trivia"). Like the rest of the principals in the cast, O'Brien's leading man days were long behind him.

Although he'd been working in films since 1939, O'Brien's career had lit up after returning from military service during World War II with major roles in classic *film noirs* like *White Heat* (1949) and *D.O.A.* (1950). But by the mid–1950s, as he began putting on weight, he was increasingly cast in supporting character parts although typically to critical praise. He earned a Supporting Actor Oscar for his work in *The Barefoot Contessa* (1954), and another Oscar nod for his role in the tense political drama *Seven Days in May* ("Edmond").

A heavy drinker, he began suffering a variety of health problems as early as the 1950s. By the time he was cast in *The Wild Bunch*, cataracts, ill health, the toll of years of drinking had him looking considerably older than 53, but perfect for the part of Sykes, a dinosaur among dinosaurs (Eggert).

There was one point, however, where Peckinpah must have wondered if he'd made a mistake in casting O'Brien. At a pre-shooting table read of the script, O'Brien read his part flatly, causing Peckinpah to ask, "Eddie, is that the way you're going to do it? Let me see something," at which O'Brien went into full Freddie Sykes "They? Who the hell is ... *they*?" mode, leaving Peckinpah more than satisfied (Word, "A Word on Westerns: 'Kiss...'").

* * *

Most of the supporting cast were actors with whom Peckinpah had worked in the past; he knew what he could get out of them, and they understood the director's opaque, on-the-fly work process (Francis).

Filling out the Bunch were Ben Johnson and Warren Oates as Tector and Lyle Gorch, respectively.

When it came to Western authenticity, Johnson was hard to beat. A one-time rodeo champion, Johnson had gotten into the movies first as a horse-wrangler and stuntman. He later became one of John Ford's stock company of supporting actors, his leathery face looking as natural a part of the Western landscape as the buttes and plains of Monument Valley, a favored Ford location (Parkinson 146). Fittingly, as Ford's era closed and Peckinpah's began, beginning with *Major Dundee* Johnson became one of Peckinpah's stock company.

Oates had been a favorite of Peckinpah back to the director's TV days, and the director went on to cast him in *Ride the High Country* and *Major Dundee* before turning to him again for *The Wild Bunch*. Oates' rumpled face was capable of a unique combination of, as actor Peter Fonda once recalled, an "innocence lightly engraved with a little bit of decadence" (Thurman, "Warren"). Many of the scenes between Johnson and Oates are touched with an air of adolescent bickering and childlike petulance, and even flashes of the innocence Fonda talked about. During one moment during the interlude in Angel's village, one of the village elders, watching how Oates and Johnson are chasing after a young girl like crushing teens, observes, "We all dream of being a child again, even the worst of us. Perhaps the worst most of all"—a duality Oates often captured in his roles, and with exquisite precision in *Bunch*.

* * *

As the key members of Deke Thornton's posse, Peckinpah cast Strother Martin as Coffer, and L.Q. Jones as T.C.

After a decade or so of small parts in TV and film, Martin had become something of a star among character actors with his role as a chain gang warden in *Cool Hand Luke* uttering one of the most famous lines in moviedom: "What we got here is failure to communicate." It says something of the value filmmakers placed on what Martin could bring to even the smallest of parts that he was cast in all three of the major Westerns released in 1969, and made each of them an unforgettable role: the self-proclaimed "colorful" mine boss in *Butch Cassidy and the*

Six. Peckinpah's Bunch

Sundance Kid, a shifty horse dealer in *True Grit*, and *The Wild Bunch* (Benson).

Peckinpah had already worked with Martin on *The Deadly Companions*, and one of his last TV efforts, an episode of *The Dick Powell Theatre* entitled "Pericles on 31st Street." But despite their years-long connection, for whatever reason, Peckinpah made a habit of tormenting Martin on the *Bunch* shoot. Martin, who, in real life, was a much more sensitive soul than the villains he often played, wound up, according to L.Q. Jones, "totally petrified of Sam" (Fine 133).

L.Q. Jones was another prolific character actor whose rangy looks and authentic Texas twang made him a natural for Westerns. Peckinpah knew Jones from his days working for Don Siegel, and had first used him in *Ride the High Country*, and then came back to him for *Major Dundee* where, ironically, he played Warren Oates' brother (Fine 71).

One of the elements which makes the Jones/Martin pairing so memorable is the interplay between the characters, driven by a subtext not created by Peckinpah or Walon Green, but dreamed up by Jones and Martin. According to Jones: "The understory, the backstory is what makes most really good pictures good. *The Wild Bunch* is an action piece, and yet it's character-driven. So Strother and I ... we decided to make [Coffer and T.C.] a little bit gay ... and Sam went along with it" (Seydor, "*The Wild Bunch*").

* * *

For the sadistic, morally bankrupt General Mapache, Peckinpah chose Emilio Fernandez. In his native Mexico, Fernandez—a veteran of the Mexican revolution—was a major figure in Mexican cinema, internationally-recognized as a top-caliber director and writer. North of the border, because of his real-life reputation for violence, he began accruing acting credits usually in Bad guy roles like Mapache (Hopwood, "Emilio"). Peckinpah was already acquainted with Fernandez who had worked with him on *Major Dundee* (Fernandez had done second unit work on a number of American films shooting in Mexico) (Fine 124).

* * *

Another member of the Peckinpah stock company was Dub Taylor. Taylor had come up in vaudeville in the 1930s before moving over to film where he immediately became a go-to character actor, especially by directors of Westerns. By the 1960s, his "leathery presence, often grizzled, came to embody the Old West not only as it was lived but how it had been presented onscreen" ("Dub Taylor"). Taylor had been cast in an episode of "The Westerner," and then Peckinpah had cast him in a 1963 episode of *Dick Powell Theater*—"The Losers"—which revisited some of the characters of his cancelled series. Taylor would become a part of Peckinpah's theatrical outfit when the director cast him as a cackling horse thief in *Major Dundee*.

* * *

Gray-haired, weather-beaten, thick in the middle—it was, by and large, an ensemble cast one would never see today in a major studio mainstream release. That was by design, Peckinpah looking for that prevailing, permeating air of a generation in decay witnessing its own passing.

Into their midst, Peckinpah threw two relative newcomers.

For Angel, the Mexican member of the Bunch, Peckinpah cast Puerto Rican actor Jaime Sanchez. Peckinpah had first asked Robert Blake, but Blake—coming off his breakout role in *In Cold Blood* (1967)— priced himself out of the role. At the time, Sanchez had done only a handful of movies and TV roles, but Peckinpah had been struck by his performance in Sidney Lumet's 1964 Holocaust drama, *The Pawnbroker* ("*The Wild Bunch:* Trivia").

Sanchez was a good fit for Peckinpah's demanding style of working. His first professional acting gig had been in the original 1957 Broadway production of *West Side Story* working under director/choreographer Jerome Robbins, "a man driven, a man who also said, 'I want it *this* way!' Sam had that" (Weddle 45).

But Sanchez' youthful exuberance could grate. According to Ernest Borgnine: "He was barely thirty at the time, and he was like a kid in a candy store. He just loved playing with his gun.... But it got to be irritating, having him constantly pull his six-shooter on us" (Ferrara).

The other newcomer was Bo Hopkins cast as Crazy Lee, a role not originally part of the script but which Peckinpah added to the opening robbery scene (Ferrara). At the time, Hopkins had only done a handful of TV roles. Hopkins was just 26 when Peckinpah cast him in his first feature film.

Perhaps because of his youth, his novice status, or his willingness to take on any chore—firing off guns to spook horses for a shot, say— Hopkins didn't suffer any of the wars with the director the major stars

Six. Peckinpah's Bunch

did (Weddle). Years later, Hopkins would reflect on how even the veteran actors seemed to look after him, Dub Taylor staying up all night to help him memorize the hymn "Shall We Gather at the River" for the robbery scene, and Ernest Borgnine acting "like a father to me" (Word, "A Word on Westerns: 'Kiss My...'").

But there were times when Hopkins paid for his inexperience. For the robbery sequence, where he was wired with "squibs" to simulate gunshot hits, Hopkins was asked by the special effects man if he wanted to wear an undershirt under the squibs. Hopkins, never having worked with squibs before, declined, feeling—with fresh-out-of-acting-school eagerness—that "I wanted to feel it" so he could better react to the hits. It was a mistake Hopkins never repeated after becoming blistered and bruised from being squibbed 26 times (Word, "A Word on Westerns: Baptism").

* * *

Sam Peckinpah's road back to Hollywood began in Mexico. In the spring of 1968, with his cast in place, a more-or-less finished screenplay in hand, a budget of $3.4 million and a 75-day shooting schedule, Sam Peckinpah led his troupe south of the border to begin filming *The Wild Bunch*. For at least some of the cast and crew, it would be an experience like none other, and would convince even some of the director's friends that he was "an absolute madman" (Thurman, "Warren Oates").

Seven

Mexico Lindo

> *"We're all idealists. You think we do it for the money?"*
> —George Hansen (Robert Duvall) in *The Killer Elite*

From the outset, Sam Peckinpah was committed to shooting *The Wild Bunch* in Mexico, partly out of his affection for the country, partly for reasons of authenticity, but it's hard not to suspect also—at least to some extent—to put a goodly distance between himself and the executives back at Warner Bros.-Seven Arts. Despite his rapport with Ken Hyman and his productive relationship with Phil Feldman, Peckinpah's paranoia about front office interference had abated not a whit (Ferrara). So insecure was he about the footage he was producing that he ordered Lou Lombardo not to show any of it to anyone without his direct approval, even going so far as to tell his editor to "pull the plug on the moviola" if producer Phil Feldman showed up in the editing room (Fine 139).

There had been something of a production learning curve for Peckinpah since his experiences on *Major Dundee*. *Dundee*'s far-flung locations had made a hard shoot harder, so this time Peckinpah kept his locations grouped around the towns of Parras de la Fuente and Torreon (Eggert). From his research for *Villa Rides!*, Peckinpah, who in his own rough-edged way, was something of a romantic, no doubt realized Parras had a particular historic resonance with his story. Parras had been the birthplace of Francisco Madero, the Mexican president who had supported the revolution against the Diaz government, and also, at one point, been Pancho Villa's headquarters (Redman).

Despite whatever comparative convenience this may have provided logistically, by all accounts the shoot was still a grueling, uncomfortable experience with cast and crew enduring baking heat, choking dust, and a severe lack of creature comforts in Mexico's high desert (Fine 131). Said one of Peckinpah's stunt crew, "We were out in an area that was so dry the cactus had dried up and the horned toads carried canteens" (Ferrara).

Seven. Mexico Lindo

To give some idea of the circumstances, at that time the city of Parras had no electricity. In fact, the production paid the city to put off electrifying the town so as not to ruin its period-authentic look with utility poles and power lines (Snider).*

Peckinpah's improvisational work style could be taxing at the very least, infuriating—as in the case of Robert Ryan—at its worst, and pushed the production behind schedule (Weddle 50–51). But it was not just his on-the-fly style of directing which could drive an actor or crew insane. Peckinpah regular L.Q. Jones would explain in an interview years later that part of the trick to working with the director was realizing he'd already been dealing with the material for maybe a year in advance of the actual shooting; he already saw the film in his head. If you did something he hadn't seen in that mental version of his movie, "he'd chew your ass totally out." But while Peckinpah may have known specifically what he wanted for his camera, "the problem was he wouldn't tell *you*." Actors with a track record with the director learned to more-or-less divine what Peckinpah wanted, but the experience could be holy hell for newcomers (Francis).

Peckinpah's demand for perfect execution of a vision he sometimes couldn't express resulted in a virtual blood-letting of the crew roster. By the time shooting in Mexico had ended, 22 people had been fired from the crew (Weddle 48).

If Peckinpah demanded a lot from his cast and crew, he demanded no less from himself. His typical routine began at 4:00 a.m. with the director looking over material to be filmed that day, then a few hours later, he would join Lucien Ballard for the drive to that day's location, the two men taking that time to discuss how they would handle the day's shooting. The production would film for nine hours after which Peckinpah would screen the newest delivery of dailies, following which he would have production meetings before turning in around midnight (Seydor, "*The Wild*"). During filming, he developed a case of bleeding hemorrhoids, but refused treatment and went through the remainder of the shoot taking shots for the pain and sometimes working with blood running down his leg (Fine 137).

---

*If you look closely at some of the wider shots—particularly down angles—of the main street of Parras, which is standing in for Starbuck, Texas, you can see that the street has been filled with dirt up to the top of the curb to give the town a rustic, unpaved look. The production trucked in tons of dirt along with building out building fronts to give the street the desired period look (Redman).

Peckinpah could be improvisational, but many on the shoot were impressed with the fountain of information he could keep in his head. One stuntman—no more than an extra, really—who, à la Robert Ryan, had spent days on the set without being called for a shot, began showing up on the set without his fake beard. The director immediately noticed the missing facial decor when he finally turned to him and came close to firing the man (Fine 135).

What breaks Peckinpah's work out from that of so many other directors was his eye for specific, even tiny details which were like the small tiles in a big mosaic; they filled in the bigger picture, giving it a unique, distinctively Peckinpahesque feel (135). There was, for example, the matter of Edmond O'Brien's costume. When O'Brien got into the wardrobe which had been made up for him back in Los Angeles, "Sam just ripped [the clothes] off me and said, 'You're gonna wear one suit that was taken off a dead man's body" (Weddle 46).

Similarly, when Strother Martin showed up for shooting garbed in a way Peckinpah had approved weeks before, the director balked. "I want to make him a 1913 Hell's Angel," Peckinpah told wardrobe supervisor Gordon Dawson. Dawson added a large cross hanging down Martin's chest on what looks like a string of rosary beads, with the image of Christ replaced with a .38 cartridge (Weddle 48–49).

When Peckinpah's improvisations jelled, they seemed such a full-bodied, organic part of the whole, in retrospect it awes that they were not originally part of the script or that there'd been no kind of pre-planning. The Gunman's Walk and exit from Angel's village may be among the most memorable such moments, but hardly the most complex. Phil Feldman would latter recall, with some amazement, how Peckinpah put together the opening act of the Bunch's raid on an Army train of rifles the morning he first showed up on the location for shooting (Weddle 53). More impressive was Peckinpah's execution of the final shootout; what the members of the production came to dub "The Battle of Bloody Porch" (Fine 142).

* * *

Peckinpah had his Gunman's Walk which got the Bunch into the hacienda courtyard where they face off with Mapache who defiantly slits Angel's throat when the Bunch demand the release of their comrade. Pike and Dutch pump pistol and shotgun rounds into the Mexican general, Mapache drops to the ground, there's a moment where the Bunch and Mapache's troops are frozen, awaiting the next move, and then.... And

Seven. Mexico Lindo

then nothing. The three pages of the screenplay dedicated to the final confrontation afforded no help on how to actually choreograph the battle. Peckinpah was stumped (Weddle 51–52; Fine 142).

After sitting by himself for several hours—time in which the answer evidently percolated in his head—the director came out of his creative coma to confer with Lucien Ballard to work out a plan (Weddle 51–52; Fine 142). Ultimately, the Battle of Bloody Porch would take twelve days to film; approximately 15 percent of the eventual shooting schedule, longer than it took to film any other single scene in the movie including the opening shootout and the bridge-blowing sequence following the raid on the arms train.

That there was no advance plan for what is easily one of the most complicated action sequences in American film, and that Peckinpah never storyboarded or diagrammed his shots is a testament to the man's directorial skill when viewing the approximately six minutes of elegantly constructed chaos.

The architecture of the battle isn't just men running here and there and blasting away. There's an overall build to the fight, from the first individual pistol shots from Pike which ignite the battle to the enormous volume of gunfire and explosions which mark its climax. Similar to what they did with the opening shootout, Peckinpah/Ballard/Lombardo alternate the maelstrom of running and shooting men to break for memorable moments: Dutch exchanging fire at close range with soldiers pushing through a doorway, holding a woman in front of him as a shield; or, in one of the film's most infamous moments, when Pike, shot in the back by one of Mapache's soldiers' whores, whips around, spits out, "Bitch!" then hits her with a shotgun blast that throws her against a wall.

For all the sound and fury of the battle, what gives its construction a certain elegance is the way Peckinpah & Co. create peaks during the fight through a recurring use of escalating patterns of three:

Dutch ramps up the violence by throwing three hand grenades;
When Tector takes over the heavy machine gun which commands the hacienda courtyard, Lyle covers his back, at one point shotgunning three of Mapache's soldiers as they charge through a door onto the hacienda porch, the final soldier going down in the most violent fashion after his head explodes in blood;
Three of the Bunch take a turn at the machine gun, but each handoff comes with an escalation of the violence: when Lyle takes the gun from his wounded brother, he rakes Mapache's dining table and a shower and din of shattering glassware is added to the gunfire along with a raw, savage scream from Lyle; Pike takes the gun

from a fallen Lyle and brings the battle to its highest pitch when he touches off, sequentially, three cases of dynamite.

The battle ends seconds later when Pike is brought down by three rifle shots, the first by a uniformed young boy so small he can barely sight his rifle.

Not only does each triplet have its own escalating arc, but each takes the kinetic action in the courtyard to a higher level. The violence of *The Wild Bunch* has often been described as ballet-like, but perhaps more accurately—at least as far as the Battle of Bloody Porch goes—in its deliberate use of recurring patterns and breakout moments, the battle's composition might be viewed as more orchestral, broken up into movements and phrases which take the overall piece to an emotional and kinetic peak.

* * *

One of the details on which Peckinpah seemed most fixated—and which was a cornerstone of the project—was in getting the violence, by his judgment, done right. It wasn't morbidity or visceral excitement Peckinpah was after. "I use violence as it is," he said of its depiction in *The Wild Bunch*. "It's ugly, brutalizing and bloody fucking awful. It's not fun and games … it's a terrible ugly thing" (Ferrara).

He had real-life models to draw on. There had been, for one, what he'd seen during his military service in China. But he also long held onto a "haunting image" from a time before that, from his younger days, out hunting in the high country around his home, bringing down his first deer and seeing "its blood blossoming out with the bullet across a patch of white snow" (Weddle 47).

Fringe horror films aside, that level of graphic realism had never been accomplished in a mainstream commercial film. Not to take anything away from *Bonnie and Clyde*, but as controversially violent as that film was in its day, it stands as surprisingly bloodless next to *The Wild Bunch*. Even during the final "death ballet"—brilliantly edited by the great Dede Allen—as the titular characters writhe under a hail of machine gun fire, for all the squibs detonating on Warren Beatty and Faye Dunaway, there's more holes than blood.

Similarly, during a face-off between the antiheroes of *Butch Cassidy and The Sundance Kid* and a group of Mexican *bandidos*, director George Roy Hill films the incident in slow motion to capture the trauma of the moment, but, again, even though Hill himself described the sequence as

Seven. Mexico Lindo

"the bloodbath scene" and a "massacre," there's little visible blood-letting (Crawford).

To that end, Peckinpah pushed his special effects crew to extremes from the first day when the crew began shooting on the main streets of Parras. What kicks off the opening shoot-out are two of the Bunch blasting out the windows of the railroad office with shotguns. Peckinpah thought the standard squibs weren't enough to give him the effect he wanted, so he had the windows re-rigged with dynamite (Weddle 49). The end of the first day of shooting saw the production company having already exhausted its stores of blank ammunition and movie blood (Eggert). The studio would later claim that the production used more ammunition than had been fired off during the actual Mexican Revolution (Eggert).

Again dissatisfied with standard squibs when the effects crew organized a demonstration of how they'd play on actors, Peckinpah produced a gun and fired real bullets into the demo targets, declaring, "That's the effect I want" (Weddle 46).

The on-set action could be frighteningly intense in a real-life way. Years later, Ernest Borgnine remembered his stand-in breaking down in tears. A veteran of World War II, the heavy fusillades of gunfire "brought back too many memories" for the man (Greenberg 26).

Simply rupturing a blood bag wasn't enough. Peckinpah had his effects team put thin slices of uncooked steak across the bags so that when a squib blew open the bag, small bits of meat would fly out along with the blood (Fine 142). Peckinpah also had actors squibbed front and back so bullets would appear to completely pierce a body—a Hollywood first (Weddle 46). Borgnine would later recount watching Peckinpah go around the Bloody Porch location between shots carrying a can of movie blood and sprinkling it around the set (Greenberg 26).

The level of destruction during the Bloody Porch scene was stratospheric. Wardrobe supervisor Gordon Dawson had to set up a "uniform repair factory" during the scene's shooting to rehabilitate the 350 uniforms he had available as they became squib-holed and bloodied. Dawson would later claim "we blew up 6,000 [uniforms]" (Weddle 52).

Even in post-production—and beyond—Peckinpah continued to push, to make sure the violence he presented on screen fulfilled the vision in his head. After the film was previewed in Kansas City, he ordered the gunshot effects redone, louder and with each kind of weapon in the film having a distinct sound, "whereas most Warner Bros. productions had used the same gunshot sounds since the 1930s" (Fine 148; Eggert). One story has it that Peckinpah also wanted to include the sounds of buzzing flies over the footage of the dead littering the hacienda courtyard (Ferrara).

Filming, which had been scheduled for 70 days, ran over to 81 days. No studio likes overages, but considering the complexity and scale of *The Wild Bunch*, this was not a frightening overage. A little more eyebrow-raising was that, ultimately, the $3.4 million budget would nearly double to $6.4 million (Eggert). Peckinpah was cushioned against any studio wailing by Phil Feldman, and also by the director's wisely having allowed some visiting studio execs to see a polished cut of a section of the film. It was enough to buy their enthusiastic tolerance, at least for the moment (Ferrara).

But the end of shooting is not the end of movie-making.

* * *

Despite the fast pace Lou Lombardo had developed editing for television, there was no way for him to keep up with the miles of footage Peckinpah was generating. He spent an additional three months editing in Mexico after shooting was completed, then continued to edit the film back in Los Angeles, working with the director while Peckinpah was simultaneously involved in pre-production for his second contracted feature for Warner Bros.-Seven Arts, *The Ballad of Cable Hogue*. Editing would continue into the beginning of shooting for *Cable Hogue*. All told, Lombardo would spend six months in L.A. shaping and refining *The Wild Bunch* (Fine 145).

Peckinpah was as demanding in the editing phase as he'd been during production, with the director sometimes calling for his editor to shave or add as little as a single frame to a shot (Eggert).

Lombardo's and Peckinpah's first cut of the film ran a clearly unacceptable five hours. Months of work, of frame-cutting, revising, refining, and tweaking finally got the film to a length with which Peckinpah was content: 2:24 (Fine 145–146). It had been a mammoth editing job; while most films in those pre-Michael Bay days averaged 600 cuts, *The Wild Bunch* boasted an astronomical 3,642 (Eggert).

* * *

On the eve of *The Wild Bunch*'s release, Sam Peckinpah was satisfied. Not only was he certain the film would be a commercial success and

Seven. Mexico Lindo

re-establish his serious filmmaker bona fides, but he viewed the film as a personal accomplishment as well. "A good picture is usually 70 percent of your intentions," he told an interviewer. "*The Wild Bunch* was about 96 percent" (Fine 154). "Of all the projects I have ever worked on," he would tell others, "this is the closest to me" (Ferrara).

So it was, right up to the film's first preview. And then … not quite as much.

Eight

Missing Pieces

"Do you think that they will ever forgive us for what we've done?"
—Sergeant Steiner (James Coburn) in *Cross of Iron*

Which *The Wild Bunch* did you see? *The Wild Bunch* one saw depended very much on where and when one saw the movie.

Paul Schrader, a film critic in 1969 who would go on to become the provocative screenwriter and writer/director of works like *Taxi Driver* (1976) and *American Gigolo* (1980), saw a pre-release 3:45 cut of the film he thought "absolutely brilliant," judging every subsequent cut—presumably even Peckinpah's version—a diminishment (Fine 146). *Filmfacts* reported at the time of the film's release that the cut previewed in Kansas City ran 190 minutes ("*The Wild*" 217). Thereafter, more than once, Warner Bros. would pull Peckinpah's 2:24 version from distribution and make still more cuts (Fine 154). Again according to *Filmfacts*, when screened in Los Angeles the film ran 148 minutes; 140 in Manhattan; 135 in Washington, D.C. ("*The Wild*" 217). Even when the film began showing up in revival houses in subsequent years, there was no standard print in distribution; go to three different revival theaters and it was possible to see three different versions. It would not be until the film's 25th anniversary re-release that Peckinpah's cut was restored and thereafter became *The Wild Bunch* (Hunter).

Peckinpah, of course, was furious over the cuts and never forgave Phil Feldman whom he held responsible (Snider). "I thought that [the cuts] were excessive for the point I wanted to make," he told an interviewer. "I have a story to tell ... and I do not want the violence per se to dominate what's really happening with the people" (Axmaker). The thinking behind the studio's re-editing was sadly simple. Warner Bros. may have been enthused about the prospects for the film before its release, but once it began playing in front of paying audiences, they had reason to worry

EIGHT. Missing Pieces

from a purely dollars-and-cents point of view. Despite Warner Bros.' pre-release excitement, *The Wild Bunch* did not open strongly. Worried about less than impressive box office, the studio hoped shortening the film might allow theater owners to cram an additional showing into prime exhibition hours thereby possibly boosting the box office take (Ebert).

While there is a widely-held opinion the film suffered from the deletions, the sentiment is not unanimous. Critic Stephen Hunter, for example, writing for *The Baltimore Sun* on the re-release of the restored *Bunch*, said:

> Is it better? Is it deeper? Is it fuller? Is it more violent? Is it any less the most difficult masterpiece in movie history?
>
> No, no, no, no and no.
>
> The additions feel incidental ... they don't deepen motive, they simply slow down the pace [Hunter].

There were five sequences that, at one time or another, were deleted from Peckinpah's cut. Let's take a close look at them and try to assess a fair value to their loss/inclusion.

#1 and #2

It's the night after the botched railroad office robbery which opens the film. The Bunch are encamped somewhere across the Mexican border. On the other side of the line, Deke Thornton and his ragtag posse of lowlifes are also settling down for the night.

The film cuts back and forth between the two camps, switching from a conversation between Pike and Dutch, to Deke Thornton sitting apart from the rest of his posse. It is a long, dialogue-heavy scene running approximately five minutes in the restored version. In the truncated *The Wild Bunch*, two sections from the scene are deleted.

The Pike/Dutch dialogue begins with Dutch asking Pike what their next move might be. Pike brings up the possibility of hitting an Army payroll. When Dutch points out the authorities will probably be waiting for the Bunch's next move, Pike replies, "I wouldn't have it any other way."

In a deleted sequence, the scene then begins to cut back and forth between Pike and Deke Thornton, intercut with a flashback: Pike and Deke some years previous cavorting in a whorehouse, there's a knock on the door, Pike thinks it's some requested champagne, the door opens and there's a group of lawmen in the hall. One of the lawmen fires his pistol, bringing Deke down with a wounded shoulder while Pike escapes.

Peckinpah doesn't integrate his flashbacks all that smoothly. Earlier in the film, after the opening shootout, when Thornton tells railroad exec Harrigan (Albert Dekker) that he'll keep his word because "I don't want to go back to prison," Peckinpah drops in a quick flash of Thornton being flogged as if he doesn't trust us to understand why Thornton so much fears being returned to custody. It's an awkward and unnecessary bit, and the whorehouse sequence feels the same. There's a bit too much cross-the-t's-dot-the-i's to it. One could argue from a purely creative point of view, *not* being so specific and letting the audience make the connections—an exercise in Keatsian "negative capability"—would actually be a more engaging way to go, and more in keeping with *The Wild Bunch* as a whole; a work in which most of its deeper themes emerge and/or are suggested rather than hammered home ("Negative").

Illustrating the point: just prior to the opening shootout, as the Bunch prepare to make their break, Peckinpah cuts between the Bunch and Thornton's posse waiting on the rooftops around the railroad office. The posse smell blood; they're eager for the killing to begin. They smile in anticipation, one of them—Strother Martin's Coffer—looks almost pained in his anticipation, kissing his rifle at one point.

Thornton, in contrast, is clearly unhappy with the situation.

And the Bunch? Once the ambushers are spotted, they move about the railroad office like a well-practiced team, Pike having only to give clipped orders. In purely visual terms, Peckinpah has told us that there are Bad Guys and there are Bad Guys, and the difference between them is night and day.

And so it is throughout the film: in action—during the railroad office robbery, when the Bunch raid the munitions trains—the group always moves with a cool efficiency, a marked contrast with the raggedy posse chasing them, and, during the train sequence, the bumbling green soldiers guarding the train. By the time Thornton reprimands what's left of his posse—"We're after *men* ... and I wish to God I was with them"— we understand Thornton's elevation of the Bunch over his motley gang of "egg-sucking, chicken-stealing gutter trash." The caliber of these men is evident enough that the threat of being left behind—which Thornton makes to his posse, and which, earlier, Pike makes to Angel when the younger man looks to become obsessed with revenging himself against

Eight. Missing Pieces

Mapache, the man who has killed his father and stolen his woman—is enough to bring a return to obedience.

Similarly, the second deleted sequence—a piece of dialogue between Pike and Dutch following the whorehouse flashback—may also hit the thematic nail too squarely on the head. Pike talks about how he's hit the same railroad that was the day's target several times in the past, infuriating railroad exec Harrigan (which explains Harrigan's homicidal zeal in bringing down the Bunch). The dialogue turns into a lecture on pride, the inability of some men to learn from their wrong moves. When Dutch asks, "How about us, Pike? You reckon we learned, being wrong today?" Pike answers, "I hope to God we did."

Again, I would argue it's a point which emerges naturally from the film without this kind of italicized emphasis, and since both the whorehouse and pride-goeth-before-a-fall dialogue extend what is already a heavily expository scene, it's understandable why Warner Bros. felt the footage could be sacrificed.

#3

More debatable is the deletion of a scene coming not long after the camp scene. The Bunch are crossing the Mexican desert, and there's been a mishap; old Freddie Sykes has caused most of the Bunch to become unhorsed and tumble down a sand dune. An irate Tector Gorch, who has already questioned the value of having the old man along, threatens to kill Sykes, but is stopped by Pike: "When you side with a man, you stay with him!"

The deleted sequence follows. Sykes rides up alongside Pike to thank him for the unifying speech, and then asks him about Clarence Lee aka Crazy Lee, the Bo Hopkins character left behind in Starbuck during the opening shootout. Sykes reveals Lee had been his grandson. When an upset Pike asks why Sykes hadn't told him of the relationship, Sykes shrugs it off: "You had enough things on your mind. 'Sides, he had to pull his weight like the rest of us."

It doesn't bother Sykes that the boy was killed, and it's an open question about whether or not he knows Pike deliberately left Crazy Lee behind. All that matters to him is that Lee performed well. Pike's "He did fine. Just fine" is all the solace the old man needs.

Does it move the plot along? Does it deepen motivations, add to characters' pasts? No, but it *does* add a texture, an idea of the warped moral universe in which these characters live. It doesn't matter to Sykes that Crazy Lee, his grandson, was deemed too crazy by Pike to be worth saving. All that matters is that the boy did his job.

That code of the professional is something which surfaces again and again in the film. Earlier, when Dutch wonders how Pike came to bring a crazy old coot like Freddie Sykes into the Bunch, Pike grants the old man pedigree enough when he explains, "He used to run with Thornton and me. Did his share of killing and more."

Part of what makes *The Wild Bunch* work—what makes us, eventually, connect with a band of ruthless Bad Guys—is the dynamic that within an amoral universe, they live by a moral code. True, it's a *warped* moral code, one justifying killing and thievery, yet one which still breaks them out from the scavenging posse, the obsessed Harrigan who shows not a shred of regret over the innocents killed in his badly-planned ambush, and the ravaging, sadistic Mapache and his equally brutal troops.

#4

By the time the Bunch is on their way to rob an Army munitions train for Mapache, we've had several nods toward an old leg injury of Pike's. After his "When you side with a man" speech, Pike attempts to climb back on his horse, his stirrup strap breaks and he falls to the ground, his left leg giving him obvious pain. Later, after making the deal for the raid on the train with Mapache, Pike, Dutch, and Sykes are basking in a steam bath and we see the deep scar on Pike's leg.

The deleted sequence takes place as the Bunch are riding to intercept the train and begins with Dutch saying, "You never told me how you got all tore up like that," meaning Pike's leg. There then follows one of Peckinpah's awkwardly handled flashbacks as Pike narrates an incident from his past: his involvement with a woman he wanted to marry; a married woman whose husband evidently was gone and, according to the woman, never coming back. But the husband does return, walks in on Pike and the woman, kills her, wounds Pike, then runs off. "There isn't a day or an hour that passes that I don't think about it," Pike muses.

What makes the flashback even more awkward is that Pike's voiceover narration does the job well enough, and the flashback—while hardly

EIGHT. Missing Pieces

a deft piece of cinematic storytelling—also does the job, but together they produce a clumsy narrative redundancy.

For all that, there is still value to the scene. The Bunch are always seen as detached, rootless, men whose only personal connection is to each other. But with Pike's memory we see a possibility, a might-have-been, and it gives his character another fine, subtle layer of melancholy. There are, even in the truncated versions of the film, small moments which now make sense: the way Pike seems to sink into a more reflective attitude toward the tail end of the fiesta sequence in Angel's village; the way he looks at one of Mapache's camp followers when the Bunch first arrive at the hacienda; his morose anger around a whore and her infant before rallying the Bunch for the Gunman's Walk. In the edited version of the film, those looks can be taken simply as an older man's eye drawn to a pretty young girl. With the integration of the sequence, it's an older man's memory sparked by a pretty young girl, and rueful thoughts of a life denied.

#5

The Bunch have successfully raided the munitions train and escaped. The deleted sequence which follows those events concerns Mapache receiving word the Bunch have his guns.

Mapache and his troops are at a train/telegraph station, buckling under an artillery barrage and attack by Pancho Villa's forces. It is a sequence both extravagant (the barrage, a train full of troops, charging men on horseback) and bizarre (Mapache stands oblivious to the hail of gunfire as the men around him are hit, and on the rear platform of the caboose of his train, a mariachi band led by a female vocalist blithely and vigorously perform the Mexican Revolution ballad "El Corrido de Santa Amalia"). It's a Western as directed by Fellini; something more out of George Miller's *Mad Max* films than John Ford's West.

It's the only action sequence among the deleted footage, and one certainly has to question why the studio would cut such an obviously expensive bit of spectacle.

Still, it's a scene which actually provides very little plot information. Mapache receives a telegram that the Bunch have accomplished their mission, and he orders one of his lieutenants to intercept the Bunch and their cargo.

But the textural point of the scene is not its expository value. It is the only scene in the film which shows us Mapache as someone other than a morally decadent, self-indulgent brute. He is all those things, but we see in the way he stands unflinchingly against Villa's troops, initially resisting the call of his second-in-command to save himself, that he is also fearless. In the way his troops unswervingly follow him, the way the young boy in uniform who delivers the telegram looks admiringly to him, we can see how Mapache inspires those around him, might even appear heroic to someone like the boy who might be blind to the general's voracious vices.

Like the scene of Freddie Sykes' concern about how his doomed grandson performed when the shooting started, the value here is not narrative but something more subtle. *The Wild Bunch* is a story about unabashedly bad men, but not all bad men are equal in the film, and not all bad men are simply bad. The Bunch has a warped code of honor, one shared by Deke Thornton, but both the Bunch and Thornton stand apart from the bounty hunters who are no more than vultures ("trash," Thornton calls them several times). They also stand apart from Mapache (described by Thornton as "a killer for Juerta who calls himself a general," and by Dutch as "just another bandit") who is both brave but so utterly morally corrupt the Bunch stand as honorable men in comparison. When Pike jokes Mapache and the Bunch are in the same line of work, a repulsed Dutch declares, "Not so's you'd know it, Mr. Bishop, we ain't *nothin'* like him. We don't *hang* nobody."

Part of the uniqueness of *The Wild Bunch* is this moral twilight zone, one in which the audience is forced to commit its sympathies not on clear rights and wrongs, goods and bads, but on a gray scale of moral relativity. That was the challenge of the movie in its time, and remains its most thematically daring aspect.

* * *

The years-long discussion over the deleted sequences can make one forget an obvious fact: the standing of *The Wild Bunch* as a classic Western, as a pivotal movie and social statement in and of its time, as one of the greats in the American film canon, was largely achieved by critical and popular response to—by purists' standards—incomplete versions of the film. Put another way, the standing of the film prior to the 25th anniversary restoration amply demonstrated that *The Wild Bunch* worked quite well even without the deleted sequences.

EIGHT. Missing Pieces

But maybe the proper way to consider the worthiness of the cut scenes isn't what the movie lost by their deletion, but what it gains by their inclusion. As Stephen Hunter wrote, the gain certainly isn't in plot or motivation, but is textural; a greater sense of the complexity and multifaceted quality of a universe which may be less immoral than amoral, and where codes of conduct are arbitrary standards set by each character, but it is those codes which give each character their own, odd sense of self-worth.

Martin Scorsese put it best to Peckinpah biographer Marshall Fine: "There was no attempt to ingratiate (the characters); the audience had to accept them on their own terms.... And when they're all gone—how moving that is. It was savage poetry" (Fine 153).

Perhaps that best describes what was lost in the deletions. Actor Ned Beatty, talking about *The Wild Bunch* in a documentary about Warren Oates, noted that Warner Bros. "did not cut violence. They cut poetry" (Thurman, "Warren Oates").

Nine

The Wild Bunch

> *"Think of them as fleas on a dog hit by a car driven by a drunken teenager whose girlfriend just gave him the clap. It will help your sense of perspective."*
> —Lawrence Fassett (John Hurt) in
> *The Osterman Weekend*

Synopsis

(This synopsis is based on Peckinpah's 2:24 cut of the film. Scenes that were deleted during its original theatrical release are in italics.)

C. 1914, southern Texas. A squad of U.S. cavalry rides into the town of Starbuck. Leading them: Pike Bishop. At his side: Dutch Engstrom. This is the Old West in transition: the uniforms the cavalrymen wear aren't Federal blue, but olive drab fatigues; they are armed with .45 automatic pistols and pump-action shotguns. They pass a group of children gathered around a small pit they've made where they've set an army of ants against several scorpions. They pass a temperance meeting, Starbuck's mayor railing on about the evils of drink. The Old West is fading.

The cavalrymen meet up with other soldiers waiting for them and proceed to a railroad office. They don't see that eyes are on them; on a roof overlooking the railroad office are a scruffy bunch of ambushers led by railroad officer Harrigan and Deke Thornton. They have been waiting for the men below. Harrigan has specifically been waiting for Pike. When asked, a grimly resigned Thornton replies, "He's there."

Once inside the railroad office, the apparent soldiers manhandle the staff and one customer, holding them at gunpoint as Pike snarls, "If they move, kill 'em!" As the Bunch empty the safe, one of their number—Angel—on lookout spies the guns of the antsy ambushers on the roof

Nine. The Wild Bunch

above. Several other members of the Bunch situated here and there on Starbuck's main street also spy the riflemen above. Pike orders one of the band—Crazy Lee—to stay behind with their prisoners while the rest make a break. Showing just how crazy he is, Crazy Lee responds enthusiastically: "I'll hold 'em here 'til hell freezes over or you say different!"

The temperance meeting is now marching down the main street. Pike waits until they pass by the railroad office, then throws the office manager out into the street. The ambushers are so eager for a kill they don't bother to identify the man and open fire. The Bunch blast out the windows of the railroad office, leap out into the street, and a bloody battle ensues, the temperance marchers caught in the middle. "They're blowin' this town all to hell!" a giddy Crazy Lee tells his hostages. At one point in the melee, Pike and Thornton spy each other. They each take a shot at the other but miss. Several of the Bunch are killed during the fighting along with a number of civilians, and one of the Bunch is horribly wounded when he is shot in the face.

As the Bunch ride out of town, the children "playing" with the ants and scorpions bury their "game" under blazing straw, consuming all.

Crazy Lee's hostages try to escape but he blasts them, then, in turn, is shot down by three of Thornton's posse, but not killed. Thornton and Harrigan appear in the office. "Why don't you just kiss my sister's black cat's ass," Crazy Lee gasps out defiantly, then shoots down the three men who wounded him before Harrigan finishes him. As the furious mayor of Starbuck lambastes Harrigan for "using our town as a battlefield," a disgusted Thornton walks back out into the body-littered street where his vulture-like posse is stripping the dead and arguing over credit for kills, while children re-enact the shootout.

Outside of town, the Bunch take a halt when their wounded man, his face a bloody pulp, topples from his horse. Realizing he can't go on any further, he asks, "Finish it, Mr. Bishop," and Pike does with a pistol shot. He offers the survivors—the Gorch brothers, Lyle and Tector—the option of burying the man, but Dutch shames them into forgoing the waste of valuable escape time.

Back in Starbuck, Thornton faces off with Harrigan. We learn that Thornton has been freed from prison but on the condition he bring down Pike. Harrigan shows no concern at all for the innocent blood spilled on the Starbuck streets nor the ineptitude of the men he's saddled Thornton with. "You're my Judas goat," he tells Thornton. When Thornton calls

The Wild Bunch

him out, about how it feels "to sit back and hire your killings with the law's arms around you," a grinning Harrigan purrs, "Good."

The Bunch cross into Mexico and rendezvous with Freddie Sykes who is waiting for them with fresh horses. The Gorches object to sharing equally with rookie Angel and old Sykes but when the argument comes close to guns coming out, they back off. They cut into the sacks taken from Starbuck. "Silver rings!" Lyle Gorch says in amazement. "Silver rings your butt!" says an angry Dutch, "Them's *washers!*"

They realize they've been baited into the ambush, lost a number of their men, all for "a dollar's worth of steel holes!" "We've got to start thinking beyond our guns," muses Pike, "Those days are closing fast." They come to realize the absurdity of their situation and laugh at their own haplessness.

That night, Thornton and his posse bed down on the Texas side of the border, the Bunch on the Mexican side. One of the posse—Coffer—asks Thornton about Pike Bishop, the kind of man he is. "The best," Thornton tells him. "He never got caught."

Then Thornton and Pike remember the incident which separated them; the two of them in a whorehouse, Pike enjoying himself, Thornton wary. A knock at the door, one of the prostitutes opens it and outside a posse of lawmen. There's a shot and Thornton goes down wounded, but Pike bounds away escaping.

Pike and Dutch discuss next moves. When Pike brings up the possibility of taking on an Army payroll, Dutch warns that the law will be waiting for them. "I wouldn't have it any other way," Pike says.

Pike tells how in the past he's burned the railroad more than once infuriating a railroad officer named Harrigan. Pike says how Harrigan's pride wouldn't let him learn from his mistakes, and Dutch wonders if they, the Bunch, learned anything from the day's disaster. "I sure hope to God we did," says Pike.

As they turn over to go to sleep, Dutch says, "I wouldn't want it any other way either."

With the new day, the Bunch head south, across the Mexican desert. Riding atop the dunes, Sykes bumps into the mounts of the others and causes them all—except a grinning Angel—to fall off their horses. Tector, who was first to object to paying Sykes a full share, declares, "I'm gonna get rid of him." Pike stops him: "We're not getting rid of anybody! We're gonna stick together, just like it used to be. When you side with a man, you stay with him! And if you can't do that, you're like some animal!

NINE. The Wild Bunch

You're finished! *We're* finished! *All of us!*" But when Pike goes to climb back on his horse, his stirrup strap snaps and he falls to the ground. "How the hell you gonna side anybody when you can't even get on your horse?" taunts Tector, but with great effort and despite the pain in his leg, Pike manages to pull himself back into his saddle even without his stirrup. With a certain admiration, Tector and the others watch Pike get back on the trail, slump-shouldered and worn, but continuing on across the desert.

The Bunch ride into Angel's home village, a small place that Pike is told has already been pillaged for anything of value. When Pike asks one of the village elders, Don Jose, why they didn't call federal troops for help, Don Jose tells them, "They *were* Federal troops!" For Angel, the wound to his home is personal: his father was murdered by the raiders, and his woman has willingly run off with them to become the woman of their leader: General Mapache.

Pike watches the Gorch brothers playing cat's cradle with one of the young women of the village, chasing after her like schoolboys with a crush. Observes Don Jose, "We all dream of being a child again. Even the worst of us. Perhaps the worst most of all." And in this Pike realizes Don Jose has figured out the kind of men the Bunch are. How? Because it seems Don Jose is a member of the same fraternity.

A fiesta follows, the Bunch and the villagers, for the moment, forgetting their respective miseries. Except for Angel, fixated on Mapache. "Either you learn to live with it," Pike warns him, "or we'll leave you here." That's threat enough for Angel: "I go with you, *jefe*."

The next day, the villagers line the road out of town saluting the Bunch as they pass.

The Bunch ride to the town of Agua Verde, the base for Mapache and his troops. The Bunch witness the entry of the general into the town in his new automobile; the kind of machine only some of them have even heard about. Mapache retires to a hacienda courtyard where he dines with his officers. Angel's woman, Teresa, appears in the courtyard with the gift of a lavishly equipped horse for Mapache. Angel steps up to her, asking why she left the village. She had no choice, Teresa tells him, she was going hungry, but now, as the woman of Mapache she is happy. She brushes past Angel, taunts him by sitting in Mapache's lap and tonguing the general's ear. It's too much for Angel. Screaming, "*Puta!*" ("Whore!") Angel shoots her. The Bunch quickly disarm Angel and before Mapache's men can turn on them, the Bunch make it clear they're not looking for a fight. Mapache's men have mistakenly thought Angel had tried to assassinate the general but Pike explains he was simply jealous over the girl; something the blood-spattered Mapache and his men think is quite comical. One of two German civilians dining with the general notice the Bunch's .45 automatics; at the time, a military-only firearm. The Germans express their interest in "Americans who do not share their government's naïve sentiments." "Well, we share very few sentiments with our government," Pike says dryly.

That night, the Bunch dine with Mapache, his lieutenants and his German advisors and strike a deal for $10,000 to raid an American munitions train and steal rifles for the general. Dutch, who doesn't think much of Mapache, expresses some reluctance: "Getting pretty close to home, ain't it?" but the deal is struck, and Pike convinces Mapache to let Angel go: "I need him."

That night, the Gorches cavort with several whores provided by Mapache while Pike, Dutch, Angel and Sykes retire to a steam bath. Angel doesn't want to participate in the raid: "Would you give guns to someone to kill your father or your mother or your brother?" Says Pike, "Ten thousand cuts an awful lot of family ties." Dutch offers a compromise: Angel gives up his share of the bounty in return for keeping some of the rifles to give to the anti-government rebels.

Back in Starbuck, Thornton tells Harrigan he anticipates that Pike will have met with Mapache and probably make a try at the munitions train. Harrigan refuses Thornton's demand for better men than the "trash" he's been assigned, or the green Army recruits guarding the train.

The raid on the train goes off meticulously at a water stop with the Bunch separating the cargo-carrying part of the train from the cars carrying the posse and soldiers. Thornton spies the front part of the train steaming off and leads his posse in pursuit. The soldiers, thinking Thornton's posse has stolen the train, chase off after Thornton's men. Down the line, the Bunch load the guns onto a wagon and take off for the border river and a bridge they've rigged with dynamite to cover their escape. The wagon gets stuck when a wheel falls through a weak spot in the bridge but the dynamite fuses are already lit. With Thornton's posse firing down on them and the soldiers firing on Thornton's men, the Bunch finally get the wagon free. Thornton's posse ride down onto the bridge. Pike pauses downriver to make a grand gesture; tipping his hat and bowing. Just as Thornton sights his rifle on Pike, the dynamite explodes, the bottom falls out of the bridge, and Thornton and his men

NINE. The Wild Bunch

go into the river. The Bunch salute the success of the raid passing a bottle among themselves, dissolving into laughter when it finally gets to Lyle ... empty!

Fending off an attack by Villa's troops, Mapache receives word that the Bunch have successfully robbed the train. He sends some of his men to intercept them.

Thornton and the surviving members of his posse, much of their equipment lost, are now on the Mexican side of the river. There's no going back to the United States without Pike and the Bunch to prove they weren't part of the robbery.

After some of Angel's friends come for their share of the stolen rifles, the Bunch proceed back to Agua Verde. On the way, they are stopped by the men Mapache sent to intercept them, but, having anticipated the general might not want to honor his part of the bargain, Pike reveals to the Mexicans that the wagon is rigged to explode. The troops withdraw.

The Bunch take the stolen rifles to Mapache in separate lots: each pair bringing several crates, and getting their share of the gold in return. But when Dutch shows up with Angel, Mapache takes Angel prisoner, Teresa's mother having informed on him about giving rifles to the rebels. There's nothing Dutch can do and leaves Angel behind.

Holed up on a hilltop outside of Agua Verde, Dutch has given the news to the rest of the Bunch. Below, they see Freddie Sykes, returning with horses from the last delivery of rifles, ambushed by what remains of Thornton's posse. When Dutch damns the persistent Thornton, Pike defends his old riding partner: "He gave his word!" "That's not what counts!" Dutch comes back, "It's who you give it *to*!"

Pike elects it's better to let Thornton busy himself hunting down Sykes while the Bunch return to the safety of Agua Verde where Mapache is entertaining himself torturing Angel amidst a massive celebration. When Pike sees the laughing Mapache dragging Angel behind his automobile, Pike offers to buy Angel back, but Mapache will have none of it. Tired, humiliated, dejected, the Bunch retreat to a whorehouse.

While the Gorch brothers argue with a shared whore about price, Pike, disgusted with himself, sits with his own whore, notices her baby in a crib. His anger reaches a point where he stands in the doorway to the Gorches' room: "Let's go." Lyle looks to Tector, then back to Pike: "Why not?" Tector leaves behind the swallow he's been toying with: La Golondrina.

Outside the whorehouse, a glum Dutch has been sitting whittling,

The climax of the *Gunman's Walk* as the Bunch enter the courtyard of Mapache's hacienda. From left to right: Ben Johnson, Warren Oates, William Holden, Ernest Borgnine.

but when the other men exit, and Dutch catches the smile on Pike's face, it's his turn to smile. The four go to their horses, arm themselves, and march to the hacienda courtyard. "We've come for Angel," Pike demands of the general.

At first, Mapache appears to agree and leads bleeding Angel toward them only to slit his throat in front of the Bunch. Pike and Dutch open fire and down Mapache goes. And then…

Silence. Mapache's troops freeze, the Bunch freeze, no one willing to make a first move. Dutch laughs, the other men smile. It's their game to call. With a look of distaste on his face, Pike looks over at one of the

Opposite, top: The Gorch brothers go down together during the Battle of Bloody Porch: Warren Oates (left) and Ben Johnson.
Bottom: The Battle of Bloody Porch: Ernest Borgnine (left) and William Holden.

NINE. The Wild Bunch

The Wild Bunch

German advisors, raises his pistol and drops him. The courtyard becomes a maelstrom of gunfire, the Bunch against Mapache's 200 troops, with Tector, Lyle, then Pike taking a turn at the machine gun that was part of the booty from the munitions train. One by one, the Bunch fall, Pike finally brought down by three rifle shots, is hand still gripped around the trigger of the machine gun as he falls to his knees, as if his hand is raised in a fist.

Thornton's posse arrives, tickled at the scavengers' bounty splayed across the courtyard. Before they discover the bodies of the Bunch, Thornton finds Pike and takes his revolver, the one gun Pike hadn't gotten to use. The posse load up with the bodies of the Bunch and all the loot they can carry but see Thornton sitting by the village gates. "You

Deke Thornton (Robert Ryan) stands over the body of his friend Pike (William Holden), whose hand is still clutched, like an upraised fist, around the grip of the machine gun. Ernest Borgnine's Dutch lies dead near his riding partner. In the finished cut, Peckinpah smartly keeps the faces of the Bunch from the camera once they're dead to bring home the finality of their passing.

NINE. The Wild Bunch

ain't comin'," Coffer concludes. Thornton's reply is that he gave his word to bring the Bunch back and that's what he's doing. The posse ride off, leaving Thornton behind. Sometime later, Thornton hears shots in the distance. Still later, Sykes—who evidently was able to escape the posse—shows up in the company of some rebels. "Me and the boys got some work to do," Sykes says to Thornton. "You want to come with us? It ain't like it used to be … but it'll do." Thornton smiles, climbs on his horse and joins Sykes. They ride off with the rebels, Sykes cackling.

As "La Golondina" plays on the soundtrack, images of each of the Bunch, laughing, then their exit from Angel's village into a white light.

Ten

Undying Echoes and Dying Fires

"Well, second's better than third."
—J.R. Bonner (Steve McQueen) in *Junior Bonner*

An Echo Louder Than the Gunshot

In 1999, the Library of Congress selected *The Wild Bunch* for preservation as "culturally, historically, or aesthetically significant" ("Mission"). The American Film Institute has ranked the movie as one of the best of all American films, one of the 100 best thrillers, and one of the ten best Westerns of all time. Rotten Tomatoes gives the film a 94 percent positive rating. Google the film, and by general consensus, it's clear the film is both an acknowledged genre classic as well as an important entry in the American film canon; in the words of Roger Ebert, "one of the great defining moments of modern movies."

All that in mind, it can be a bit of a surprise to look back at the film's actual box office numbers when released in 1969 and learn it was not a particularly impressive performer. In his book *Peckinpah: The Western Films*, Paul Seydor claims *The Wild Bunch* did well enough to pay Warner Bros.' bills for a year (142). Still, of the three major Westerns released in 1969—*True Grit* which came out in June, along with *Bunch* and *Butch Cassidy and the Sundance Kid* released that October—*Bunch* was easily the weakest performer of the group earning $10.5 million (calculating admissions by the average ticket price at the time, this would translate to a current box office value of approximately $67.7 million, putting it within the annual top 50 earners of recent years—what's considered a "midrange" performer).

True Grit—a much more traditional Western with a touch of (no pun intended) 1960s grit down to starring that most traditional of Western icons, John Wayne—and *Butch Cassidy*—which took on some

Ten. Undying Echoes and Dying Fires

of the same Death of the West themes as *Bunch* but in a more whimsical, light-hearted fashion—not only were among the top performers of 1969, but among the top-earning movies of the *decade*, *True Grit* coming in at #45 among all releases 1961–1970, and *Butch Cassidy* #8 ahead of such films as *Patton* (1970), *Bonnie and Clyde, 2001: A Space Odyssey*, and *Lawrence of Arabia* (1962) (Finler 277).

Nor was the movie universally lauded on its release. Years later, Ernest Borgnine could still recall an incident when *The Wild Bunch* was first presented to reviewers at a promotional junket in the Bahamas at which Warner Bros. was previewing its upcoming releases. At a post-screening press conference, an appalled journalist from *Reader's Digest* stood up and asked, "Why was this film ever made?" (Ebert *"The Wild"*; "Ernest") According to a canvas of sixteen major reviewers taken by *Filmfacts* at the time, the movie's score was eight positive against four mixed and four negative; a win but not a resounding herald (*"The Wild"* 219).

But, in retrospect, maybe that shouldn't be a surprise.*

There'd never been a movie like *The Wild Bunch* before, at least not in the commercial mainstream. The titular characters of *Butch Cassidy and the Sundance Kid* are outlaws, but outlaws who only resort to violence once (before the final shootout) and then only to kill the *bandidos* who've murdered a man they've been working for. Otherwise, they're played more as lovable scamps rather than true Bad Guys ... and they're played by Paul Newman and Robert Redford; as handsome a bromantic couple as has ever graced the big screen.

Even *Bonnie and Clyde*—the movie one could argue opened the door to *The Wild Bunch*—soft-pedals its subject. The movie's Bonnie Parker and Clyde Barrow are played by Faye Dunaway and Warren Beatty; infinitely more attractive than their real-life counterparts. They dote on each other, care about each other, and the only time in the movie they kill a civilian—a shopkeeper who attacks Clyde—Clyde is distraught over having been forced—I emphasize, *forced*—to have to shoot the man. Otherwise, the only other targets of the Barrow Gang's violence are cops and posse members portrayed as, within the context of the movie, "legitimate" targets.

---

*Yet another parallel between *The Wild Bunch* and *The Magnificent Seven*. On its release, UA considered *Seven* a flop. It was only after its success overseas which led to a re-release domestically followed by constant revivals and re-showings on TV that the movie eventually became one of the most persistently popular of Westerns and an acknowledged genre classic (Prince). *The Magnificent Seven* was added to the National Film Registry in 2013.

117

But the Bunch, ah, the Bunch: pot-bellied middle-aged men, who may kill only as a practical matter, but are ruthless when doing so, and seem to have no second thoughts about shooting—and on occasion trampling—the men and women, civilian or not, who get in their way. And the violence they inflict is brutal, bloody, and truly, truly *violent*.

It may be more surprising that *The Wild Bunch* did as well as it did.

But it was not the sound of Sam Peckinpah's amplified gunshots that made the biggest cultural impact. It was their ongoing echo.

* * *

It's hard to break out the individual impact of the three successful Westerns of 1969 from what they may have done collectively, but certain is that they kicked off a surge in the genre's popularity through much of the 1970s that hasn't been equaled since. The already demonstrated pliability of the Western showed even more elasticity. John Wayne continued to punch out Bad Guys in the likes of *Chisum* (1970), *Big Jake* (1971), and *The Cowboys* (1972), but traditional Westerns stood alongside such twists on the genre as rock musical Western (*Zachariah*, 1971), surreal Biblical allegory (*Greaser's Palace*, 1972), and a brutally in-your-face comic attack on racism in Mel Brooks' classic anything-goes Western parody *Blazing Saddles* (1974).

All three of those 1969 Westerns may have integrated Death of the West themes into their stories to some degree or another, but it was obviously the visual tropes of *The Wild Bunch* which seemed to push the genre from the classical post-Civil War period into the early 20th-century culture clash of automobiles and horses, encroaching civilization and the last vestiges of the wild in the Wild West in movies like *Tell Them Willie Boy Is Here* (1969), *McCabe & Mrs. Miller* (1971), *Bite the Bullet* (1975), *Big Jake* ("The Latter").

That idea of the Death of the West as symbolizing something larger in the then present day—a loss of something pure and noble in the American spirit—wasn't restricted to this re-set Western period. Peckinpah himself successfully transposed the same themes to the present in his story of a modern-day rodeo star in the genial, gentle *Junior Bonner* (1972), and Sydney Pollack managed the same feat in his thematically melancholy, visually lyrical *Jeremiah Johnson* (1972), which was set in the pre-Civil War frontier.

Perhaps that's why *The Wild Bunch* resonated so strongly beyond its middling box office performance and thereafter through the years.

Ten. Undying Echoes and Dying Fires

Butch Cassidy, and to a much lesser extent, *True Grit*, used the passage of an era as background, a plot point. It was, however, the essence of *The Wild Bunch*; something not only reflecting a feeling of the time, but that, sadly, tragically, remains relevant to this day.

* * *

The film clearly had an impact on cinematic violence and filmmakers who specialized in action. Spurting blood became routine, and hardly a major action piece today—fireballs with the hero jumping clear in the foreground, spectacular car crashes, high falls, shattered windows, etc.—isn't filmed in slow motion (Greenberg 27). Walter Hill's *The Long Riders* (1980) is virtually a pastiche of *The Wild Bunch*, even lifting specific images from the film, and the bullet-riddled climax of his *Extreme Prejudice* (1987) is an obvious riff on the Battle of Bloody Porch. You can see Peckinpah's influence in the years after in the work of action directors like John Woo, macho posturers like John Milius, and specialists in over-the-top violence like Quentin Tarantino.

It's not hard to argue this has not generally been a positive thing. Peckinpah had meant to repulse people, and instead, he upped the ante (Fine 156). By the time of *Die Hard 2* (1990), hero Bruce Willis is stabbing a Bad Guy through the eye with an icicle, *Total Recall* (1992) has villain Michael Ironside meeting his just end by falling to his death after an elevator amputates both his arms, and *Starship Troopers* (1997) treated its audience to any variety of dismemberments, impalings, incinerations, and eviscerations as futuristic soldiers battle it out with giant bugs, all in the spirit of a fun night's bit of movie entertainment.

The muse behind the Marvel universe, Stan Lee, opined in one of his "Stan's Soapbox" columns that "a story without a message is like a man without a soul" (Feige 20). The reason *The Wild Bunch* still stands apart from the long line of imitators and acolytes and occasional remakers is the violence in Peckinpah's movie *means* something; the movie has a soul.

The Tarantinos and even the Woos are playing a game of telephone. Violence, for them and their like, has become eye candy, visceral excitement. How much meaning can it have in what are essentially comic books for adults like *Kill Bill Vols. 1 & 2* (2003, 2004) and *Face/Off* (1997) and *Mission: Impossible II* (2000)? Peckinpah rooted *The Wild Bunch* and, for that matter, all his other Westerns, in a West he felt he knew and understood, a West which had—at least so he believed—actually existed, populated with knowable human beings with real knowable concerns. The universes of, say, Tarantino's *Django Unchained* (2012) and *The Hateful Eight* (2015) can *only* exist in the movies; their characters are pure cinematic invention. They are movies made with undeniable skill and, admittedly, a passion of sorts, but it is a passion for celluloid fun; they are not movies about the West, but "movies ... about movies" (D. Murray). Peckinpah's passion was for a time and a place and a breed of men buried by change; men he felt were, in many ways, just like himself.

Career-Maker

In a very real, pragmatic way, the movie had an immediate impact on the careers of a number of its creative personnel. There were several careers which could be divided into Before and After *The Wild Bunch*.

Lucien Ballard had already been a respected cinematographer, but *The Wild Bunch* elevated him to a kind of superstar status in the trade ("Lucien"). He would shoot several more films for Peckinpah: *The Ballad of Cable Hogue, Junior Bonner,* and *The Getaway* (1972).

Jerry Fielding's Oscar-nominated score for the movie—one of the only two Academy Award nominations the film received—not only cemented his comeback from the blacklist, but granted him permanent access to big screen composing and would lead to two more Oscar noms: one for his second feature score for Peckinpah, *Straw Dogs* (1971); and for Clint Eastwood's *The Outlaw Josey Wales* (1976), another filmmaker with whom, post-Peckinpah, Fielding would develop a long-running collaboration (Michael Winner was another). Fielding would do several more scores for Peckinpah: *Junior Bonner, The Getaway* (which the producers replaced with one by Quincy Jones much to Peckinpah's dismay [Terrill 244]), *Bring Me the Head of Alfredo Garcia* (1974), and *The Killer Elite* (1975). It was after this last that Fielding, tired of the stress of dealing with Peckinpah, decided it would be his last collaboration with the filmmaker (Burlingame).

The Wild Bunch certainly provided a booster rocket for co-writer Walon Green. He would work on other high-profile projects like William Friedkin's *Sorcerer* (1977) and *The Brinks Job* (1978), and uncredited work on John Badham's *WarGames* (1983), but he would have a greater impact in television as co-producer/co-executive producer on such TV classics as *Hill Street Blues, NYPD Blue, ER,* and the original *Law & Order.*

TEN. Undying Echoes and Dying Fires

But, of course, the biggest professional impact was on the man whose name came above the title: Sam Peckinpah.

What Goes Up...

The Wild Bunch may not have been the smash hit Warner Bros. had been hoping for, but it earned well enough that, combined with the disproportionate amount of buzz generated by the film, it put Sam Peckinpah's name back on the bankable directors list. The film kicked off a five-year production spree as remarkable in its quantity and overall quality as it is in its creative ambition; a body of work which would, forever after, reinforce and define the Sam Peckinpah brand established with *The Wild Bunch.*

Even before *Bunch* had been released, Peckinpah was at work filling out his two-picture contract with Warner Bros. with *The Ballad of Cable Hogue* (1970). Set a little earlier than *Bunch* but in the same turn-of-the-century period, *Cable Hogue* took many of the same Death of the West themes of its predecessor and recalibrated them for a bittersweet, humorous, and often romantic story about a "desert rat" (Jason Robards) who finds prosperity in his beloved western wastes, and love with a prostitute in a nearby town (Stella Stevens).

Peckinpah pushes a little too hard to make his story likable and his occasional use of slapstick comedy and fast-motion chases is as awkward as his *The Wild Bunch* flashbacks. But if *Bunch* is an angry, pained, defiant cry over the loss of something in the American spirit, then \ *Cable Hogue* is its eloquent, loving eulogy. Its flaws did not outweigh its overall great strengths, and the film would come to be considered a "neglected ... masterpiece" (Nachbar 119).

Unfortunately, Peckinpah's relationship with his producer Phil Feldman, as well as with Warner Bros., had soured over the re-editing of *The Wild Bunch*, and deteriorated even further when *Cable Hogue* ran over budget and behind schedule largely because of bad weather (Fine 184). The last straw for Peckinpah was when the studio screened an unrefined, overlong, unscored print for distributors who, unsurprisingly, were less than enthused by what they saw (182). With little faith in the film and eager to be finished with the increasingly troublesome director, Warner Bros. gave the film a minimal release and it quickly disappeared (Seydor, *The Western* xiv).

The Wild Bunch

Dustin Hoffman in *Straw Dogs* (1971), one of Peckinpah's best and most controversial post–*Wild Bunch* films.

Peckinpah came roaring back with *Straw Dogs* (1971). Based on Gordon Williams' novel *The Siege of Trencher's Farm* and informed by the writings on territoriality by social anthropologist Robert Ardrey, violence is not an element of *Straw Dogs* as it was in *The Wild Bunch*, but its subject. The film was a change for Peckinpah in that it was his first modern-day feature, one plugging directly into the social turmoil of the times, and up until its last act, was a drama-driven rather than action-driven piece. But because of its brutal third act—which may have offered less violence quantitatively than *The Wild Bunch*, but made up for it in excruciating intensity—and a controversial rape scene, *Straw Dogs* generated even more heated conversation than *Bunch* (Fine 213). Reviewers were divided with a *Filmfacts* canvas showing an almost even split between positives and negatives ("Straw Dogs" 3). The critical reception seemed to have little impact on box office, however, and *Straw Dogs* out-earned *The Wild Bunch* (Fine 207).

As with *The Ballad of Cable Hogue*, Peckinpah again tried to show

Ten. Undying Echoes and Dying Fires

there were more colors to his palette than the red of spilt blood and reunited with his *The Cincinnati Kid* star Steve McQueen for *Junior Bonner*, a quiet, warm drama set in the contemporary West about a one-time rodeo star dealing with his fading career, dysfunctional family, and a dying West. Reviewers were generally impressed, considering *Bonner* "a jewel of the kind that does not appear very often" (Siegel 58). The box office was less kind. It may have been that McQueen and Peckinpah, both associated with action films, disappointed audiences with *Junior Bonner*'s low-key charms, or that the film suffered from being one of a raft of rodeo flicks all released within the same three-month window in 1972 (*J.W. Coop*, *The Honkers*, *When Legends Die*), all of which flopped (Siegel 58; Terrill 216).

Ali MacGraw and Steve McQueen in *The Getaway* (1972). Although evaluation of the film has risen over the years, especially after Roger Donaldson's misbegotten 1994 remake, at the time critics were not impressed. Moviegoers, however, were and gave Peckinpah the biggest hit of his career. Unfortunately for Peckinpah, his success in films like *The Getaway* while films like *The Ballad of Cable Hogue* (1970) and *Junior Bonner* (1972) failed at the box office branded him as "Bloody Sam."

Still, McQueen and Peckinpah had both been so pleased with *Junior Bonner* that they re-teamed for *The Getaway* (1972), a robbers-on-the-lam action thriller loosely adapted from Jim Thompson's novel. While the shoot went smoothly, trouble orbited the production. There was bad blood between Peckinpah and producer Robert Evans over a previous deal gone bad, and then McQueen began an affair with his leading lady, Ali MacGraw, who, at the time, was Evans' wife (Fine 228, Terrill 228). McQueen, whose production company was backing the film, had final cut approval and had edits made which flattered the star but irritated Peckinpah, and then McQueen had Jerry Fielding's score replaced with a "jazzier" one by Quincy Jones which so aggravated the director he took out a full-page ad in trade paper *Daily Variety* complimenting Fielding on his score (Terrill 244).

Reviewers were generally hostile, not because the movie was executed poorly, but apparently objecting that for the first time Peckinpah had made a film which was about nothing more than it was about (Fine 231–232). It was considered a disappointment for Peckinpah to do a movie that was merely entertaining ... but entertaining it was. Not only was *The Getaway* the only one of a string of couple-on-the-run crime thrillers (Terry Malick's *Badlands* [1973], Robert Altman's *Thieves Like Us* [1974], Steven Spielbeg's *The Sugarland Express* [1974]) to find success at the box office, it would be the biggest hit of Peckinpah's career, his only blockbuster, grossing nearly $20 million (232). With the same formula used in calculating *The Wild Bunch*'s box office in today's terms, that would translate to approximately $110 million today.

But the film also damned the filmmaker as "Bloody Sam" (Fine xiii). The introduction for an *Esquire* photo spread on the filming of *The Getaway* read: "The last time Sam Peckinpah directed a movie [was *Straw Dogs*]. It was a violent movie ... and so was *The Wild Bunch* before it" ("Cahiers").

As if *The Ballad of Cable Hogue* and *Junior Bonner* had never existed.

Peckinpah seemed to be trying to split the difference on his next project, using his new box office cachet to return to the source material behind his first screenplay, "The Authentic Death of Hendry Jones," with *Pat Garrett and Billy the Kid* (1973). The film was intended as a more elegiac, lyrical treatment of the same themes of *The Wild Bunch*, but circumstances and Peckinpah's own increasingly self-destructive flaws came together to permanently derail a career which had only recently been resurrected with *The Wild Bunch* (Fine 240).

Ten. Undying Echoes and Dying Fires

Richard Jaeckel (left) and James Coburn in *Pat Garrett & Billy the Kid* (1973). Studio-mangled masterpiece? Overlooked cinema poetry? Directorial fumble? An ongoing debate although it's undeniable that individual scenes from the film do achieve the lyrical quality Peckinpah was after.

Peckinpah and producer Gordon Carroll and MGM, the studio backing the film, never agreed on a shooting schedule even after production had begun (Seydor, *The Western* 184). MGM chief James Aubrey, who had been brought in to turn the debt-ridden studio around with a ruthless cost-cutting mandate, was not only constantly on the director to speed up shooting, but also wanted bloody action whereas Peckinpah was going for something more poetic and reflective (Fine 251). After Peckinpah delivered his cut, MGM recut the film with Peckinpah publicly yowling that the studio had removed "the heart of the film" (*"Pat Garrett," Filmfacts* 87). Peckinpah went so far as to sue (unsuccessfully) to have his name removed from the movie (Seydor, *The Western* 198). Peckinpah also lost the services of his usual composer, Jerry Fielding, who pulled out when tasked with having to compose music around songs written for the film by Bob Dylan who also had a small role in the film (*"Pat Garrett,"* Crimetv.com).

But Peckinpah's hands were not clean. Always a heavy drinker, booze was finally getting in the way of his work (Fine 252–253). It also seemed as if he had lost control of his distinctive process. Screenwriter Rudy Wurlitzer would complain at the time of constant rewrites leaving the script a mess (Seydor, *The Western* 190). In an interview years later, Peckinpah regular L.Q. Jones, who had a role in *Pat Garrett*, recalled that Peckinpah's process was to take a project apart—pit actors against each other, rework a script even through a shoot—and then reassemble it. Said Jones: "He did that up through, it stopped when we did *Pat Garrett and Billy the Kid.* He was too sick. So he took it apart, but he couldn't put it back together" (Francis).

Opinion then was and remains divided over *Pat Garrett and Billy the Kid:* studio-mangled masterpiece, overlooked classic, intriguing but flawed curio, but at the time it was a high-profile failure with both reviewers and ticket-buyers ("Peckinpah's Cut" 110).

Warren Oates (against the car) in *Bring Me the Head of Alfredo Garcia* (1974). Dismissed when released, *Alfredo Garcia* has, over time, come to be viewed as one of Peckinpah's best and possibly most personally expressive films. Some suspect it's an allegory for Peckinpah's own trials in the film industry.

Ten. Undying Echoes and Dying Fires

Peckinpah reacted by going off to Mexico to make *Bring Me the Head of Alfredo Garcia* (1974), a tequila-fueled fever dream about a third-rate barroom piano player (Warren Oates) and his prostitute girlfriend (Isela Vega) on a quest for a $10,000 bounty offered for the eponymous head. Years later, the film would be considered something of a cult classic, possibly one of Peckinpah's best and most personal films, an allegory for his own quixotic artistic aspirations and crucifixions (Thurman, *Sam Peckinpah's*; Murphy 14). But at the time, too nihilistic and grotesque for reviewers or audiences, some declaring it one of the worst movies of all time, *Alfredo Garcia* handed Peckinpah his second box office flop in a row (Medved 55).

Alfredo Garcia marked the end of Peckinpah's best, and the beginning of the director's long, painful fade to black. Both his career and his person now began to suffer from the cumulative damage of too many years of too much liquor, a developing cocaine habit, too many studio battles.

… Flies Too Close to the Sun, Catches Fire and Crashes

Sam Peckinpah had fought with producers and/or studio execs on most of the ten features he had directed to that point. He had been fired from one project, almost fired from another. The word was out that his combative attitude and conduct on the set, made worse by his escalating drinking and drug use and his increasingly chaotic work methods, made for ignored schedules and busted budgets; he was, in short, more trouble than he was worth.

And as for his worth? Of the ten films he'd directed, and the three others (including uncredited work on *One-Eyed Jacks*) he'd written, only three had been winners at the domestic box office.

His toxic reputation pushed him out of the higher circles of the motion picture industry, relegated him to lesser projects for lesser producers, and he became branded exclusively as an action director. His first film after the back-to-back flops of *Pat Garrett* and *Alfredo Garcia* was the modern-day political thriller *The Killer Elite* for first-time producer Arthur Lewis (Fine 281). Peckinpah, now wrestling with a cocaine habit as well as liquor, wrangled constantly with Lewis and execs at United Artists, home of the project (Simmons, "The Peckinpah" 61). Again, Peckinpah's deconstruction/reconstruction methodology failed him and the script, nominally by Stirling Silliphant who had won an Oscar for *In the Heat of the Night*, was constantly being rewritten. In a later magazine profile, actor Burt Young, who had a supporting role in the film, said the screenplay had fallen into such a mess "that they would take a baloney like me" and even give Young a crack at rewriting it (Lester, "Actor" 74).

The movie was intended to capitalize on the post-Watergate paranoia about Washington moral bankruptcy, but next to other films in that vein released around the same time, like *The Parallax View* (1974) and *Three Days of the Condor* (1975), *The Killer Elite* seems both stylistically and dramatically a weak sibling. Although the movie did make its money back, reviewers generally considered the film lesser Peckinpah (Fine 292–293).

Then came World War II–set *Cross of Iron* (1977), Peckinpah's only war film, for Wolf Hartwig, a producer of cheap, often sleazy T & A flicks trying to up his industry pedigree. It was a troubled shoot with Hartwig's financing spotty throughout the production, and Peckinpah ultimately having to improvise an ending when the money ran out before a proper one could be filmed. Peckinpah's health also suffered throughout the shoot, a combination of the production's stresses and his heavy drinking (Niemi 67). The film received a minimal release in the United States (although it did well enough overseas to justify a sequel with which Peckinpah had no involvement), and while estimation of the film has risen over the years and *Cross* easily represents the best of the director's late career work, the critical consensus at the time was that Peckinpah was in decline (Fine 304–305).

James Coburn in *Cross of Iron* (1977), easily the best of Peckinpah's late career films, a body of work generally reflecting his ostracization from the major Hollywood production circles as well as his own faltering skills thanks to alcohol and cocaine.

Ten. Undying Echoes and Dying Fires

The director seemed to only confirm that appraisal with *Convoy* (1978), a nonsensical piece about a trucker rebellion based on the gimmicky hit song by C.W. McCall which kicked off the CB craze. Peckinpah's attempts to shoehorn his favored Death of the West themes into the movie, with his independent truckers as stand-ins for the Wild Bunch, only succeeded in turning a silly movie into a silly and pretentious one (Fine 306). Peckinpah's increasingly erratic behavior drove the film over-budget and behind schedule, but the film still managed to be a money-maker (Fine 319). Still, that didn't compensate for the overwhelming opinion among reviewers that Sam Peckinpah had—in the words of his nephew David—"forfeited his credentials as a serious director [with *Convoy*]" (320).

Peckinpah wouldn't work for another four years and when he did, he was again working for producers attempting their first major film with an adaptation of Robert Ludlum's political thriller, *The Osterman Weekend* (1983). Peckinpah had no illusions about the project, taking the job only because it was "the least despicable option available," even refusing to exercise his right to a proprietary credit (Jameson 28, 30). Working with a screenplay even screenwriter Alan Sharp knew was unworkable, and constantly tangling with the producers over the story and costs, the end product unsurprisingly was panned by critics and a box office dud.

The Osterman Weekend would have made for an ignominious end to a career in which, until those last few years, Peckinpah's failures—*Major Dundee*, *Pat Garrett and Billy the Kid*—had been as notable in their almost-but-not-quite ambitions as his successes. To complete an arc which had begun with the promise of *Ride the High Country* and reached a zenith in *The Wild Bunch* with the likes of *The Osterman Weekend* would have been a Hollywood tragedy of the highest order. Thankfully, Fate provided Peckinpah with the opportunity to—literally—go out on a high note.

In mid–1984, Peckinpah was improbably approached about a documentary project with Beatle John Lennon's son Julian, to support the release of Julian's debut album, *Valotte*. This evolved into shooting a pair of videos for the album (Fine 366, 368). Although Peckinpah, in typical Peckinpah fashion, continually drove the record execs overseeing the project to distraction, he delivered what were universally considered elegantly simple yet moving and poetic pieces of mini-cinema: one for the single "Valotte," the other, the ironically titled "Too Late for Goodbyes" (371).

This last would serve as his cinematic eulogy. The body he had so long abused finally failed him. Just a few months after the Julian Lennon shoot, on the morning of December 28, 1984, two months short of his sixtieth birthday, David Samuel Peckinpah died at Cetinela Medical Center of heart failure.

Eleven

A Moment Come and Gone

> "The day of the Forty-Niner is gone. The day of the steady businessman has arrived."
> —Luther Sampson (Percy Helton)
> in Ride the High Country

By the time of *Pat Garrett and Billy the Kid* and *Bring Me the Head of Alfredo Garcia*, the buzz from *The Wild Bunch* had long since dissipated, and the industry's verdict was in: Sam Peckinpah was a money-losing pain in the ass.

He was a self-admitted alcoholic who had multiplied his problems by getting involved with cocaine as a supposed cure for his drinking with the expected disastrous results (Fine 278). He was combative, rebellious, abusive, undisciplined, and regularly went over-schedule and over-budget. He'd fought with producers and/or studio executives on most of his films, could be needlessly provocative when dealing with the press if he felt criticized.

An even worse sin in Hollywood's eyes: the overwhelming majority of his movies didn't make money.

For the sake of argument, let's take the problematic elements out of the equation. Let's say Sam Peckinpah had not been erratic, paranoid, amplifying his psychological flaws with alcohol and cocaine. Let's say producers had loved working with him, that he'd delivered his films more-or-less on time and on budget, that he didn't get into verbal brawls with members of the press who took issue with some of the content in his films. Let's go further and say that *Major Dundee* and *Pat Garrett and Billy the Kid* hadn't been taken away from him and recut, that MGM had done justice to *Ride the High Country* in its marketing and distribution of the film in the United States, and Warner Bros. had done the same with *The Ballad of Cable Hogue*.

It's possible, even probable, that with that change in circumstances, he would've done more and better films in the later part of his career, but other than that… It can only be seen in retrospect, but, as I said in the Introduction, Peckinpah, like his Wild Bunch, had had his career breakthrough by being a desperate man in a desperate time who—also like the Bunch—would eventually be out of step, out of place, and desperately out of time. Even if Peckinpah had managed to continue to make good movies, as long as they were *his* kind of movies, the issue would've been: who was going to come out to see them?

The movie-going audience isn't static.

Taking a macro view of the state of the industry at the time Sam Peckinpah was experiencing his at-long-last career breakthrough with *The Wild Bunch*, his sands were already running out. Consider the top 10 movies of the 1960s were

The Sound of Music (1965)
Love Story (1970)
Airport (1970)
The Graduate
Dr. Zhivago (1965)
Mary Poppins (1964)
M*A*S*H
Butch Cassidy and the Sundance Kid
Thunderball (1965)
Patton (1970)

It is, to say the least, an eclectic collection (which is a statement about the era in itself), dominated by films—good and bad—intended for an adult sensibility, i.e., for grown-ups. Say what you will about treacly *Love Story* and the soapy melodrama of *Airport*, they were not movies for the 15- to 24-year-old demographic. Along those same lines, other top earners of the decade included *Bonnie and Clyde* (#15), *2001: A Space Odyssey* (#16), *The Dirty Dozen* (#19), *Bullitt* (#24), *The Longest Day* (1962, #26), *Lawrence of Arabia* (#30), and *Midnight Cowboy* (1969, #31) (Finler, 277).

Contrast this with the top 10 earners of the 1970s

Star Wars (1977)
The Empire Strikes Back (1980)
Jaws (1975)
Grease (1978)
The Exorcist (1973)
The Godfather (1972)

Eleven. A Moment Come and Gone

Superman—The Movie (1979)
The Sting (1973)
Close Encounters of the Third Kind (1977)
Saturday Night Fever (1977)

Also among the top earners of the decade: *Smokey and the Bandit* (1977, #13), *Star Trek* (1979, #17), *Jaws II* (1978, #20) (Finler 277–278). And then come the 1980s.

E.T.: The Extra-Terrestrial (1982)
Home Alone (1990)
Return of the Jedi (1983)
Batman (1989)
Beverly Hills Cop (1984)
Ghostbusters (1984)
Ghost (1990)
Raiders of the Lost Ark (1981)
Indiana Jones and the Last Crusade (1989)
Indiana Jones and the Temple of Doom (1984)

Among the top 10 moneymakers of each year of the decade are a significant number of sequels: *Superman II* (1981), *Rocky III* (1982), *Rambo: First Blood—Part II* and *Rocky IV* (both 1985), *The Karate Kid II* and *Star Trek IV: The Voyage Home* (both 1986), *Beverly Hills Cop II* (1987), and *Lethal Weapon 2* (1989).

And now let's look at the top earners of the last five full years, 2014–2018.

Star Wars: The Force Awakens (2015)
Black Panther (2018)
Avengers: Infinity War (2018)
Jurassic World (2015)
Star Wars: The Last Jedi (2017)
Incredibles 2 (2018)
Rogue One: A Star Wars Story (2016)
Beauty and the Beast (2017)
Finding Dory (2016)
Avengers: Age of Ultron (2015)

There's not a single film in the group that's not related to an existing franchise, and/or is a direct sequel, or a remake. There's also not a single title—not one—that's aimed squarely at an adult sensibility. The eclecticism of the 1960s has been replaced by a thematic monochromaticism. Reinforcing both points, the annual top 10 earners over the same period include *Jurassic World: Fallen Kingdom, Aquaman, Deadpool 2, Mission: Impossible—Fallout, Ant-Man and the Wasp, Solo: A Star Wars Story* (all 2018); *Wonder Woman, Guardians of the Galaxy Vol. 2, Spider-Man: Homecoming, Thor: Ragnarok, Justice League, Logan* (all 2017); *Captain America: Civil War, Deadpool, Batman v. Superman: Dawn of Justice, Suicide Squad* (all 2016); *Furious 7, The Hunger Games: Mockingjay—Part 2, Mission: Impossible—Rogue Nation* (all 2015), *The Hunger Games: Mockingjay—Part 1, Captain America: The Winter Soldier, Guardians of the Galaxy* (all 2014).

As early as the late 1970s, one can see a tectonic change in the cinematic terrain; a shift in moviegoing sensibilities that has gone into overdrive over the last twenty years or so. In his 1993 article "The Decade When Movies Mattered," critic David Thomson looked back on what many consider one of the most creative periods in American cinema (a period Thomson posits actually begins in the mid–1960s): "In the films of the '70s, the curtain called "happy ending" was ripped away by the life force of the people, and by the actual conditions of America. So many kinds of dismay and disenchantment made for the short-lived but still beguiling *honesty* of the '70s (Thomson 45, italics mine). "For a few years at least, our movies spoke to us with unaccustomed candor [but] by the end of the decade ... pictures got smaller" (90).

Smaller not in spectacle; in that area, they grew ever *more* spectacular each year thanks to advances in special effects technology and the demands of an audience who wanted each new effects/action extravaganza to be more extravagant than the last. Smaller, in that they became bigger productions *about* less.

Contrast Thomson's comments with *Entertainment Weekly*'s 2018 end-of-year sum-up by Chris Nashawaty: "While we continued to wrestle with issues of identity, equality, and representation in what we watch, read, and listen to, we also beat a hasty retreat into the comfort food of the past, taking refuge in the cozy familiarity of reboots, sequels" (Nashawaty 16).

Nashawaty goes on to point out how, in the midst of "the most divisive national-identity crisis in recent memory," the box office that year—as in most years since the beginning of the new century—was dominated by superhero flicks, franchise sequels, reboots and remakes, and a general trend toward escapism (16).

ELEVEN. A Moment Come and Gone

Demographics shift as certainly and inexorably as the ocean's tides and can similarly re-sculpt the shorelines of popular culture. The irony—bitter irony, depending on your tastes—is that the same social/cultural/demographic dynamics which made *The Wild Bunch* possible have also, over time, created a growth culture for the overwhelming popularity of tales of derring-do by men in tights, chosen young wizards, plush-toy-adorable questers on a trek through magical lands, vampires and their gloomy high school girlfriends, and, in the same process, made *The Wild Bunch* kind of filmmaking and Sam Peckinpah kind of filmmaker nearly impossible in the commercial mainstream at the major studio level.

Even if Peckinpah had not made himself a *persona non grata* in Hollywood in the mid–1960s, a few years earlier and *The Wild Bunch* could not have been made; the tolerances for Peckinpah's kind of unvarnished storytelling—both in the unmitigated and adamant antiheroism of its main characters as much as in its extreme violence—wasn't in place yet. And a few years later...

Almost as soon as that great creative window David Thomson wrote about was opening to its max to let in *The Wild Bunch*—the era of *Five Easy Pieces* (1970), *Shampoo* (1975), *All That Jazz* (1979), *The Godfather I* and *II*, *Chinatown* (1974), *Taxi Driver* (1976), *Klute* (1971), *All the President's Men* (1976), *A Clockwork Orange* (1971), *The Last Picture Show* (1971), *Mean Streets* (1973), etc., along with Peckinpah's own *Straw Dogs* and *Bring Me the Head of Alfredo Garcia*—another wind was coming along soon to blow it closed. Like his avatar, Pike Bishop, Peckinpah—at the very time he was experiencing the career breakout in 1969 promised years before with *Ride the High Country*—needed to be thinking past his "guns"; those days were closing fast.

In the summer of 1975, less than a year after *Alfredo Garcia* had crashed and burned soon after opening, Universal released the film adaptation of Peter Benchley's potboiler *Jaws*, only the second feature by a young Steven Spielberg whose first feature, *The Sugarland Express*, had stiffed at the box office (grossly out-earned by Peckinpah's similar *The Getaway*), and who had done most of his work in TV. *Jaws* set records earning more money and earning it faster in its initial release than any movie in history, and did so at a time of the year which had previously been a junkyard of cinematic pap for kids out of school (Knauer, *TIME: American Legends* 143). *Jaws* co-producer Richard Zanuck would claim that he earned more from *Jaws* than his father—legendary 20th Century-Fox chief Darryl Zanuck—earned in his *entire lifetime* (Biskind 278)!

The Wild Bunch

The shark that devoured the creative explosion of the 1960s–1970s. Richard Dreyfuss (left) and Robert Shaw face off with a massive sea-going predator in *Jaws* (1975), the movie that sent Hollywood on a still-ongoing quest for similarly massive hits.

Proving *Jaws*' success was not, in the jargon of the industry, a "non-repeating phenomenon," two years later *Star Wars* rocketed past *Jaws*' earnings, and then with its sequel, *The Empire Strikes Back* and its nearly equal box office returns, destroyed the Hollywood rule-of-thumb about sequels—make them cheap, make them quick, and hope for 40 percent of the original's take (Dempsy 31)—and set the industry on course toward the concept of The Franchise: the property which becomes a brand name for sequels and spinoffs across the spectrum of media platforms—from features to TV cartoons to videogames—and earns as much, if not more, in merchandising as in ticket sales (Biskind 341).

Those kinds of returns on those kinds of films signaled a massive cultural turning away from Thomson's "honesty" of the 1970s toward a "culture [that] is about distraction, numbing oneself.... There is no

Eleven. A Moment Come and Gone

George Lucas proved the outsized success of *Jaws* was no fluke but a new paradigm with *Star Wars* (1977); the death knell for Peckinpah's kind of filmmaking at the major studio level. Shown here are Mark Hamill (left) and Harrison Ford.

self-reflection, no sitting still" (Lester, "We're Hooked" 42). As long ago as the early 2000s, years before the current saturation of the top-end of the box office charts by special effects-laden spectacles, critic Pete Rainer was lamenting, "Escapism is fine, but where are the films that capture, if only indirectly, the frights we are escaping *from*?" (64). The documentary-like grit of *The French Connection* (1971) gave way to the near–James Bondian action of the *Lethal Weapon* series and the gloss and laughs of the *Beverly Hills Cop* flicks; the nightmare of Vietnam in *Apocalypse Now* (1979) surrendered to the upbeat revisionist revisiting of *Rambo* and ultimately the MTV-styled flag-waving of the likes of *Top Gun* (1986) and *Pearl Harbor* (2001). And as for Sam Peckinpah's beloved West.... Like Pike Bishop said, those days closed fast ... frighteningly fast.

The Wild Bunch

Movie sensibilities changed because moviegoers' sensibilities changed. The near-documentary grit of *The French Connection* (top) (1971), with Gene Hackman, gave way to the almost cartoonish over-the-top-ness of action-stuffed movies like the *Lethal Weapon* (bottom) series (Danny Glover [left] and Mel Gibson in the 1987 original).

The reflective moral ambiguity/ambivalence of the 1960s–1970s in which Peckinpah reveled was steam rollered by an artificial and simplistic moral clarity in super-patriotic actioners like *Top Gun* (top) (1986) (Val Kilmer [left] shaking hands with Tom Cruise) and the *Rambo* movies (Sylvester Stallone takes on the Vietnamese single-handed—and wins—in *Rambo: First Blood Part II* [bottom] [1985]).

The Wild Bunch

The Western may not be dead, but it's been on life support since its great flowering of the late 1960s-early 1970s (Bach, 197). Since that time, only a handful of Westerns have made any serious impact at the box office: *Silverado* (1985), *Young Guns* (1988) and its 1990 sequel, *Dancing with Wolves* (1990), umpteenth re-telling of the OK Corral shootout *Tombstone* (1993), the spoof *Maverick* (1994), soap operish *Legends of the Fall* (1994), lark *The Mask of Zorro* (1998), *Open Range* (2003), *Hidalgo* (2004), remake *3:10 to Yuma* (2007), Tarantino's *Django Unchained* (2012) and *The Hateful Eight* (2015), and in the work of the only committed repositor of the Western tradition, Clint Eastwood in his *The Outlaw Josey Wales* (1976), *Pale Rider* (1985), and his Oscar-winning *Unforgiven* (1992). But while *Dancing with Wolves*, *Unforgiven*, *Maverick*, and Tarantino's blood-soaked *Django Unchained* turned big box office, the rest were mid-rangers at best, while at the same time, the box office graveyard is packed with flops like the movie which sank United Artists *Heaven's Gate* (1980), *Far and Away* (1992), *Geronimo: An American Legend* (1993), *Wyatt Earp* (1994), *Bad Girls* (1994), *The Quick and the Dead* (1995), *Wild Bill* (1995), *Dead Man* (1995), *Ride with the Devil* (1999), *Wild Wild West* (1999; its $114 million box office couldn't offset its $170 million budget), *All the Pretty Horses* (2000), *Texas Rangers* (2000), *American Outlaws* (2001), *The Missing* (2003), *The Alamo* (2004), *The Assassination of Jesse James by the Coward Robert Ford* (2007), *Cowboys & Aliens* (2011), *The Lone Ranger* (2013), *A Million Ways to Die in the West* (2014), *Hostiles* (2017).

Maybe that proliferation of almost a half-century ago exhausted the genre, left nothing more to say, or maybe too many revisionists had revised the grandeur, the mystique, the *life* out of the Western. Perhaps Peckinpah himself had helped kill it with *The Wild Bunch*, celebrating the truth of the Old West by destroying the romantic mythology which had kept the genre alive for so long (Eggert).

Or perhaps it's been something more elemental.

The argument had been made by more than one critic that the traditional Western tropes, an iconography going back to the days of the 19th-century literary ancestors of the genre, i.e., Owen Wister, Ned Buntline, et al. have been transplanted to fantasy and sci fi milieus like the *Star Wars* series, to urban thrillers like Christopher Nolan's *Batman* trilogy, to actioners set against post-apocalyptic Western-like wastes as in the *Mad Max* films (D. Murray). Same tropes ... but not the same.

In such vehicles, those familiar thematic anchors have been detached

ELEVEN. A Moment Come and Gone

from their more-or-less realistic moorings—and in so doing, from their dramatic heft, from their *meaning*—to make them playable for a generation of moviegoer no longer feeling any cultural connection to the iconography of weather-beaten men on horseback out on the western expanses where the most advanced technology is the pistol on their hip and the rifle in its saddle scabbard. It is a generation which has grown up with effects-laden, hyper-paced movies about simplistically heroic heroes dashing about the cosmos, about super-powered crusaders and teen wizards (Daly 11).

The point being that even if Peckinpah had managed to rein in his vices, learned to keep his mouth shut and play nice with studio chieftains, even if, say, *Pat Garrett and Billy the Kid* had come out as the movie he'd wanted it to be, the chances are that by 1973, Peckinpah and the movies he did best—movies set in the West, both period and modern-day—had run out of time. Peckinpah had needed a Western to launch himself into features—*Ride the High Country*—and a Western to rescue him from exile—*The Wild Bunch*. Even if he'd behaved himself, Peckinpah needed a Western to bring himself back again after the failures of *Pat Garrett* and *Alfredo Garcia* because Westerns, as he'd proved throughout his career, whether set in the past or the present, were what he did best. Of the seventeen films he'd written and/or directed, only four were not set in the period or modern-day West. Peckinpah's problem was that as early as the mid–1970s, as much as he needed Westerns, Hollywood needed Westerns less and less (Munn, 157). Marshall Fine's biography, *Bloody Sam*, tells of late-career Peckinpah hustling scripts, most of them Westerns, but the studio doors were closed to him.

The change in moviegoer sensibilities paralleled a change in the movie industry. In the 1960s-1970s, the industry had re-shaped itself in a way which allowed new talent the opportunity to test, experiment, push limits. Thereafter, one by one, the major studios were absorbed by larger entities: Columbia first by Coca Cola then by Sony; Warner Bros. first by the Kinney National Company which morphed into Warner Communications which eventually merged with Time Inc. to create Time Warner which was bought in 2018 by AT&T and re-christened as the company's WarnerMedia subsidiary; 20th Century-Fox by News Corp. then by The Walt Disney Company; Paramount first by Gulf & Western then by Viacom, and so on. The endgame for such absorptions was "synergy"—the idea that each of the various divisions under the one corporate umbrella, i.e., the film studio, TV production, publishing,

Even if Peckinpah had taken better care of himself and his career, his long-term professional survivability would've been doubtful as the young moviegoers driving the top end of the movie business increasingly showed they wanted less realism and heavy drama and more special effects "eye candy" (like 1996's FX showcase *Twister* with Bill Paxton [left] and Helen Hunt)...

ELEVEN. A Moment Come and Gone

...and adventures in the realm of the fantastic and magical (left to right: Sean Astin, Elijah Wood, Billy Boyd, Dominic Monoghan in *The Lord of the Rings: The Fellowship of the Ring* [2001] the first in a series of adaptations of the J.R.R. Tolkein novels by Peter Jackson which would eventually run to six epic-sized films).

music, merchandising, etc., could work in concert to exploit a franchise brand name to the fullest extent possible. For example, when Warner Bros. acquired the Harry Potter property, two years before the franchise's first film appeared on movie screens in 2001, *all* of Time Warner's division heads were laying out marketing and ancillary strategies for the franchise *ten years out* (Fierman 27)!

Along with this corporatization of the motion picture industry came studio hierarchies both more bureaucratic and labyrinthine, with tiers of "creative executives" whose job often seemed to be, in the eyes of many filmmakers, to massage any element of risk out of material, and to market test every element of a project from posters to trailers to the actual finished product, insuring that every aspect of a project conformed to proven forms (Biskind 402; Svetkey 22). Robert Evans, who had headed up Paramount during the days of *Love Story* and *The Godfather* films, would, in a 1993 interview, remember that in his day the studio had been run by "four people," in contrast to the then present-day, when the same company was managed by "a hundred executives" (Grobel 54).

As of the day the film community was buzzing about the lightning bolts Sam Peckinpah had shot from movie screens with *The Wild Bunch*, his days were numbered. Had he taken better care of himself and his career, it wouldn't have mattered; there would never have been another *The Wild Bunch*. That he was given the chance to make the movie he did took something on the order of an alignment of planets to happen. We can look at this as a tragedy; that this great director only made one film as memorable—as legendary—as *The Wild Bunch*. Or, we can look at it from the perspective that he was lucky—that *we* were lucky—one was made at all.

Epilogue:
Riding into the Light

"Lord, as the day draws towards evening, this life grows to the end of us all, we say, 'Adieu' to our friend. Take him, Lord, but knowing Cable, I suggest you do not take him lightly. Amen."

—Josh (David Warner) in
The Ballad of Cable Hogue

And so, at last, we are back where we began, wondering why after fifty years we are still talking about *The Wild Bunch*.

Of all Sam Peckinpah's films, why *The Wild Bunch?* It was not his first film (that would be *The Deadly Companions*), nor was it the film which established his feature director bonafides (that would be *Ride the High Country*). Stylistically and thematically, *Straw Dogs* is a more mature work, *The Ballad of Cable Hogue* more lyrical, to some eyes *Bring Me the Head of Alfredo Garcia* more personally expressive and certainly more daring. Some argue that the unmutilated *Pat Garrett and Billy the Kid* is more poetic, and certainly *The Getaway* was more popular.

So, again, why *The Wild Bunch?* Why does every essay, article, book, discussion of Sam Peckinpah quickly and early on identify him first and foremost as the director of *The Wild Bunch*? Any overview of his career typically breaks his timeline down into the movies that came before and those that came after *The Wild Bunch*. It may not have been his most successful or even best made film, but it has, over time, come to be looked at as his defining work.

Why?

In part, like the best narrative work, peel back a layer of text and subtext, and there's something else to find.

There is, of course, the plot. *The Wild Bunch* was not, by far, the first

Epilogue: Riding into the Light

Western to deal with Death of the West themes, but none had rendered it—before or since—in the apocalyptic terms used by Peckinpah.

And Peckinpah delivers that story on a grand canvas filled with a dying American West and a Mexico torn by civil war. When that master of the epic, David Lean, crossed paths with Peckinpah who was in Europe to make *Straw Dogs*, Lean greeted him as a peer: "Sam, you and I are the only real ones left" (Hodenfield 4).

And in the film's violence and moral ambiguity/ambivalence, one can see a reflection of its time; a time when a war seemed to pointlessly and endlessly grind on, when the nation's cities burned, when one supposed political savior after another fell to an assassin's bullet, when the national leadership was viewed as misguided and/or morally bankrupt, when the country was pulling apart into racial, generational, cultural enclaves walled in by paranoia and animosity.

And there is its aesthetic catharsis. Movies seemed freed by *The Wild Bunch*, not just in how they portrayed violence, but how frankly and confrontationally they could take on any subject, any kind of characters. *The Wild Bunch* would come to be recognized as a pivot point in American cinema.

And there are its eternal and universal themes of one age dying under the wheels of another, of a generation feeling used up and spent, left behind, having outlived its time. It's a concept as applicable to aging corporate executives (see Rod Serling's *Patterns*) as it is to politically misstepping generals (*Patton*); to fading athletes (Serling, again, with *Requiem for a Heavyweight* [1962]) and graying politicians (*The Last Hurrah* [1958]); past-their-peak movie stars (*The Artist* [2011]) and modern-day lawmen feeling outgunned in the new violent anarchy of the drug trade (*No Country for Old Men* [2007]). I wager there were, undoubtedly ancient world Greeks who wistfully remembered their Hellenic greatness as they witnessed the rise of the upstart Roman Empire, and there are surely Russians of a certain age waxing nostalgic for the Soviet era, thinking that for all its flaws and oppressions, at least it was a time when they belonged to one of the world's only two superpowers. This is, surely, a key element of *The Wild Bunch*'s persistence and applicability of vision; that like much great art, it speaks to its time while also speaking to all times, telling a story that tells many stories.

And there is the man who gave *The Wild Bunch* the beating unifying heart beneath all these layers; what I referred to earlier as the film's *soul*.

Epilogue: Riding into the Light

The Last Messenger

Back in the 19th century, the most prominent French literary critic of his time, Charles Augustin Sainte-Beuve, put forth the then novel idea that understanding and assessing a literary work required "a study of the life, circumstances, and aim of the writer" ("Introductory"). In other words, the code key to decrypting an artist's work is ... the artist.

The man Sam Peckinpah was—or perhaps it might be more accurate to say the man he thought himself and/or aspired to be since, in his own life, he rarely lived up to the principles on display in his work—is stamped all over the films over which he had most control: say, from *Ride the High Country* through *Bring Me the Head of Alfredo Garcia*. But nowhere is that stamp as deep and bold as it is in *The Wild Bunch*.

For all its flaws—its awkward flashbacks, its sometime tendency to hit thematic points a little too squarely on the head—one of the reasons we still talk about *The Wild Bunch* is because it is *the* Sam Peckinpah movie. He is in every frame, every line of dialogue, he inhabits all the principle characters acting in a universe created out of his worldview and sense of self. That idea of being an outlaw, a renegade obliged to no code of conduct other than his own somewhat warped sense of what is worthy—his work—is what makes *The Wild Bunch* real, alive. This isn't one of Quentin Tarantino's game-of-telephone works inspired by a movie geek's obsession with movies, but something Sam Peckinpah believed he *lived*. "[We] were in on the last of it," he once reminisced, discussing how he and his siblings grew up in a vestigial pocket of the world of the Old West (W. Murray 72).

Maybe Peckinpah, in his mind, overly-romanticized his connection with a fading era; something that was more a wish than a reality, but *he* believed it, and it certainly had a lot to do, both for good and for ill, with the shape of his work, and how he conducted not just his career but his life. One can argue Peckinpah made, from a technical point of view, better movies than *The Wild Bunch*, maybe even a film or two that was more personally expressive, but all of the elements mentioned above combined with his own obvious passion for the story to make *The Wild Bunch* the definitive Sam Peckinpah film.

In a 1982 essay on the evolution of hardboiled detective fiction, the great crime novelist Donald E. Westlake, in showing an illustrating parallel, digressed into the evolution of the literary Western. The genre began, he posited, as "exaggerated reportage"; that even in its most puffed-up,

Epilogue: Riding into the Light

hyperbolic form, the early Westerns—from the serious literary efforts by the likes of Owen Wister to the schlock-meisters grinding out penny dreadfuls—"were lies told by people who *knew the truth* [Westlake's italics]. The first writers in the genre had been there, out West" (39).

In time came another wave; writers "who had never walked that ground." Their fiction did not come out of the West, but derived from the work of the authentic Westerners who had come before them. Out of this second generation came the genre rituals—shootouts at high noon on a dusty main street and the like—and then, in time, as the rituals became codified, "the very ritual itself leads to art, with ritualized refried fiction leading to the possibility of art; that's the Western" (39–40).

The chronology of the movie Western is not as neatly linear, with Western moviemakers tumbling into the genre randomly: a ritualist like John Ford as early as the silents, and someone who had "walked the ground" like Delmer Daves in the 1940s.

But Peckinpah had walked the ground, or at least believed he had. David Lean may have been more right than he knew when he'd dubbed Peckinpah one of the "last ones left"; by the time Peckinpah had made *The Wild Bunch*, he may very well have been one of the last makers of Westerns who had actually come from the West. He knew the real West, and he (and Walon Green) knew the rituals, and the artistry of *The Wild Bunch* is in its twisting, inverting, exploding those rituals with a dirty, messy honesty.

All of this goes to why *The Wild Bunch* is, fifty years after its premiere, considered a great Western, and beyond that, a great movie by a great filmmaker, and part of why it's still as vital today as it was a half-century ago.

But there's something else...

And here I confess to becoming highly subjective. Part of the movie's enduring popularity—and online discussions and rating sites like Rotten Tomatoes indicate the movie is more popular and certainly more highly thought of than it was in 1969—is that it's Peckinpah's most *watchable* movie.

Let me put it another way: it's *fun*. A hell of a lot of fun.

Why We Go to the Movies

In a two-part TV documentary, *The Cowboy*, which traces the evolution of the movie Western and its shaky relationship with the historical

Epilogue: Riding into the Light

West, actor Bruce Dern—who has certainly performed in his share of Westerns and holds a special place in the canon as the villain who shoots John Wayne in the back in *The Cowboys*—presented with a Dernish grin the documentary's summarizing idea that "movies should be fun. Westerns are fun" (D. Murray).

Along with all those elements discussed above—all those ingredients that not only make *The Wild Bunch* cinematic art, but *great* cinematic art—goes the sheer visceral enjoyment of the movie. It would be the worst form of reverse snobbery not to admit (at least in my case) some of the appeal of the movie is watching manly men galloping across the Western scrubland, clever capers, jaw-dropping stunts (speaking for myself, I find the bridge-blowing sequence every bit as oh-my-God impressive as the destruction of *The Bridge on the River Kwai*), the humor both droll ("Well, we share very few sentiments with our government") and bawdy (the Gorch brothers cavorting with their cherubesque whores under a shower of wine after they've shot holes in centuries-old wine barrels), and some of the most intense and complex action sequences in American film.

After a half-century of cinematic carnage, as well as an increasing penchant for the grotesque, the violence of *The Wild Bunch* may no longer appall the way Peckinpah had intended; too much Karo syrup movie blood has flowed under the bridge since 1969. But the violence of *Bunch* still has an impact, in part because the action *means* something, something is at stake. And, in part, because—and Peckinpah would chafe under this reputation for the rest of his career—nobody did movie violence better than Sam Peckinpah, and Peckinpah never did it better than he did in *The Wild Bunch*.

One of the pleasures we get from movies is the vicarious thrill; the excitement, the catharsis, the danger of things we would never do but get to experience through the characters on screen. It's the rare human being whom, at least at some point in their life, hasn't felt pushed around by factors greater than themselves ... like the Bunch: passed over for a promotion, unjustly fired, the one car among a stream of speeding cars to be ticketed, locked in a no-win argument with a customer, or perhaps more seriously—also like the Bunch—to feel that opportunities have been missed or never came our way, that we feel left behind, forgotten. *The Wild Bunch* ends with one of the greatest kick-the-other-guy-in-the-nuts visual statements of "Fuck me? Noooo, fuck *you!*" in American cinema.

There's a moment in the final scene oft written about; that silent few

Epilogue: Riding into the Light

beats after Pike and Dutch have pounded Mapache with lead after he's slit the throat of Angel. Mapache's body thuds to the ground, the soldiers in the hacienda courtyard begin to go for their guns, the Bunch turn to face them, and everyone in the courtyard freezes. There have been those who say that in that moment, the Bunch have the chance to walk out of the courtyard but choose not to do so (Seydor, "*The Wild*").

I disagree.

I have always believed that from the moment of "Let's go," "Why not?" the Bunch know that long walk to the courtyard is a one-way trip; that they know they're never coming out of Mapache's lair alive. The electric majesty of that frozen moment isn't that they elect to stay instead of leave; it's that knowing this is the end of their story, *they* get to decide when to end it.

I've mentioned several times the connection between *The Wild Bunch* and *The Magnificent Seven*, and this is another one. The Seven have been captured and escorted out of the little Mexican village they've been protecting by bandit leader Calvera's minions. In the hills far from the village, their guns are tossed to the ground and they are left presumably to head back to the United States. One of the first to pick up his gun belt and strap it back on is the knife-throwing Britt (James Coburn), mostly silent for the entire film. He's the first to announce his intention to go back to the village—a quite probably suicidal move—not out of some pure-heart sentiment to save the villagers, to "do the right thing," or for any other high-minded altruism. "Nobody throws me my own guns and says run," Britt says, "nobody" (Sturges). At the end of wasted lives, the Bunch, too, have nothing left but their pride, and intend to take it with them.

The Bunch don't go into the hacienda courtyard for Angel; he's an excuse, not a reason. They've gone in there to raise a bloody middle finger to the 20th century as they pass on their way out the door.

* * *

Grappling with the question of "What is a classic?" our 19th-century French *ami* Sainte-Beuve defined the term and the artist behind the work as follows:

> A true classic ... is an author who has enriched the human mind, increased its treasure, and caused it to advance a step; who has discovered some moral and not equivocal truth, or revealed some eternal passion in that heart where all seemed known and discovered; who has expressed his thought, observation, or intention,

in no matter what form, only provided it be broad and great, refined and sensible, sane and beautiful in itself; who has spoken to all in his own peculiar style, a style which is found to be also that of the whole world, a style new without neologism, new and old, easily contemporary with all time.

Such a classic may for a moment have been revolutionary; it may at least have seemed so, but it is not; it only lashed and subverted whatever prevented the restoration of the balance of order and beauty [Sainte-Beuve].

Eternal passion of the heart, easily contemporary with all time.

That's why we're talking about *The Wild Bunch* fifty years later.

That's why we'll still be talking about *The Wild Bunch* fifty years from now.

Appendix A: *The Wild Bunch* Production Credits

Running Time: 2:58 (current restored cut)
Release Date: June 18, 1969
Budget: $6.24 million (approximately $43.3 million in 2018 USD)
Box Office Gross: $10.5 million
MPAA Rating: R
Released By: Warner Bros.-Seven Arts

The Production

Cast

Pike Bishop	William Holden
Dutch Engstrom	Ernest Borgnine
Deke Thornton	Robert Ryan
Freddie Sykes	Edmond O'Brien
Lyle Gorch	Warren Oates
Angel	Jaime Sanchez
Tector Gorch	Ben Johnson
Mapache	Emilio Fernandez
Coffer	Strother Martin
T. C.	L. Q. Jones
Harrigan	Albert Dekker
Crazy Lee (C. L.)	Bo Hopkins
Mayor Wainscoat	Dub Taylor
Lieutenant Zamorra	Jorge Russak

Appendix A

Herrera	Alfonso Arau
Don Jose	Chano Ureueta
Jess	Bill Hart
Buck	Rayford Barnes
McHale	Stephen Ferry
Teresa	Sonia Amelio
Aurora	Aurora Clavel
Ignacio	Enrique Lucero
Rocio	Elizabeth Dupeyron
Yolis	Yolanda Ponce
Juan Jose	Jose Chavez
Juan	Rene Dupeyron
Benson	Pedro Galvan
Emma	Graciela Doring
Perez	Major Perez
Mohr	Fernando Wagner
Ernst	Ivan J. Rado
Paymaster	Ivan Scott
Margaret	Senora Madero
Luna	Margarito Luna
Gonzalez	Chalo Gonzalez
Lilia	Lilia Castillo
Carmen	Elizabeth Unda
Julio	Julio Corona

Uncredited:

Alyce Allen	Buck Holland
Archie Butler	Walt La Rue
Tap Canutt	Erwin Neal
Gordon T. Dawson	Matthew Peckinpah
Dennis Feldman	Bill Shannon
Mickey Gilbert	Jim Sheppard
Robert "Buzz" Henry	Jack Williams
"Chico" Hernandez	Joe Yrigoyen

Production Credits

Crew

Director	Sam Peckinpah
Producer	Phil Feldman
Screenplay	Walon Green
	Sam Peckinpah
Story	Walon Green
	Roy N. Sickner
Associate Producer	Roy N. Sickner
Music	Jerry Fielding
Cinematography	Lucien Ballard
Editing	Louis Lombardo
Associate Film Editor	Robert L. Wolfe
Assistant Editor	Joel Cox (uncredited)
Art Direction	Edward Carrere
Wardrobe Supervisor	Gordon Dawson
Costume Design	James R. Silke (uncredited)
Makeup	Al Greenway
	Keester Sweeney (uncredited)
Production Management	William D. Faralla
Assistant Directors	Cliff Coleman
	Fred Gammon
Second Unit Directors	Buzz Henry
	John "Bud" Cardos (uncredited)
Second Assistant Director	Howard G. Kazanjian (uncredited)
First Assistant Director	Phil Rawlins (uncredited)
Property Master	Phil A. Ankrom (uncredited)
Assistant Property Master	John Barton (uncredited)
Poster Designer	Bill Gold (uncredited)
Props	Arnold Losey (uncredited)
Art Department	Tyros Wong (uncredited)
Sound	Robert J. Miller
Sound Effects Editors	Joe Kavigan (uncredited)
	Stanley Martin (uncredited)
	Billy Mauch (uncredited)

Appendix A

	Bill Rivol (uncredited)
	John O. Young (uncredited)
Supervising Sound Effects Editor	Ed Scheid (uncredited)
Re-recording Mixer	Dan Wallin (uncredited)
Special Effects	Bud Hulburd
	Ralph Ayres (uncredited)
	James Rugg (uncredited)
Stunt Coordinator	Archie Butler (uncredited)
Stunts	Denny Arnold (uncredited)
	Norman Bishop (uncredited)
	Joe Canutt (uncredited)
	Tap Canutt (uncredited)
	John "Bud" Cardos (uncredited)
	Gary Combs (uncredited)
	Louie Elias (uncredited)
	Tony Epper (uncredited)
	Chad Evans (uncredited)
	Jim Feazell (uncredited)
	Joe Finnegan (uncredited)
	Mickey Gilbert (uncredited)
	Bill Hart (uncredited)
	Robert "Buzz" Henry (uncredited)
	"Chema" Hernandez (uncredited)
	Bob Herron (uncredited)
	Billy E. Hughes (uncdredited)
	Whitey Hughes (uncredited)
	Gary McLarty (uncredited)
	Erwin Neal (uncredited)
	Bob Orrison (uncredited)
	Danny Sands (uncredited)
	Bill Shannon (uncredited)
	Jim Sheppard (uncredited)
	Roy N. Sickner (uncredited)

Production Credits

	Jack Williams (uncredited)
	Joe Yrigoyen (uncredited)
Key Grip	Bud Gaunt
Still Photographer	Bernie Abramson (uncredited)
Assistant Camera	Dave Friedman (uncredited)
Grip	Reggie Jones (uncredited)
Camera Operator	Thomas Laughridge (uncredited)
Generator Operator	James F. Reber (uncredited)
Gaffer	Don Stott (uncredited)
First Assistant Camera	Richard Tim Vanik (uncredited)
Wardrobe Supervisor	Gordon Dawson
Location Auditor	Morrie Nierenberg (uncredited)
Music Supervisor	Sonny Burke
Music Film Editor	Donald Harris (uncredited)
Supervising Music Film Editor	Richard C. Harris (uncredited)
Scoring Mixer	Dan Wallin (uncredited)
Transportation Gaffer	Bud Dawson (uncredited)
Drivers	Chet Jan (uncredited)
	Joe Lessner (uncredited)
	Charles Misere (uncredited)
	Frank Olmstead (uncredited)
	Earl Pierson (uncredited)
	Rex Schroetter (uncredited)
Script Supervisor	Crayton Smith
Ramrod	Tony Faehnle (uncredited)
Production Coordinator	Stanley Feldman (uncredited)
Assistant to Producer	Anthony Goldschmidt (uncredited)
Secretaries	Gay Hayden (uncredited)
	Alyce S. Miller (uncredited)
Head Wrangler	"Chema" Hernandez (uncredited)
Unit Publicist	Robert Joseph (uncredited)
Secretary to Executive Producer	Greta Shepherd (uncredited)
Weapon Specialist	Branko Wohlfahrt (uncredited)

Appendix B: The Songs

La Adelita

After the Bunch escape Starbuck and meet up with Freddie Sykes, they camp for the night. Angel serenades some children with this popular ballad of the Mexican Revolution composed to honor the women who had joined the fight (Norris):

*In the heights of a steep mountainous range
a regiment was encamped
and a bright woman bravely follows them
madly in love with the sergeant.*

*Popular among the troop was Adelita
the woman that the sergeant idolized
and besides being pretty she was brave
that even the Colonel respected her.*

And it was heard, that he, who loved her so much, said:

*If Adelita would like to be my girlfriend
If Adelita would be my wife
I'd buy her a silk dress
to take her to dance to the quarter.*

*If Adelita would leave with another man
I'd follow her by land and sea
by sea in a war ship
by land in a military train.*

La Golondrina

One of the most memorable moments from *The Wild Bunch* is the gang's exit from Angel's village. The music accompaniment for the scene is the Mexican folk song "La Golondrina (The Swallow)."

Appendix B

Composed by Narciso Serradel Sevilla in 1862, who fought against the French Imperial troops occupying Mexico at the time (the setting for Peckinpah's *Major Dundee*), "La Golondrina" became, for many Mexicans, a song of farewell, and, as such, a favorite of Mexican expatriates. It is also often requested at funerals of Mexican-Americans.

Note: the first two verses are traditionally omitted (Barrow).

To far off lands, the swallow now is speeding
For warmer climes and sun-drenched foreign shores
While cooler breezes tell of summer fading
My heart with you, into the heavens will soar.

Oh graceful swallow bear a message of love
For on your journey, lies the land of my heart
As down you sweep, shed my blessings upon them
That tell of love which in my heart still burns

To far off lands, the swallow now is speeding
For warmer climes and sun-drenched foreign shores
While cooler breezes tell of summer fading
My heart with you, into the heavens will soar

Among those shores are all that I care or live for
My home my loved ones, waiting for my return
Then glide downwards as you see from above
A sea swept isle from which we had to part

To far off lands, the swallow now is speeding
For warmer climes and sun-drenched foreign shores
While cooler breezes tell of summer fading
My heart with you, into the heavens will soar

Each winter long console me in my dreaming
And you fond swallow on your gleaming wings
Will speed as I would wish I could go speeding
Straight to their hearts, and with you my love bring.

Corrido de Santa Amalia (The Ballad of Santa Amalia)

The song is played by a mariachi band behind Mapache during his faltering stand against Villa's forces at a train station, and heard again as the Bunch take their final walk toward the hacienda courtyard to face off with the general, this time from a group of soldiers drunkenly warbling their way through the tune, another popular ballad during the Mexican Revolution (Takis).

The Songs

In Santa Amalia there lived a young girl
Cute and beautiful as a jasmine
She alone was kept
Sewing clothes to live

The bad brother tells her one day
Oh! Little sister of the heart
Your beauty has me crazy
And your husband wants to be me

The poor young woman was amazed
And in the instant he answered
I'd rather die a thousand times
Before you get to stain my honor

The bad brother took out the revolver
And in the instant he shot
Giving him a shot in the senses
That the whole skull destroyed him

By "ay" they ask who it was?
Then ask the authority
People came from everywhere
To see the crime of that place

The judge declares that he had been
I am the man who killed her
Go sister, go to heaven
That I will pay in jail

Appendix C:
A Collage of Reviews

To give some idea of the impact of *The Wild Bunch* in its time, and its continuing—and even ascendant—status, following are excerpts from some representative reviews during the film's initial 1969 release, reviews from the film's 25th anniversary re-release, and a canvass of contemporary views of the movie.

Then

The Wild Bunch contains faults and mistakes, but its accomplishments are more than sufficient to confirm that Peckinpah, along with Stanley Kubrick and Arthur Penn, belongs with the best of the newer generation of American filmmakers.—*Time* ("*The Wild Bunch*")

The Wild Bunch has become this year's controversial film about violence.... It is also, many critics agree, an extraordinary film.—Roger Ebert, *The Chicago Sun-Times*

... a brilliantly made, thought-provoking movie ... it is beautifully made and full of spectacular visual images ... [Peckinpah] makes movies which are real movies, and which ripple with power and crackle with energy.—Charles Champlin, *The Los Angeles Times* ("*The Wild*" 218)

... one of the few American films of recent memory that doesn't seem to have been concocted by a market research computer. Even when he is most awkward and wrongheaded, Peckinpah is wildly original and individualistic. And though I prefer directors who make beautiful things look easy rather than directors (like Peckinpah) who make beautiful things look hard, not all that many directors can do beautiful things at all, and Peckinpah has done enough beautiful things ... to qualify as an authentic original...—Andrew Sarris, *The Village Voice*

Appendix C

... may someday emerge as one of the most important records of the mood of our times and one of the most important American films of the era.—Richard Schickel, *Life*

25 Years Later

The hard action, bracing wit and mournful grace of Peckinpah's cowboy classic shames every new movie around ... a bruising and brilliant work of art.—Peter Travers, *Rolling Stone*

It's a tribute to Peckinpah's corrosive genius that, 25 years later, *The Wild Bunch* still won't go down easy.—David Ansen, *Newsweek*

...an American masterpiece, one of the greatest films ever produced in the Hollywood system ... the supreme modern American action film.—Michael Wilmington, *The Chicago Tribune*

...one of the best westerns ever made, and the best film of any kind to come out in 1969.—Jay Boyar, *The Orlando Sentinel*

It's astonishing how harrowing *The Wild Bunch* is more than 25 years after it blasted its way onto the big screen to become maybe the best shoot-'em-up ever made ... even people who hate the film can't dismiss its visceral impact, its twisted ethos, its balletic imagery. It must be art.—Peter Stack, *The San Francisco Chronicle*

...one of the great, arrogant take-it-or-leave-it jobs in history ... the ultimate end-of-the-road western ... all these years later, the movie retains it almost seductive grandeur ... one of the best-written and best-performed American films of all time.—Stephen Hunter, *The Baltimore Sun*

Reflecting from Today

As of this writing, *The Wild Bunch* has a Rotten Tomatoes rating of 88 percent positive among "Top Critics," 94 percent among "All Critics," and a 91 percent positive audience score.

I was in college in Minneapolis when *The Wild Bunch* came out and it barely played the city. I didn't catch up with it until a year or so later, when I saw it at a drive-in.
  Even with tinny sound and a scratchy print, I was blown away right from the start. I'd seen *Bonnie and Clyde*, and *Butch Cassidy*, but this used slow-motion in a new way. You felt this violence in a more visceral, impactful way. It was thrilling but also unsettling.

A Collage of Reviews

There was much, much more in this story of bad men who lived by a code that the times had bypassed. Unfortunately too many filmmakers saw only the superficial—the slo-mo blood spurting—and missed the rest. Eventually even Peckinpah himself succumbed to that impulse and began to parody himself

No matter. *The Wild Bunch* stands as one of the greatest Westerns of all time.—Marshall Fine

---

How can a bunch of *alta cockers* be so much fun to watch? They are old, ugly, and probably smell as bad as they look. *Pride* is what keeps popping in my head, and that's something that never goes away. The violence, the blood—it's *great!!!*—Abraham Gordon

---

I saw *The Wild Bunch* countless times and if it was on TV right now, I would stop writing this and go watch it.

I thought it reached a new level of violence on film. I don't remember it for that, but for how good it was, and how perfect the cast was.

As an aside, when I was in Durango scouting locations for a film where some of *The Wild Bunch* was shot, one of the houses I was shown was one where Peckinpah stayed. It was as close to a grand whorehouse [as you] could get, and from the stories I heard from the townspeople, he was wilder than his films.—Bill Persky

---

My husband Larry and I were fortunate to see Sam Peckinpah's *The Wild Bunch* when it was released back in 1969. What an unforgettable movie experience that was! Although we had different opinions about the film, both of us realized it was something special—and we argued about it for several days. Larry absolutely loved the graphic violence on screen, but I started scrunching down in my seat as soon as I saw that scorpion fighting those millions of ants! Still, the movie drew me in more intensely than any other Western I had seen before. I didn't even want to blink!

And afterwards, Larry convinced me that showing extreme graphic violence in films might help viewers realize how horrible such actions are in real life. Now I'm not so sure about that. But I do know *The Wild Bunch* holds up as an excellent example of entertaining and thought-provoking cinema.—Betty Jo Tucker

---

I saw *The Wild Bunch* a long time ago, but just like the first time I saw *Star Wars*, I remember loving the movie and the characters in it and the actors who played those roles.—Gerald Abrams

---

Some we're appalled by it, others saw it as a masterpiece of unvarnished acting and unforgettable camerawork.

Now that we [Warner Bros.]) have restored the missing nine minutes and thereby made the characters and plot more coherent, it's clear that the scenes should never have been edited in the first place.—Jeff Bewkes

---

For me, there is nothing like a fresh take on a familiar genre. Just when you think it's safe to project what's going to happen, the nuance of the characters and the arc of the story take what is familiar and make it fresher, richer, and more memorable.

On TV, *The Sopranos* was a mob story, *Mad Men* was an office drama, but both were much more. Peckinpah made Westerns that had the depth of Dostoevsky.

There may have seemed to be less apparent nuance to Peckinpah because of his use of explicit violence, but his stories were about ideals and the way values are compromised by the pragmatics of living, and his characters were often isolated and more complex than heroes or bad guys.—Josh Sapan

---

Appendix D: Film Critic Stephen Whitty on *The Wild Bunch*

The Wild Bunch came out when I was about ten, and so it didn't make an immediate impression on me. I was still deep into my monster-movie love (haven't quite grown out of that, yet), and Westerns still just meant hour-long dramas that took up too much of the TV schedule, like *Gunsmoke* and *Bonanza*, or the once-a-year John Wayne pictures my mother or grandfather took me to at Radio City. I didn't experience *The Wild Bunch* then as the ground-breaking movie it was.

Instead, I caught up with it when I was eighteen, in college. New York City was still full of retro movie houses back then—not just artsy, carefully curated ones that would do all-Lubitsch festivals, but dank, dirty shoeboxes that always smelled of dope, and programmed double-features like *Candy* (1968) and *The Magic Christian* (1969), or *Harold and Maude* (1971) and *Brewster McCloud*. And *The Wild Bunch* was a regular feature, although always shown on its own.

That was when and where I first saw it, and immediately recognized its power.

First of all, there was Sam Peckinpah's complete understanding, and reverence, for living Hollywood iconography. It had been clear right from *Ride the High Country*, when he cast those old titans Joel McCrea and Randolph Scott—not to burlesque them as aging cowpokes, but to salute who they were and mourn what was fading away with them. It's an instinct he truly explores here, particularly with the casting of William Holden (Hollywood's favorite, morally compromised hero) and Robert Ryan (the screen's most charismatic of bad men), along with all those great, grizzled character actors. They bring their own history to a story that's not just about a disappearing West, but a disappearing Hollywood.

Appendix D

And then there's Peckinpah's filmmaking. We'd begun to see screen violence like this before, in *Bonnie and Clyde*; very soon, the word "balletic" would become a cliché in describing this kind of slow-motion bloodletting. But there's nothing elegant about the deaths in *The Wild Bunch*. They are brutal and sadistic and senseless. They are painful, and hard to watch. Because, Peckinpah insists, they *should* be hard to watch. And if you're seeing the blasphemous savagery with which even the dead are treated here and you're not thinking, as Peckinpah was, of Vietnam—or, today, of African and Middle Eastern warzones—then you're not really seeing it.

Of course, even though much of *The Wild Bunch* is timeless, some of it is definitely of its time. No one will ever suspect Sam Peckinpah of feminism (and if today's viewers might shrink from some of this movie, they would charge the screen if they ever saw his brutal, misogynist *Straw Dogs*). And although the hero-worshipping Hemingway crowd will cheer the extraordinarily macho, simply existential resolve this movie salutes, right up to its very last lines—"Let's go." "Why not?"—that's also exactly the kind of what-the-hell self-destructiveness that has led to more than a few massive slaughters in the world.

But don't doubt that Sam Peckinpah knew these men. Or that we can learn a great deal about ourselves from knowing them too.

Appendix E: Reviewer and Pay-TV Film Programmer Youssef Kdiry—Meditations on *The Wild Bunch*

Made during the turbulent 1960s—and very much as a Hollywood response to the ongoing war in Vietnam, Sam Peckinpah's blood-soaked Western masterpiece *The Wild Bunch* (henceforth, *TWB*) hitches its bloody spurs in the pantheon of great genre films for sheer *ballsitude* (and if that's not a word, it sure is now. You're welcome, Pilgrim).

TWB inhibits its genre pedigree more akin to Sergio Leone's contemporary Spaghetti Westerns/Clint Eastwood-starrer fables—*A Fistful of Dollars* (1964), *For a Few Dollars More* (1965), *The Good, The Bad & The Ugly* (1966), and his penultimate *Once Upon a Time in the West* (1968) (and let's throw in Serio Corbucci's seminal *Django* [1966] for a good measure of prairie beans)—than to those Hollywood classics starring John "The Duke" Wayne in John Ford epics such as *Stagecoach* and *The Searchers* or Henry Hathaway's *True Grit* (which, incidentally, won The Duke his only Oscar in the twilight of his illustrious career, playing an aging gunslinger ... which is one of the central motifs in *TWB*).

Switching gears now (or horses, if you will), as I could spend more time breaking down the history and hagiography of the Western genre than the ill-fated Donner Party had for seconds servings, but rather, I shall ply you with a more personalized discourse on why Peckinpah's mid-career Western still holds up after 50 years (and countless genre movies as elegiac as Eastwood's *High Plains Drifter* [1973]; as brilliantly sketched as Mel Brooks' opus *Blazing Saddles*; as goofy as the silly *Hawmps!* [1976]; as prosaic as Eastwood's Oscar-winning *Unforgiven*

Appendix E

[1992]; or as testosterone-fueled as George Pan Cosmatos and Kevin Jarre's classic *Tombstone*).

Released theatrically by Warner Bros.-Seven Arts in 1969, I caught snippets of it as a youngster on the square TV—back in the days when fantastic widescreen movies such as *TWB* (lensed handsomely in 35mm color film stock and in the anamorphic Panavision⁰ format by legendary cinematographer Lucien Ballard) were cropped/edited for viewing displeasure.

It wasn't until the mid–1990s, that I—fully ensconced in my first film school tenure by this point—purchased *TWB* on VHS (but in widescreen format!) and sat down to fully invest in the motion picture. I did this because of my admiration for and studying of the budding auteurs of post-*New* Hollywood Cinema: John Woo (*The Killer* [1989], *Hard Boiled* [1992]), Quentin Tarantino (*Reservoir Dogs* [1992], *Pulp Fiction* [1994]), Robert Rodriguez (*El Mariachi* [1992], *Desperado* [1995]), etc., as well as the established *NH*ers like Martin Scorsese (T*axi Driver* [1976]), John Carpenter (*Assault on Precinct 13* [1976], *Escape from New York* [1981]) and Michael Mann (*Thief* [1981], *Heat* [1995]), to name but a few. Oh, and by the way: all of these auteurs count Mr. Peckinpah as a major influence on their own work, too.

To see *TWB* at this juncture of my life and nascent filmmaking career is essential, as Peckinpah's mastery of the Editing Schema influenced my short films at the time. As an early-20s chap, I admired the kinetic action and bloody violence—in fact, I recall that *TWB* (along with Beatty & Penn's 1967 opus *Bonnie & Clyde*) was the first Hollywood movie to show exit wound bullet holes in gory Technicolor red ... a cinematic corollary (and indictment) of the then-current conflict raging in Vietnam, and the bloody "Butcher's Bill" prevalent on the nightly evening news.

In 1995, Warner Bros. gave *TWB* a much-lauded theatrical re-release which I was also able to catch (courtesy of my connections as an HBO film programmer. To finally see *TWB* on the wide, silver screen was freakin' fantastic! To appreciate not only the kinetic editing (by Peckinpah's mentee, Lou Lombardo) but also the cinematography, blocking, production/costume designs; to *hear* the bullets and to delight at the gritty dialogue spoken by William Holden's Pike Bishop, Ernest Borgnine, Ben Johnson, Robert Ryan, Edmond O'Brien, Warren Oates, etc., was totally awesome!!

So now, in 2019, I had a chance to revisit *TWB* again in preparation of writing this article. I reflect even further on its themes. Now in my late 40s (and hitting the proverbial half-century mark in less time than a Stanley Kubrick production), aging, technological advancements, cultural norms shifts, marginalization, fear/resentment of the next generations have become the norm for us middle-agers.

Pause ... as I take my BP pills. *Gadzooks!!*

Much like the weary characters of *TWB*, I sense their collective despair in that by 1913, the "Old West" is as dead as Wild Bill Hickock ... horses/carriages giving way to motorized automobiles; their dated "code of honor" giving way to 20th-century industrialization and cutthroat business mentality (much like the sinking of the *RMS Titanic* the previous year heralded the end of the Gilded Age as it traveled in a downward spiral to the cold, dark depths of the Atlantic Ocean).

These men, honorable in their final intentions (though not always in their hearts), want to go out in a blaze of glory—guns blazing!! Screw this brave new world! Screw Authority!! SCREW THE MAN!!! Very indicative of Peckinpah as an individual and as a creative force, nay?

As I see it, *TWB* represents one of the bright stars in the modern cinema. It gave the MPAA and their nascent *Classification and Rating Administration* fits in rating this new style of violent cinema (launched in 1968 as the progenitor of the movie-rating classification system still in use, *CARA* replaced the draconian *Hays Code*—which dated back to the b&w 1930s).

Epic, but not operatic in the Leone way, *TWB* is defiant in its storytelling. Textured, but not as swarthy as the Spaghetti Westerns, you will not mistake this film for Fred Zinneman's *High Noon*, George Stevens' *Shane*, John Sturges' *The Magnificent Seven* or ... as if! ... *Paint Your Wagon!*, nor any of its characters molded in the Gary Cooper, Randolph Scott, Yul Brynner or John Wayne molds.

No, with these cats, you can almost smell the sweat, cheap whiskey, body odor, tobacco and leather. In the cinematography and associated mise-en-scène, you can feel the hot sun, dusty environs and ingest the aromas of firewood, gunpowder and fear. To me, Peckinpah pretty much evoked his own persona and created (with co-scripter Walon Green) a cinematic representation of his own self: defiant, prickly, brilliant, angry, ambitious, etc. I love this dude!

With the assistance/guidance/cooperation of his editor, Lou Lombardo, Peckinpah managed to (according to IMDb) incorporate over 3000 cuts in its robust 138-minute run time! His manipulation of time & space essentially helped create the music videos of our MTV

Appendix E

generation! As a side note, I noticed the Peckinpah editing style DNA evident in movies as varied as Bob Fosse's *All That Jazz* (edited by Oscar-winner Alan Heim) and Scorsese's *Raging Bull* (1980; edited by Oscar-winner Thelma Schoonmaker), to name a few masterpieces.

Every action, war, western, sci-fi and horror movie owes a cinematic debt of gratitude to *The Wild Bunch* for paving the way in making more realistic (if electrifying) movies ever since. I am a fan of some of Peckinpah's post *TWB* offerings: the solemn *Pat Garrett & Billy the Kid*; the deliciously sleazy *Bring Me the Head of Alfredo Garcia* featuring the inimitable *TWB's* Warren Oates; and the palatable *Smokey & the Bandit* rip-off *Convoy!* featuring *Garrett's* Kris Kristofferson, Ali MacGraw and *TWB's* Ernest Borgnine. But *The Wild Bunch* will always be my favorite for all of the reasons I already listed and more.

In closing, when dining out at some chain restaurants, I generally give my name on the waiting list as "Pike Bishop." William Holden and Sam Peckinpah would be proud!

Appendix F: Film Critic Brian Marks on *The Wild Bunch*—Starting at the End

There is probably an ideal Western, one that could easily be recommended to neophytes. Perhaps one of John Ford's films would do the job; the anti-racism of *The Searchers*, the demythologizing of *The Man Who Shot Liberty Valance*, or the pure bravado of *Stagecoach* could all make a compelling entrée to the genre. My first experience with a Western wasn't with one of the classic works, but with one of the key revisionist Westerns, *The Wild Bunch*.

I had been seduced by cinema at an early age—as a precocious preteen I had already jetted ahead to Fellini and Godard without spending much time exploring classic American films. A blurb on one of the many greatest films lists that popped up as the current century approached praised Sam Peckinpah's *The Wild Bunch* for its unprecedented violence and artful editing. Not yet knowing anything about editing, the violence was the main attraction.

I understood "violence" to be a shorthand for "gore"—I expected to see sprays of blood, gouged-out eyeballs, exploding heads. Instead, the violence of *The Wild Bunch* was quaint by my standards; the squibs ejected a fluid closer to red tempera paint than blood, and the balletic falls of stuntmen from street-side balconies seemed overly dramatic to me.

I catalogued my first viewing of *The Wild Bunch* as a spectacular failure and one to avoid in the future. Its two-and-a-half-hour runtime was unbearably long and peppered with stretches where nothing much seemed to happen, in contrast with the dynamic action sequences. The politics of World War I-era Mexico were completely unfamiliar to me and robbed me of the satisfaction of seeing the slaughter of the generalissimo and his bandits. And the cast, a murderer's row of Hollywood players, was completely new to me. Peckinpah was counting on viewers contrasting William Holden's character with the more noble types of his earlier roles, but I didn't benefit from the extra knowledge.

Of course, I had only scratched the surface of *The Wild Bunch*. I was too young to appreciate the movie or its place in film history. A viewing of Peckinpah's *Straw Dogs* a few years later helped me to understand (and appreciate) his jaundiced view (Dustin Hoffman's familiar presence didn't hurt). By starting with *The Wild Bunch*, I had skipped to the last page of the book on American Westerns; I knew how it would end, but without the necessary knowledge to give the outcome context. I didn't understand how unusual it was that Mexicans played such a large role in the film's story, considering Hollywood's tendency to elide them from tales of the Old West. I failed to realize just how brutal Peckinpah's use of violence was compared to the frontier justice of Ford or Howard Hawks.

Most of all, I didn't quite grasp *The Wild Bunch*'s position as Peckinpah's farewell to the Hollywood he used to know. The system in which he made his name was about as alive in 1969 as William Holden is at the end of the movie. Peckinpah had blasted its confines to smithereens with the film's Gatling gun (his aim would occasionally be as wild as the generalissimo's in some of his later features). Robert Ryan and Edmond O'Brien's riding into the sunset matches Peckinpah's own journey into a brave new world.

When I watch *The Wild Bunch* now, it's hard for me to stomach the movie's opening gunfight. The violence doesn't seem quite as old-fashioned as it once did, but the film's editing and cinematography are the real sources of its brutality. The visceral blood spurts pack a wallop, but it's the rapid cutting that does the most damage, like quick jabs of a concealed knife. When the slow-motion kicks in, it mirrors the way time can come to a standstill for those on the precipice of death. I've seen *The Wild Bunch* many times now, but that opening battle never gets any easier.

Appendix G: Author David L. Robbins on *The Wild Bunch*

My mother was a nightmare to go to the movies with. She took forever to unwrap a candy, she crinkled it like a plague of locusts in a misguided attempt at consideration. She was an overt woman by design, so an overt whisperer. At violent scenes, she pounded a fist on the arm of her theater chair, declaiming, "*Oy, oy*," with a teeth suck, and an "*Oy*." We liked popcorn and soda and she demanded value, so in the enforced quiet of a cinema, Mom wrung them to their last, tipping high the popcorn bag, snorkeling the straw.

The first time she tried to blind me by thrusting her open palm across my eyes was in 1961, at *El Cid*. I was seven. Charlton Heston took a knife in the midriff through a seam in his chainmail. Mom yelped, then cupped buttery fingers over my nose and eye sockets. I pried at her hand and stopped squirming only when she cuffed the back of my head.

"*Sha*," she hissed. That was Yiddish for "Don't move, mister."

She kept up this practice for years. I missed the boobs in *Blow-Up* (1966) and *Thunderball*. I barely heard the dialogue in *Sand Pebbles* for all my mother's sighing and oy-ing. It took years to learn that *Who's Afraid of Virginia Woolf?* (1966) had dirty words.

In 1969, when I'd turned fifteen, well past my bar mitzvah, I wasn't having it any more. Mom and I took in Sam Peckinpah's *The Wild Bunch* at the Lowe's. In this film, I had everything: curses, breasts, blood and blasts. Chair arm slapping, hand wringing, candy crinkling, slurping, sighing, tongue clicks, and *oys*. I was quick and blocked her hand before it lifted from her lap.

My mother's unconcealed reactions were even more invasive measured against the stultified silence in the Lowe's theater. This is how I remember Peckinpah's gem, *The Wild Bunch*. How loud my mother sounded when no one else made a peep.

Appendix G

Peckinpah got my mother's foot tapping with his opening scene, children watching fire ants bedevil a scorpion. As if that wasn't enough, they laid burning sticks over the struggling insects, gleeful all the while like junior demons.

My mother took me to movies because we talked about them afterward. In our family, I alone cared about films, books, and stories as deeply as she did. Early on, I became her cohort. Then, after years of her hand over my eyes, at *The Wild Bunch*, when she could not protect me from Sam Peckinpah, I became not the boy beside her in the dark but the young man.

After the film, over cones of pistachio ice cream, she complained about the lack of subtlety in *The Wild Bunch*, the depictions of such a harsh, soulless world. Lowlifes populate both sides of the chase equation, galloping through the Texas badlands into Mexico. The villains are violent, greedy and ignorant thieves, the good guys giving chase are worse. The script reserves articulate dialogue for only the two lead characters, the rest are leering tropes of bad teeth and maniacal laughter. The horses take a terrible beating in this film; it's hard to watch it with a modern eye. The film's plot is standard: the chief bad guy's old riding mate has been hired by the wicked railroad baron to hunt him down. The former comrade won't stop, and there are old vendettas to blot out loyalties.

The Wild Bunch nudges us to believe there's honor among thieves. All it achieves is to note that no one can be stupid, avaricious, and craven all the time. My mother felt this a flaw, how every character followed a dishonorable arc, and even when they tried for redemption, their dying acts did not stray beyond violence and treachery. None of the characters was worth a damn. Every one was either a gunman, a moll, a laughing Mexican, and/or a moron. They all lived and died by the Peckinpah.

No character was silent or stoic. Peckinpah had no use for the intransigent, mysterious stranger popular in the spaghetti Westerns. His characters cursed a blue streak (my favorite was this dying invective: "How'd you like to kiss my sister's black cat's ass?"). The women were stunning, dusky Latinas, another way for Peckinpah to reinforce that these bad men, these wild ones, would crush anything that got in their way, including beauty.

The back stories, when the characters had them, were bullshit. This bothered my mother. Peckinpah is the opposite of the cop waving people past an accident, intoning, "Nothing to see here." Instead, he waves his audience past all depth and emotional entanglement. He wants us to focus instead on violence, filth, earthiness, vastness, and blood. If you wander anywhere else, look for anything else, Peckinpah says, "Nothing to see there." Scenes sweep you past any soft humanness, riveting you where Peckinpah wants you, on bullets, spurts and splashes of crimson, explosions and barking weapons, curses, emptied whiskey bottles, and stuntmen earning their pay. Those opening moments of the film, the giggling children burning ants and scorpions, tell us what to expect. Peckinpah figures if you're disappointed after that, you have only yourself to blame.

The Wild Bunch holds a lofty slot in the Western oeuvre because it broke ground like a gravedigger. In 1969, we were a violent nation enduring a turbulent time. Sam Peckinpah wasn't going to give Americans more screen violence witnessed askew or through a filter or leavened by emotion or character development. No causation, no sentiment, no forgiveness. His evildoers rob and kill other robbers and killers. Maybe Peckinpah hoped we'd get violence out of our systems seated in the dark theaters, unarmed ourselves. More probably, he understood, earlier than any Hollywood director, that America liked it.

My mother stopped taking me to movies soon after *The Wild Bunch*. I turned sixteen and my driver's license let me go to the cinema on my own. Much the pity. I was left in my seat alone, not only without her candies but also her heart to object to such hardness as *The Wild Bunch*. I became, as Peckinpah intended, an aficionado of cinematic mayhem, a deadened fan needing more firepower in my films.

Peckinpah did me no service, made no worthwhile statement with *The Wild Bunch*. What he did in 1969 was to capture the American zeitgeist of violence, and with it, foretell an unfortunate future for the movies.

Appendix H: The Stock Company

Peckinpah, like many directors, and most notably that other great maker of Westerns, John Ford, had a pool of actors he regularly called on to fill out his cinematic canvases. A number of them appear in *The Wild Bunch*. Below, a trivia geek's list of those Familiar Faces which appear and re-appear in Peckinpah films over the course of the director's career*:

R. G. Armstrong—*Ride the High Country, Major Dundee, Pat Garrett & Billy the Kid.*
Richard Bright: *The Getaway, Pat Garrett & Billy the Kid.*
John Davis Chandler: *Ride the High Country, Major Dundee, Pat Garrett & Billy the Kid.*
Aurora Clavel: *Major Dundee, The Wild Bunch, Pat Garrett & Billy the Kid.*
James Coburn: *Major Dundee, Pat Garrett & Billy the Kid, Cross of Iron* (Coburn also directed the second unit for Peckinpah on *Convoy*).
Helmut Dantine: *Bring Me the Head of Alfredo Garcia, The Killer Elite.*
Jack Dodson: *The Getaway, Pat Garrett & Billy the Kid.*
Gene Evans: *Junior Bonner, Pat Garrett & Billy the Kid*
Emilio Fernandez: *The Wild Bunch, Pat Garrett & Billy the Kid, Bring Me the Head of Alfredo Garcia.*
Donnie Fritts: *Pat Garrett & Billy the Kid, Bring Me the Head of Alfredo Garcia, Convoy.*
Bo Hopkins: *The Wild Bunch, The Getaway, The Killer Elite.*
Ben Johnson: *Major Dundee, The Wild Bunch, Junior Bonner, The Getaway.*
L. Q. Jones: *Ride the High Country, Major Dundee, The Wild Bunch, The Ballad of Cable Hogue, Pat Garrett & Billy the Kid.*

---

*It's worth noting that the connection of many of these performers to Peckinpah predates his feature career, with many of them first working for him during his TV days.

Appendix H

Kris Kristofferson: *Pat Garrett & Billy the Kid, Bring Me the Head of Alfredo Garcia, Convoy.*

Strother Martin: *The Deadly Companions, The Wild Bunch, The Ballad of Cable Hogue.*

Warren Oates: *Ride the High Country, Major Dundee, The Wild Bunch, Bring Me the Head of Alfredo Garcia.*

Slim Pickens: *Major Dundee, The Ballad of Cable Hogue, The Getaway, Pat Garrett & Billy the Kid.*

Jason Robards: *The Ballad of Cable Hogue, Pat Garrett & Billy the Kid.*

Jorge Russek: *The Wild Bunch, Pat Garrett & Billy the Kid, Bring Me the Head of Alfredo Garcia, Convoy.*

Dub Taylor: *Major Dundee, The Wild Bunch, Junior Bonner, The Getaway.*

David Warner: *The Ballad of Cable Hogue, Straw Dogs* (uncredited), *Cross of Iron.*

Chill Wills: *The Deadly Companions, Pat Garrett & Billy the Kid.*

Burt Young: *The Killer Elite, Convoy.*

Gig Young: *Bring Me the Head of Alfredo Garcia, The Killer Elite.*

Appendix I:
Sam Peckinpah Filmography

Works for television are in *italics*. Feature film titles are in ***bold italics***. Rotten Tomatoes All Critics/Top Critics/Audience scores are included for features. While Rotten Tomatoes might not pass muster as a statistically valid measure, its scores do give some indication of the current critical and popular view of Sam Peckinpah's films, some of which, evidently, have improved with the years.

1955–1956

Gunsmoke	Episodes: "The Queue": d. Charles Marcus Warren; w. Sam Peckinpah
	"Yorky": d. Charles Marcus Warren; w. Sam Peckinpah
	"Cooter": d. Robert Stevenson; w. Sam Peckinpah
	"How to Die for Nothing": d. Ted Post; w. Sam Peckinpah
	"The Guitar": d. Harry Horner; w. Sam Peckinpah
	"The Roundup": d. Ted Post; w. Sam Peckinpah
	"Legal Revenge": d. Andrew McLaglen; w. Sam Peckinpah
	"Poor Pearl": d. Andrew McLaglen; w. Sam Peckinpah
	"How to Kill a Woman": d. John Rich; w. Sam Peckinpah
	"Dirt": d. Ted Post; w. Sam Peckinpah
Broken Arrow	Episode: "The Assassin": d. Frank McDonald; w. Sam Peckinpah Story. Elliott Arnold from his novel.

1957

Tales of Wells Fargo	Episode: "Apache Gold": d. Earl Bellamy; w. Sam Peckinpah
Blood Brother	Episode: "The Teacher": w. Sam Peckinpah
Have Gun—Will Travel	Episode: "The Teacher": d. Andrew McLaglen; w. Sam Peckinpah

Appendix I

1958

Trackdown	Episode:"The Town": d. Donald McDougall; w. Sam Peckinpah
Blood Brother	Episode:"The Transfer": w. Sam Peckinpah
Tombstone Territory	Episode:"Johnny Ringo's Last Ride": d. Ted Post; w. Sam Peckinpah
Man Without a Gun	Episode:"The Kidder": d. John Peyser; w. Sam Peckinpah
Broken Arrow	Episode:"The Knife Fighter": w/d Sam Peckinpah
Dick Powell's Zane Grey Theater	Episode:"Trouble at Tres Cruces": w/d Sam Peckinpah (would serve as the pilot for *The Westerner*)

1958–1959

Dick Powell's Zane Grey Theater	Episode:"The Sharpshooter": d. Arnold Laven; w. Sam Peckinpah (would serve as the pilot for *The Rifleman*)
The Rifleman	Episodes:"The Sharpshooter": d. Arnold Laven; w. Sam Peckinpah
	"The Marshall": w/d Sam Peckinpah
	"Home Ranch": d. Arnold Laven; w. Sam Peckinpah
	"The Boarding House": w/d Sam Peckinpah
	"The Money Gun": d. Sam Peckinpah; w. Bruce Geller, Sam Peckinpah
	The Baby Sitter: d. Sam Peckinpah; w. Jack Curtis, Sam Peckinpah

1959

Dick Powell's Zane Grey Theater	Episodes:"Miss Jenny": d. Sam Peckinpah; w. Robert Heverly, Sam Peckinpah
	"Lonesome Road": d. Sam Peckinpah; w. Jack Curtis, Sam Peckinpah

1960

Klondike	Episodes:"Pilot": d. Sam Peckinpah; w. Carey Wilber, Sam Peckinpah
	"Swoger's Mule": d. Elliott Lewis; w. Sam Peckinpah, Jack Garriss, Elliott Lewis
The Westerner	Episodes:"Jeff": d. Sam Peckinpah; w. Robert Heverly, Sam Peckinpah
	"Brown": d. Sam Peckinpah; w. Bruce Geller
	"The Courting of Libby": d. Sam Peckinpah; w. Bruce Geller
	"Hand on the Gun": d. Sam Peckinpah; w. Bruce Geller

Sam Peckinpah Filmography

"The Painting": d. Sam Peckinpah; w. Bruce Geller

"The Old Man": d. Andre de Toth; w. Sam Peckinpah, Jack Curtis

"School Day": d. Andre de Toth; w. Sam Peckinpah, Robert Heverly

"Mrs. Kennedy": d. Bernie Kowalski; w. Sam Peckinpah, John Dunkel *(Peckinpah was also producer for the series' 13 episodes)*

1961

One-Eyed Jacks. d. Marlon Brando
- Released by: Paramount Pictures
- Based on the novel *The Authentic Death of Hendry Jones* by Charles Neider *(Rotten Tomatoes Scores: All Critics—57 percent; Top Critics—N/A; Audience Score—72 percent)*

The Deadly Companions. d. Sam Peckinpah
- Released by: Pathe America
- Screenplay: A. S. Fleischman
- *(83 percent; N/A; 31 percent)*

Pony Express
- Episode: "The Story of Julesburg": w. Sam Peckinpah

Route 66
- Episode: "Mon Petit Chou": d. Sam Peckinpah; w. Stirling Silliphant, Herbert B. Leonard

1962

Ride the High Country aka ***Guns in the Afternoon.*** d. Sam Peckinpah
- Released by: MGM
- Screenplay: N. B. Stone, Jr.
- *(93 percent; N/A; 83 percent)*

Dick Powell Theater
- Episodes: "Pericles on 31st Street": d. Sam Peckinpah; w. Sam Peckinpah, Harry Mark Petrakis
- "The Losers": d. Sam Peckinpah; w. Sam Peckinpah, Bruce Geller; story. Bruce Geller

1965

Major Dundee. d. Sam Peckinpah
- Released by: Columbia Pictures
- Screenplay: Harry Julian Fink & Oscar Saul, Sam Peckinpah
- Story: Harry Julian Fink
- *(97 percent; 100 percent; 66 percent)*

The Glory Guys. d. Arnold Laven.
- Released by: United Artists
- Screenplay: Sam Peckinpah
- Based on the novel *The Dice of God* by Hoffman Birney.
- *(60 percent; N/A; 33 percent)*

Appendix I

1966

ABC Stage 67	Episode: "Noon Wine": w/d Sam Peckinpah
	Based on the novella by Katherine Anne Porter.

1967

Bob Hope's Chrysler Theater	Episode: "That Lady is My Wife": d. Sam Peckinpah; story. Jack Laird
	Adaptation: Halsted Welles

1968

Villa Rides! d. Buzz Kulik	Released by: Paramount Pictures
	Screenplay: Robert Towne, Sam Peckinpah
	Adaptation: William Douglas Lansford based on his novel.
	(N/A; N/A; 45 percent)

1969

The Wild Bunch: d. Sam Peckinpah	Released by: Warner Bros.–Seven Arts
	Screenplay: Walon Green, Sam Peckinpah
	Story: Walon Green, Roy N. Sickner
	(94 percent; 88 percent; 91 percent)

1970

The Ballad of Cable Hogue: d. Sam Peckinpah	Released by: Warner Bros.
	Screenplay: John Crawford, Edmund Penney
	(93 percent; N/A; 81 percent)

1971

Straw Dogs: d. Sam Peckinpah	Released by: ABC Pictures
	Screenplay: David Zelag Goodman, Sam Peckinpah
	Based on the novel *The Siege of Trencher's Farm* by Gordon M. Williams
	(91 percent; N/A; 82 percent)

1972

Junior Bonner: d. Sam Peckinpah	Released by: Cinerama Releasing
	Screenplay: Jeb Rosebrook
	(91 percent; 83 percent; 63 percent)
The Getaway: d. Sam Peckinpah	Released by: National General
	Screenplay: Walter Hill
	Based on the novel by Jim Thompson
	(85 percent; N/A; 81 percent)

Sam Peckinpah Filmography

1973

Pat Garrett & Billy the Kid: d. Sam Peckinpah	Released by: MGM Screenplay: Rudy Wurlitzer *(85 percent; 60 percent; 83 percent)*

1974

Bring Me the Head of Alfredo Garcia: d. Sam Peckinpah	Released by: United Artists Screenplay: Gordon Dawson, Sam Peckinpah Story: Frank Kowalski, Sam Peckinpah *(83 percent; N/A; 85 percent)*

1975

The Killer Elite: d. Sam Peckinpah	Released by: United Artists Screenplay: Marc Norman, Stirling Silliphant Based on the novel *Monkey in the Middle* by Robert Rostand (aka Robert Syd Hopkins) *(55 percent; N/A; 34 percent)*

1977

Cross of Iron: d. Sam Peckinpah	Released by: AVCO Embassy Pictures Screenplay: Julius Epstein, Walter Kelley & James Hamilton Based on the novel by Willi Heinrich *(80 percent; N/A; 87 percent)*

1978

Convoy: d. Sam Peckinpah	Released by: United Artists Story and Screenplay: B. W. L. Norton Based on the song by C. W. McCall and Chip Davis *(42 percent; N/A; 73 percent)*

1983

The Osterman Weekend: d. Sam Peckinpah	Released by: 20th Century–Fox Screenplay: Alan Sharp Adaptation: Ian Masters Based on the novel by Robert Ludlum *(43 percent; N/A; 37 percent)*

1984

"Valotte" (music video): d. Sam Peckinpah; artist: Julian Lennon

"Too Late for Goodbyes" (music video): d. Sam Peckinpah; artist: Julian Lennon

Bibliography

Ankeny, Jason. "Jerry Fielding." Allmusic.com. https://www.allmusic.com/artist/jerry-fielding-mn0000844461/biography
Ansen, David. "The Return of a Bloody Great Classic." *Newsweek,* March 12, 1995, rptd. Newsweek.com Sept. 9, 2018: https://www.newsweek.com/return-bloody-great-classic-180510
Axmaker, Sean. "Articles: *The Wild Bunch* (1969)." TCM.com, 2018: http://www.tcm.com/tcmdb/title/21717/The-Wild-Bunch/articles.html
Bach, Steven. *Final Cut: Dreams and Disaster in the Making of Heaven's Gate.* New York: Plume, 1985.
Balio, Tina, ed. *The American Film Industry.* Madison: University of Wisconsin Press, 1976.
Barnouw, Erik. *Tube of Plenty: The Evolution of American Television.* Revised. New York: Oxford University, 1982.
Barrow, John. "La Golondrina (The Swallow)." Purple Martin Conservation Association, April 4, 2008. https://www.purplemartin.org/forum/viewtopic.php?t=10323
Baxter, John. *Sixty Years of Hollywood.* Cranbury, NJ: A. S. Barnes, 1973.
Benson, Kit, and Morgan Benson. "Strother Martin, Jr." Find a Grave, 2001: https://www.findagrave.com/memorial/2046/strother-martin
Berman, Pat. "A Strange Fascination for Violence." *Columbia Record* (Columbia, SC), Sunday ed., Feb. 1, 1975: 1-B+.
Biskind, Peter. *Easy Riders, Raging Bulls: How the Sex-Drugs-and-Rock 'n' Roll Generation Saved Hollywood.* New York: Touchstone, 1998.
Bogdanovich, Peter. "Bogie in Excess." *Esquire* (Sept. 1964). Rptd. in *Smiling Through the Apocalypse: Esquire's History of the Sixties."* New York: Crown, 1987: 211–222.
Borneman, Ernest. "United States versus Hollywood: The Cast Study of an Antitrust Suit." *Sight and Sound* (Feb. 1951). Rptd. in *The American Film Industry.* Ed. Tino Balio. Madison: University of Wisconsin Press, 1976: 332–345.
Boyar, Jay. "Today's Westerns Pale Next to *Wild Bunch.*" *The Orlando Sentinel,* April 2, 1995. Rptd. Orlandosentinel.com Sept. 10, 2018: http://articles.orlandosentinel.com/1995-04-02/entertainment/9503300661_1_wild-bunch-butch-cassidy-new-westerns/2
Brady, John. *The Craft of the Screenwriter.* New York: Touchstone, 1981.
Brooks, Richard. (w/d). *The Professionals.* Based on the novel by Frank O'Rourke. Columbia, 1966.
_____. (w/d). *Bite the Bullet.* Columbia, 1975.
Brooks, Tim, Earle Marsh. *The Complete Directory to Prime Time Network and Cable TV Shows 1946—Present.* 6th ed. New York: Ballantine, 1995.
Buford, Kate. "Do Make Waves: Sandy—Alexander Mackendrick." *Film Comment* (May/June 1994): 41–43.
Burlingame, Jon. "*Wild Bunch* Composer Jerry Fielding Honored." Film Music Society (Nov. 13, 2009): http://www.filmmusicsociety.org/news_events/features/2009/111309.html?isArchive=111309

Bibliography

Burr, Ty. "The Actor Who Knew Too Much." *Dartmouth Alumni Magazine*, July-August 2012: https://dartmouthalumnimagazine.com/articles/actor-who-knew-too-much
"Cahiers du Peckinpah." *Esquire* (Feb. 1972): 120–122.
Carey, Gary. *All the Stars in Heaven—Louis B. Mayer's MGM*. New York: Dutton, 1981.
Champlin, Charles. "A Maverick's Violent Legacy." *The Los Angeles Times*, January 1, 1985. Rptd. latimes.com: http://articles.latimes.com/1985-01-01/entertainment/ca-10385_1_wild-bunch
_____. "The Wild Bunch." *The Los Angeles Times*, June 15, 1969. Rptd. *Filmfacts*, vol. XII, #10, 1969, 217–221.
"Closing of the American Frontier, 1870–1900." Calisphere. University of California. https://calisphere.org/exhibitions/t4/closing-frontier/
Collins, Glenn. "Lucien Ballard, Cinematographer." *The New York Times*, Oct. 6, 1988. Rptd. nytimes.com: https://www.nytimes.com/1988/10/06/obituaries/lucien-ballard-cinematographer.html
Conroy, Frank. "My Generation." *Esquire*, October 1968. Rptd. *Smiling Through the Apolocalypse: Esquire's History of the Sixties*. New York: Crown, 1987: 301–305.
Crawford, Robert L. (w/d). "The Making of *Butch Cassidy and the Sundance Kid*." Robert L. Crawford Productions, 1970.
Daly, Steve. "Saddles Soar." *Entertainment Weekly* (May 30, 2003): 10–11.
Dempsey, Michael. "The Return of *Jaws*." *American Film* (June 1978): 28+.
Dirks, Tim. "Filmsite Movie Review: *Casablanca* (1942)." AMC Filmsite. 2018.
Dougan, Clark, and Samuel Lipsman, eds. *A Nation Divided*. The Vietnam Experience. Boston: Boston Publishing, 1984.
_____. and Stephen Weiss, eds. *Nineteen Sixty-Eight*. The Vietnam Experience. Boston: Boston Publishing, 1983.
"Dub Taylor: Biography." TCM.com, 2018: http://www.tcm.com/tcmdb/person/189509%7C41654/Dub-Taylor/biography.html
Ebert, Roger. "The Wild Bunch." *The Chicago Sun-Times*, August 3, 1969. Rptd. Rogerebert.com, Sept. 10, 2018: https://www.rogerebert.com/reviews/the-wild-bunch-1969
"Edmond O'Brien: Biography." TCM.com, 2005: www.tcm.com/tcmdb/person/142848%7C44032/Edmond-O-Brien/
Eggert, Brian. *The Wild Bunch*. Deep Focus Review, July 28, 2013: https://deepfocusreview.com/definitives/the-wild-bunch/
Emery, Robert J. (p.d.w). *The Directors: George Romero*. Media Entertainment Inc. for Encore (2003).
Evans, Robert. *The Kid Stays in the Picture*. New York: Hyperion, 1994.
Everson, William K. *A Pictorial History of the Western*. Secaucus, NJ: Citadel, 1969.
Farber, Stephen. "Peckinpah's Return." *Film Quarterly*, vol. XXIII, #1 (Fall 1969): 5–11.
Feige, Kevin. "Stan Lee." *Entertainment Weekly* (Nov. 30, 2018): 18–21.
Ferrara, Greg (ed). "Articles: *The Wild Bunch*." TCM.com., 20018: http://www.tcm.com/tcmdb/title/21717/The-Wild-Bunch/articles.html
Fierman, Daniel. "*Harry Potter* and the Challenge of Sequels." *Entertainment Weekly* (Nov. 22, 2002): 24–31.
Finler, Joel. *The Hollywood Story*. New York: Crown, 1988.
_____. *The Movie Director's Story*. New York: Crescent, 1985.
Folsom, James, ed. *The Western: A Collection of Critical Essays*. Englewood Cliffs, NJ: Prentice, 1979.
Ford, John. (d) *The Man Who Shot Liberty Valance*. w. James Warner Bellah, Willis Goldbeck, based on a story by Dorothy M. Johnson. Paramount, 1962.
"Ford Motor Company Unveils the Model T." History.com. (Dec. 13, 2018): https://www.history.com/this-day-in-history/ford-motor-company-unveils-the-model-t
Francis, Patrick (d). "Interviewing Hollywood: L.Q. Jones." InterviewingHollywood.com, 2008: https://www.youtube.com/watch?v=uayweIIDG2Q

Bibliography

Freeth, Nick. *Remembering the '40s: A Decade in Words and Pictures.* London: Barnes & Noble, 2002.
Froug, William. *The Screenwriter Looks at the Screenwriter.* Los Angeles, Silman-James, 1991.
Gaita, Paul. "Jack L. Warner." TCM.com http://www.tcm.com/tcmdb/person/2020 87%7C76481/Jack-L-Warner/biography.html
Gaydos, S. "After the Falls." *Hollywood Reporter* (Feb. 10, 1992): S-10+.
Gentry, Curt. *The Last Days of the Late, Great State of California.* New York: Putnam, 1968.
Giannetti, Louis D. *Understanding Movies.* 2nd ed. Englewood Cliffs, NJ: Prentice-Hall, 1976.
Gladwell, Malcolm. *Outliers: The Story of Success.* Pbk ed. New York: Back Bay, 2011.
"Glenn Ford." TCM.com, 2005: www.tcm.com/tcmdb/person/63871%7C62323/Glenn-Ford/biography.html
Goldman, William. *Adventures in the Screen Trade: A Personal View of Hollywood and Screenwriting.* New York: Warner, 1983.
Gomery, Douglas. "Lucien Ballard." Film Reference, 2018: http://www.filmreference.com/Writers-and-Production-Artists-Ba-Bo/Ballard-Lucien.html
Greenberg, James. "Western Canvas, Palette of Blood." *The New York Times* (Feb. 26, 1995): 19+.
Grobel, Lawrence. "Glory Days." *Movieline* (Aug. 1993): 54+.
Grusin, Dave (composer). Robert Wells (lyrics). *Waterhole #3 (Code of the West).* Soundtrack album. Smash Records, 1967.
Hackett, Lawrence. "'Drawing' On Westerns: Expert Says Cowboy Films Helped Shape Recent U.S. History." *The Star-Ledger,* April 6, 1988.
Halberstam, David. *The Fifties.* New York: Villard, 1993.
Heaton, Louis (d). *Guns for Hire: The Making of The Magnificent Seven.* MGM Home Entertainment, 2001.
Heston, Charlton. *Charlton Heston: The Actor's Life—Journals 1956–1976.* New York: Pocket, 1979.
Hirshey, Gerri. "Motown at 60: Act II—The Sound That Changed the World." *AARP: The Magazine.* Dec. 2018–Jan. 2019: 43+.
Hodenfield, Chris. "Last of the Real Ones." *American Film* (March 1990): 4.
Hopwood, Jon C. "Emilio Fernandez: Biography." IMDB.com: https://www.imdb.com/name/nm02734bio?ref_=nm_ov_bio_sm
_____. "Lucien Ballard: Biography." IMDB.com: https://www.imdb.com/name/nm0005644/bio?ref_=nm_ov_bio_sm
"How to Write Photoplays (Vintage Screenwriting Series Book 1)." Amazon notes. Amazon, 2015: https://www.amazon.com/Write-Photoplays-Vintage-Screenwriting-Book-ebook/dp/B00UMSC33M/ref=sr_1_3?s=books&ie=UTF8&qid=1544056849&sr=1-3&keywords=How+to+Write+Photoplays
Hoyt, Eric. *Hollywood Vault: Film Libraries Before Home Video.* Berkeley: University of California Press, 2014.
Hunter, Stephen. "*Wild Bunch* Survives Improvements." *The Baltimore Sun,* March 31, 1995. Rptd. Baltimoresun.com, Sept. 10, 2018: http://articles.baltimoresun.com/1995-03-31/entertainment/1995090175_1_wild-bunch-depravity-bloody-murder
Huston, John. *An Open Book.* New York: Ballantine, 1980.
"Introductory Note: Charles Augustin Sainte-Beuve." *Harvard Classics, Vol. 32: Literary and Philosophical Essays.* New York: Bartleby.com, 2001.
Jameson, Richard T. "Lost *Weekend.*" *Film Comment* (April 1984): 28–30.
Jennings, Gary. *The Movie Book.* New York: Dial, 1963.
Kennedy, Burt (d). *Support Your Local Sheriff!* w. William Bowers. UA, 1969.
Knauer, Kelly, ed. *America: An Illustrated Modern History 1900–2007.* New York: Time Books, 2007.

Bibliography

———. *1968: The Year That Changed the World*. New York: Time Inc. Home Entertainment, 2008.

———. *1969: Woodstock, the Moon and Manson: The Turbulent End of the '60s*. New York: Time Inc. Home Entertainment, 2009.

———. *TIME: American Legends—Our Nation's Most Fascinating Heroes, Icons, and Leaders*. Special Edition. New York: Time Books, 2001.

———. *Visions of the '60s: The Images That Define the Decade*. New York: Time Home Entertainment, 2010.

Knudsen, Tyler (w/d). "The Bizarre Process of Writing *North by Northwest*." Cinema Tyler: Making Film. March, 2018. https://www.youtube.com/watch?v=lltazliRp58

———. "How Kubrick Adapted *The Shining* into a Cinematic Masterpiece." Cinema Tyler: Making Film. September 2017. https://www.youtube.com/watch?v=fHvk2zgUBpY

Lapin, Nicole, and Jason Hanna. "1969 Alcatraz Takeover 'Changed the Whole Course of History.'" CNN. CNN.com. http://www.cnn.com/2009/CRIME/11/20/alcatraz.indian.occupation/

Lawrence, Jerome, and Robert E. Lee. *Inherit the Wind*. http://msbarcena.weebly.com/uploads/6/3/1/9/6319509/inherit_the_wind-full_text_electronic_version.pdf. 1955.

Lester, Peter. "Actor-Write Burt Young Has an Ex-Pug's Mug, But He Can Knock Out Scripts in Three Weeks," *People* (July 17, 1978): 71–74.

Lester, Will. "We're Hooked on High Tech." Associated Press. Rptd. In *The Star-Ledger* (Dec. 22, 2005): 42.

LoBrutto, Vincent. *Selected Takes: Film Editors on Editing*. New York: Praeger, 1991.

"A Look at the 1940 Census." Census.gov. https://www.census.gov/newsroom/cspan/1940census/CSPAN_1940slides.pdf

Maclear, Michael. *The Ten Thousand Day War—Vietnam: 1945–1975*. New York: Avon, 1981.

Manning, Robert, ed. *A Nation Divided*. The Vietnam Experience. Boston: Boston Publishing, 1984.

Marx, Grouch, with Tor Arce. *The Secret Word Is Groucho*. New York: Putnam, 1976.

Medved, Harry, with Randy Dreyfuss. *The 50 Worst Films of All Time (and How They Got That Way)*. New York: Warner, 1984.

Mesce, Jr., Bill. "What Makes a Classic Movie Classic?" *Sound on Sight*, 3/27/12, rptd. *Reel Change: The Changing Nature of Hollywood, Hollywood Movies, and the People Who Go to See Them*. Albany, GA: BearManor Media, 2014: 228–230.

———. "The World's First Screenwriter: Aristotle." *Sound on Sight*, 12/8/10, rptd. *Reel Change: The Changing Nature of Hollywood, Hollywood Movies, and the People Who Go to See Them*. Albany, GA: BearManor Media, 2014: 351–353.

"Mission." Library of Congress. National Film Preservation Board. https://www.loc.gov/programs/national-film-preservation-board/about-this-program/mission/

Munn, Michael. *Gene Hackman*. London: Hale, 1997.

Murphy, Kathleen. "Blood of a Poet: The Cinema According to Sam Peckinpah." The Film Society of Lincoln Center, The Walter Reade Theater Program (March 1995): 7+.

Murray, Dick (d); Steve Burgess (w). *The Cowboy*. "Episode 2: Hollywood *vs.* History." Discovery Channel, 2016.

Murray, William. "Interview: Sam Peckinpah." *Playboy* (August 1972): 65+.

Nachbar, Jack, ed. *Focus on the Western*. Film Focus. Englewood Cliffs, NJ: Prentice, 1974.

Nashawaty, Chris. "Politics and Pop Escapism." *Entertainment Weekly* (Dec. 14/21, 2018): 16–17.

"Negative Capability." Keats' Kingdom, 1/16/19: http://www.keatsian.co.uk/negative-capability.php

Niemi, Robet. *100 Great War Movies: The Real History Behind the Films*. Santa Barbara, CA: ABC-CLIO, 2018.

Norris, Laura, and Joseph Reiss. "Las Soldaderas." University of Michigan, December 15, 2006: http://www.umich.edu/-ac213/student_projects06/joelan/index.html

Bibliography

"1968: The Year That Shattered America." Cover. *Smithsonian* (Jan./Feb 2018).
O'Brien, Patrick K., ed. *Philip's Atlas of World History*. London: Philip Ltd., 1999.
Parkinson, Michael, and Clyde Jeavons. *A Pictorial History of Westerns*. London: Hamlyn Publishing, 1973.
Parks, Rita. *The Western Hero in Film and Television: Mass Media Mythology*. Studies in Cinema. Ann Arbor, MI: UMI Research Papers, 1982.
"Pat Garrett and Billy the Kid." Crimetv.com: http://www.crimetv.com/page/movies/westerns/pat-garrett-and-billy-the-kid/1047
"Pat Garrett and Billy the Kid." *Filmfacts* XVI (Feb. 1973): 86–89.
Patterson, John. "'Bloody' Sam Peckinpah: Wasted, Insane and Indestructibly Pure." *The Guardian*, March 30, 2016. https://www.theguardian.com/film/2016/mar/30/bloody-sam-peckinpah-wasted-insane-wild-bunch
"Peckinpah's Cut of *Pat Garrett* Finally Emerges for a Screening." *Variety* (May 7, 1986): 110.
"Phil Feldman; Hollywood Producer." *The Los Angeles Times*, Oct. 11, 1991, rptd. latimes.com: http://articles.latimes.com/1991-10-11/news/mn-230_1_phil-feldman
Prince, Stephen. "*The Magnificent Seven*." https://www.loc.gov/programs/static/-national-film-preservation-board/documents/magnificent_seven.pdf
Quantrill, Jay Alan. "Original Motion Picture Sound Track: *The Wild Bunch*." Liner notes. Varese Sarabande Records, 1980.
Rainer, Pete. "Blood Sport." *New York* (April 19, 2004): 64–65.
Redman, Nick (w/d). "A Simple Adventure Story: Sam Peckinpah, Mexico, and *The Wild Bunch*." Warner Bros., 2005.
Roessing, Walter. "Scribes of the Scrimmage." *American Way*, Oct. 15, 1985: 70–74.
Rossen, Robert (d). *The Hustler*. w: Sydney Carroll, Robert Rossen, based on the novel by Walter S. Tevis. 20th Century Fox, 1961.
Sainte-Beuve, Charles Augustin. "What Is a Classic?" *Harvard Classics, Vol. 32: Literary and Philosophical Essays*. Translation by E. Lee. New York: Bartleby.com, 2001.
Sander, Gordon F. *Serling: The Rise and Twilight of Television's Last Angry Man*. New York: Dutton, 1992.
Sapan, Josh. *The Big Picture: America in Panorama*. New York: Princeton Architectural Press, 2013.
Sarris, Andrew. *The American Cinema: Directors and Directions 1929–1968*. New York: Dutton, 1968.
_____. "*The Wild Bunch*." *The Village Voice*, July 3, 1969. Rptd. Letterboxd.com, Dec. 29, 2016: https://letterboxd.com/notandrewsarris/film/the-wild-bunch/
Schaffner, Franklin J. (d). *Planet of the Apes*. w: Michael Wilson, Rod Serling, based on the novel *Monkey Planet* by Pierre Boulle. 20th Century Fox, 1968.
Schnall, Marianne. "Interview with Gloria Steinem." *Ms.* (April 3, 1995). Eleanor Roosevelt National Historical Site.
Server, Lee. *Robert Mitchum: "Baby, I Don't Care*.*"* New York: St. Martin's Griffin, 2002.
Seydor, Paul. *Peckinpah: The Western Films*. Urbana: University of Illinois Press, 1980.
_____. (w/d/p) "*The Wild Bunch: An Album in Montage*." Tyrus Entertainment, 1996.
Shickel, Richard. "Master of the 'Dirty Western.'" *Life* (July 25, 1969): 8.
Siegel, Mike. "Restoring *Junior*." *Cinema Retro*, vol. 14, issue 41, 2018: 56–60.
Simmons, Garner. "The Peckinpah Tapes," *American Film* (May 1985): 59–61.
_____ "Sam Peckinpah's Television Work." *Film Heritage* (Winter 1974–1975): 1–16.
Simon, Roger. "Philadelphia Story," *U.S. News & World Report* (August 7, 2000): 32.
Sklar, Robert. *Movie-Made America: A Cultural History of American Movies*. New York: Vintage, 1975.
Snider, Eric D. "13 Bullet-Riddled Facts About *The Wild Bunch*." Mental Floss (March 2, 2016): http://mentalfloss.com/article/76406/13-bullet-riddled-facts-about-wild-bunch
Stack, Peter. "*Wild Bunch* Rides Again/Director's Cut of '69 Classic." *San Francisco*

Bibliography

Chronicle (March 3, 1995), rptd. Sfgate.com (9/17/18): https://www.sfgate.com/movies/article/Wild-Bunch-Rides-Again-Director-s-cut-of-69-3042790.php

Stafford, Jeff. "*You're a Big Boy Now* (1966): Articles." TCM.com., 2018: http://www.tcm.com/tcmdb/title/96592/You-re-a-Big-Boy-Now/articles.html

Steinem, Gloria. "I'm Not the Women In My Mind." *Parade* (January 12, 1992): 1.

"Stonewall Riots." The History Channel. History.com. https://www.history.com/topics/-the-stonewall-riots

"*Straw Dogs.*" *Filmfacts* XV (Feb. 1972): 1–5.

Sturges, John (d). *Bad Day at Black Rock*. Millard Kaufman (w). Adapted by Don McGuire from Howard Breslin's story, "Bad Day at Honda." MGM, 1955.

_____. (p/d). *The Magnificent Seven*. William Roberts, Walter Newman (uncredited) (w). Adapted from Akira Kurosawa's *Seven Samurai* (1954). United Artists, 1960.

Svetkey, Benjamin. "America Is from Mars, Hollywood Is from Venus." *Entertainment Weekly* (Nov. 26, 2004): 18+.

Takis, John. "*The Wild Bunch:* FSM Online Liner Notes." Film Score Monthly, 2013: http://www.filmscoremonthly.com/notes/wild_bunch.html

Terrill, Marshall. *Steve McQueen: Portrait of an American Rebel*. New York: Donald Fine, 1993.

Thomson, David. "The Decade When Movies Mattered." *Movieline* (Aug. 1993): 43+.

Thurman, Tom (p/d). Tom Marksbury (w). *Sam Peckinpah's West: Legacy of a Hollywood Renegade*. Starz/Encore Entertainment, 2004.

_____. "Warren Oates: Across the Border." Fly by Noir Productions, 1992.

"A Time of Tumult." *Life: 50th Anniversary Collector's Edition 1936–1986* (Fall 1986): 187–195.

Travers, Peter. "*The Wild Bunch*." *Rolling Stone* (March 3, 1995). Rptd. Rollingstone.com (9/17/18): https://www.rollingstone.com/movies/movie-reviews/the-wild-bunch-101877/

Trumbo, Mitzi. "Trumbo Family: Kirk Douglas Overstates Blacklist Role." Salon, August 7, 2012: https://www.salon.com/2012/08/07/trumbo_family_kirk_douglas_overstates_blacklist_role/

"Vietnam War U.S. Military Fatal Casualty Statistics." National Archives. https://www.archives.gov/research/military/vietnam-war/casualty-statistics, 4/29/08.

Weales, Gerald. "The Bogart Vogue: Character and Cult." *Commonweal, 83* (March 11, 1966). Rptd. in *Sense of the 60's*. Edward Quinn, Paul J. Dolan, eds. New York: The Free Press, 1968: 163–168.

Webb, Michael, ed. *Hollywood: Legend and Reality*. Boston: Little, Brown, 1986.

Weddle, David. "Dead Man's Clothes: The Making of *The Wild Bunch*." *Film Comment*, May-June 1994: 44–57.

Westlake, Donald E. "The Hardboiled Dicks." Speech, Smithsonian Institution, May 13, 1982. Rptd. *The Getaway Car: A Donald Westlake Nonfiction Miscellany*. Ed. Levi Stahl. Chicago, U. of Chicago Press, 2014: 31–52.

Wicking, Christopher, and Tise Vahimagi. *The American Vein: Directors and Directions in Television*. New York: Dutton, 1979.

"*The Wild Bunch:* Man and Myth—*Time Magazine* Review." *Time* (June 20, 1969). Rptd. Scraps from the Loft (8/19/17): http://scrapsfromtheloft.com/2017/08/19/wild-bunch-man-myth-time-magazine-review/

"*The Wild Bunch*: Trivia." IMDB.com. https://www.imdb.com/title/tt0065214/trivia?ref_=tt_trv_trv

"*The Wild Bunch.*" *Filmfacts*, vol. XII, #10, 1969, 217–221.

Wilmington, Michael. "*The Wild Bunch* Back in the Saddle Again." *The Chicago Tribune*, March 17, 1995. Rptd. Chicagotribune.com, Sept. 10, 2018: http://www.chicagotribune.com/news/ct-xpm-1995-03-17-9503170365-story.html

Word, Rob (w/d/p). "A Word on Westerns: 'Kiss My Sister's Black Cat's Ass'—Bo Hop-

Bibliography

kins on *The Wild Bunch*." Autry National Center, 2014: https://www.youtube.com/watch?v=GMk5SARS5vs

_____. "A Word on Westerns: Baptism in Blood—Bo Hopkins Gets Squibbed on *The Wild Bunch*." Autry National Center, 2014: https://www.youtube.com/watch?v=VBjGP7sldnU

Wright, Will. *Sixguns & Society: A Structural Study of the Western*. Paper ed. Berkeley: University of California Press, 1977.

"WW II Casualties." World War 2. Oct. 4, 2009. http://worldwar2-database.blogspot.com/2010/10/world-war-ii-casualties.html

Index

Numbers in ***bold italics*** indicate pages with illustrations

Abrams, Gerald (producer) 165
Across the Pacific (1942) 3
"La Adelita" (song) 78, 159
Advise and Consent (1962) 77
Airport (1970) 132
The Alamo (2004) 140
Alcatraz Native American occupation 10
Aldrich, Robert (director) 17, 41
Alice's Restaurant (1970) 20
All That Jazz (1979) 135, 172
All the President's Men (1976) 135
All the Pretty Horses (2000) 140
Allen, Dede (editor) 94
Altman, Robert (director) 18, 75, 124
American Gigolo (1980) 98
American Outlaws (2001) 140
Anderson, Michael (actor) ***35***
Angels with Dirty Faces (1938) ***11***
Ant-Man and the Wasp (2018) 134
Apache (1954) 49
Apocalypse Now (1979) 137
Aquaman (2018) 134
Armstrong, Neil (astronaut) 2
Arness, James (actor) 28
The Artist (2011) 146
The Assassination of Jesse James by the Coward Robert Ford (2007) 140
Assault on Precinct 13 (1976) 170
Astaire, Fred (actor) 12
Astin, Sean (actor) ***143***
AT&T (media corporation) acquisition of Time Warner 14, 141
Attack! (1956) 46
Aubrey, James (studio executive) 125; *see also* MGM
The Authentic Death of Hendry Jones (novel) 31, 34, 124; *see also* One-Eyed Jacks
Avengers: Age of Ultron (2015) 133
Avengers: Infinity War (2018) 133

Bad Day at Black Rock (1955) 84
Bad Girls (1994) 140
Badham, John (director) 120
Badlands (1973) 124

Baker, Joe Don (actor) 75
The Ballad of Cable Hogue (1970) 1, 39, 41, 96, 120, 121, 122, ***123***, 124, 131, 145
The Ballad of Josie (1967) 24
Ballard, Lucien (cinematographer) 70–75, 77, 78, 80, 91, 92, 120, 170
Bandido! (1956) 37, 52
The Barefoot Contessa (1954) 85
Bates, Charles (actor) ***60***
Batman (1989) 133
Batman v. Superman: Dawn of Justice (2016) 134
Bay, Michael (director) 96
The Beatles (rock band) 1
Beatty, Ned (actor) 105
Beatty, Warren (actor) ***16-17***; *Bonnie and Clyde* 40, 94, 117, 170
Beaumont, Francis (playwright) 4
Beauty and the Beast (2017) 133
The Bedford Incident (1965) 19
Benchley, Peter (author) 135
Bergman, Ingmar (director) 22
Berkeley, Busby (director) 12
Beverly Hills Cop (1984) 133, 137
Beverly Hills Cop II (1987) 133
Bewkes, Jeff (former Time Warner CEO) 165–166
The Big Country (1958) 49, 50
Big Jake (1971) 118
The Big Steal (1949) 46
Birney, Hoffman (author) 31; *see also The Glory Guys*
Biskind, Peter (author) 40
Bite the Bullet (1975) 47, 118
Black Like Me (1964) 19
Black Panther (2018) 133
Blake, Amanda (actress) 28
Blake, Robert (actor) 88
Blazing Saddles (1974) 118, 169
Blood on the Moon (1948) 47
Blowup (1966) 21, 175
The Body Snatcher (1945) 46
Boetticher, Budd (director) 47
Bogart, Humphrey (actor; aka "Bogie") ***11***, 12, 23, 39

195

Index

Bonanza (TV series) 1, 167
Bonnie and Clyde (1967) **16-17**, 18, 20, 21, 22, 23, 67; box office 117, 132; climax 73, 94, 164, 168, 170; Jack Warner 40; Warren Beatty 40
Boone, Richard (actor) 81
Boorman, John (director) 17–18, 74
Borgnine, Ernest (actor) 54, 61, 84–85, **84**, 88, 89, 95, **112**, **113**, **114**, 117, 170, 172
Boyd, Billy (actor) **143**
Brando, Marlon (actor) 31, 34
The Bravados (1958) 52
Brennan, Walter (actor) 85
Bresler, Jerry (producer) 34, 35
Brewster McCloud (1970) 20, 167
The Bridge on the River Kwai (1957) 81, 149
Bring Me the Head of Alfredo Garcia (1974) 26, 120, **126**, 127, 131, 135, 141, 145, 147, 172
The Brinks Job (19780 120
Broken Arrow (1950) 49
Broken Arrow (TV series) 26
Bronson, Charles (actor) 54, 83
Brooks, Mel (director) 169
Brooks, Richard (director) 24, 47
Brown, Jim (actor) 83
Brynner, Yul (actor) 37, 53, 171
Bullitt (1968) 20, 21, 78, 132
Buntline, Ned (author) 44, 45, 140
Butch Cassidy and the Sundance Kid (1969) 34, 51, 52, 58, 86–87, 119; box office 116–117, 132; slow motion violence 74, 94–95, 164

Cagney, James (actor) **11**, 39
Calley, John (studio executive), as Warner Bros. chief 17
Camelot (1967) 40
Candy (1968) 167
Cape Fear (1962) 21
Captain America: Civil War (2016) 134
Captain America: The Winter Soldier (2014) 134
The Caretakers (1963) 71
Carpenter, John (director) 54, 170
Carroll, Gordon (producer) 125
Casablanca (1942) 3–4, 12, 15, 23, 59
Cassavetes, John (actor) 74
Cat Ballou (1965) 80
Catch-22 (1970) 22
CBS (TV network) cancellation of *The Smothers Brothers Comedy Hour* 1–2
The Charge of the Light Brigade (1968) 19
Chase, Charlie (film comedian) 71
Cheyenne Autumn (1964) 49
Chinatown (1974) 135
Chisum (1970) 118
Cimarron (1931) 49

Cimarron (1960) 49, 50
The Cincinnati Kid (1965) 20, 36, 41, 122
A Clockwork Orange (1971) 135
Close Encounters of the Third Kind (1977) 133
Clyde, Andy (actor) 85
Cobb, Lee J. (actor) 85
Coburn, James **125**, **128**, 150
Cody, Buffalo Bill (showman) 44
Cohn, Harry (movie studio executive) 12, 40, 83
Columbia (movie studio) 12, 13, 83; *Major Dundee* 35, 36; part of Sony 14, 141
The Comancheros (1961) 52
Connors, Chuck (actor) 29, **29**
Convoy (1978) 43, 129, 172
Cool Hand Luke (1966) 20, 78, 86
Cooper, Gary (actor) 171
Coppola, Francis Ford (director) 18, 64
Corbucci, Serio (director) 169
Cord, Alex (actor) 83
Corman, Roger (producer) 64
Cosmatos, George Pan (director) 170
Cotten, Joseph (actor) **60**
Cowboy (1958) 47
The Cowboy (TV documentary) 148–149
The Cowboys (1972) 118, 149
Cowboys & Aliens (2011) 140
Crawford, Joan (actress) 12, 39
Cross of Iron 7, 98, 128, **128**
Cruise, Tom (actor) **139**
Culp, Robert (actor) 83

Dancing with Wolves (1990) 140
D'Antonioni, Michaelangelo (director) 18, 22
Daves, Delmer (director) 47, 148
Davis, Bette (actress) 12, 39
Davis, Sammy, Jr. (actor) 83
Dawson, Gordon (wardrobe supervisor) 60, 64, 92, 95
Day, Doris (actress) 39
Dead Heat on a Merry-Go-Round (1966) 20
Dead Man (1995) 140
The Deadly Companions (1961) **31**, 32, 34, 37, 56, 82, 87, 141
Deadpool (2016) 134
Deadpool 2 (2018) 134
Death of a Salesman (stage play) 50
Dekker, Albert (actor) 68
Demarest, William (actor) 85
DePalma, Brian (director) 18
Derek, John (director) 74
Dern, Bruce (actor) 149
Desperado (1995) 170
The Detective (1968) 21
The Dice of God (novel) 31, 37; *see also The Glory Guys*
Dick Powell's Zane Grey Theater (TV anthol-

196

Index

ogy series) 29–30; "The Losers" 88; "Pericles on 31st Street" 87
Die Hard 2 (1990) 119
The Dirty Dozen (1967) 17, 20, 21, 41, 69, 84, 132
Dirty Harry (1971) 17
Django (1966) 169
Django Unchained (2012) 120, 140
D.O.A. (1950) 85
Dr. Strangelove or: How I Learned to Stop Worrying and Love the Bomb (1964) **13**, 17, 19, 22
Dr. Zhivago (1965) 132
Dodge City (1939) 49
Donaldson, Roger (director) **123**
Dorsey, Tommy (band leader) 77
Douglas, Kirk (actor), breaking the blacklist 78
Dreyfuss, Richard (actor) **136**
Dunaway, Faye (actress) **16-17**, 94, 117
Dylan, Bob (songwriter/actor) 125

Eastwood, Clint (actor/director) 81, 120, 140, 169
Easy Rider (1969) 20–21, 50, 67
Ebert, Roger (film critic) 116
Eisenhower, Dwight D. (U.S. president) 7
El Cid (1961) 175
"El Corrido de Santa Amalia" (song) 72, 80, 103, 160–161
El Dorado (1967) 24
El Mariachi (1992) 170
The Empire Strikes Back (1980) 132, 136
ER (TV series) 120
Escape from New York (1981) 170
E.T.: The Extra-Terrestrial (1982) 133
Evans, Robert (studio executive) 17, 124, 144
Executive Suite (1954) 50
Exodus (1960) 19, 78
The Exorcist (1973) 132
Extreme Prejudice (1987) 119

Face/Off (1997) 119
Fail-Safe (1964) 18, 19
Far and Away (1992) 140
Feldman, Phil (producer) 63–64, 70, 75, 78, 81, 90, 92, 96, 98, 121
Fellini, Federico (director) 22, 103
The Felony Squad (TV series) 75
Fernandez, Emilio (actor) 61, 87
Fielding, Jerry (composer) 68, 77–80, 120, 124, 125; TV career 78
Fields, W.C. (actor) 23
film noir 46–47, 48, 49
Finding Dory (2016) 133
Fine, Marshall (biographer) 56, 73, 74, 105, 141, 164–165
A Fine Madness (1966) 20

A Fistful of Dollars (1964) 169
FitzSimons, Charles (producer) 32, 34; see also *Ride the High Country*
Five Easy Pieces (1970) 20, 135
Fix, Paul (actor) 85
Flap (1970) 24
Fleischman, A.S. (screenwriter) 32; see also *Ride the High Country*
Fletcher, John (playwright) 4
The Flim Flam Man (1967) 20
Flynn, Errol (actor) 39
Fonda, Henry (actor) 82
For a Few Dollars More (1965) 169
Ford, Glenn (actor) 47, 82, 83
Ford, Harrison (actor) **137**
Ford, John (director) 45, 48, 62, 86, 103, 148, 169, 179, 173, 174
Forty Guns (1957) 49
Fosse, Bob (director) 172
The Fox (1967) 21
Frankenheimer, John (director) 18, 30–31, 41
The French Connection (1971) 18, 137
Friedan, Betty (feminist writer) 10
Friedkin, William (director) 18, 120
Furious 7 (2015) 134

Gable, Clark (actor; "The King") 12
Garfield, John (actor) **11**
Geronimo: An American Legend (1993) 140
The Getaway (1972) 120, **123**, 136, 145
The Getaway (1994) **123**, 124
Ghost (1990) 133
Ghostbusters (1984) 133
Giant (1956) 50
Gibson, Mel (actor) **138**
Gladwell, Malcolm (author) 55, 56
Gleason, Jackie (actor) 36
The Glory Guys (1965) 37, 57
Glover, Danny (actor) **138**
The Godfather (1972) 132, 135, 144
The Godfather: Part II (1974) 64, 135, 144
Goldman, William (screenwriter) 34
Goldwyn, Sam (producer) 15
"La Golondrina" (song) 62, 78–79, 111, 115, 159–160
Gone with the Wind (1939) 12
The Good, the Bad, & the Ugly (1966) 169
Gordon, Abraham (production company development executive) 165
The Graduate (1967) **16-17**, 19, 20, 21, 23, 132
Grease (1978) 132
Greaser's Palace (1972) 118
The Great Escape (1963) 20
The Great Train Robbery (1903) 23, 44
Green, Walon (screenwriter) 58, 65, 68, 120, 148, 171; slow motion violence 74; see also *The Wild Bunch*

Index

Gries, Tom (director) 47
Guardians of the Galaxy (2014) 134
Guardians of the Galaxy Vol. 2 (2017) 134
Guess Who's Coming to Dinner? (1967) 19
Gugarin, Yuri (Russian astronaut) 2
Gunfight at the O.K. Corral (1957) 49
The Gunfighter (1950) 50
Guns in the Afternoon 32; see also *Ride the High Country*
Gunsmoke (TV series) 1; Peckinpah 26, *28*, 167

Hackman, Gene (actor) *138*
Hamill, Mark (actor) *137*
Hamlet (play) 4
Hard Boiled (1992) 170
A Hard Day's Night (1964) 20
"Hard Hats" (demonstrators) 8, 10
Harold and Maude (1971) 167
Harper (1966) 20
Harris, Frank (author) 47
Harris, Richard (actor) *35*, 82
Harry Potter property 144
Hartwig, Wolf (producer) 128
The Hateful Eight (2015) 120, 140
Hathaway, Henry (director) 169
Have Gun—Will Travel (TV series) 26
Hawks, Howard (director) 170
Hawmps! (1976) 169
Hayden, Sterling (actor) 81
Heat (1995) 170
Heaven's Gate (1980) 140
Heim, Alan (editor) 172
Heston, Charlton (actor) 34, 35, *35*, 81, 175
Hidalgo (2004) 140
High Noon (1952) 50, 171
High Plains Drifter (1973) 169
The Hill (1965) 41
Hill, George Roy (director) 74, 94–95
Hill, Walter (director) 119
Hill Street Blues (TV series) 120
His Girl Friday (1940) 12
Hitchcock, Alfred, work process 59, *60*
Hoffman, Dustin (actor) *16-17*, *122*, 174
Hogan's Heroes (TV series) 78
Holden, William (actor) 33, 54, 62, 73, 76, 79, 81–82, *82*, 83, *112*, *113*, *114*, 167, 170, 172, 174
Hollywood anti-trust suit 14, 15; attendance 14–15; changing demographics 15, 17, 132–137; collapse of studio system 11–12, *14*, 17; competition from TV 15; cultural revolution 19; rise of studio system 13–14; vertically integrated studio system 14, 141, 144; Western popularity 42, 45, 118, 137, 140, 141
Hombre (1967) 24
Home Alone (1990) 133

The Honkers (1972) 123
Hopkins, Bo (actor) 88–89, 101
Hostiles (2017) 140
Hour of the Gun (1967) 24, 52, 71
House Un-American Activities Committee (HUAC), McCarthy era blacklist 77
How the West Was Won (1964) 24, 49
The Hucksters (1947) 50
Hud (1963) 24, 50
Human, Eliot (studio chief) 41
The Hunger Games: Mockingjay—Part 1 (2014) 134
The Hunger Games: Mockingjay—Part 2 (2015) 134
Hunt, Helen (actress) *142*
Hunter, Stephen (film critic) 99, 105
The Hustler (1961) 20, 36
Huston, John (director) 41
Hyman, Kenneth (studio executive) 38, 41, 42, 64; approaches Peckinpah 41; hires Phil Feldman 63, 80, 90

If... (1968) 20
In Cold Blood (1967) 88
In the Heat of the Night (1967) 19, 23, 128
The Incredible Sex Revolution (1965) 75
Incredibles 2 (2018) 133
Indiana Jones and the Last Crusade (1989) 133
Indiana Jones and the Temple of Doom (1984) 133
Inherit the Wind (stage play) 48
Invasion of the Body Snatchers (1956) 26, 46
Invitation to a Gunfighter (1964) 24
The Iron Horse (1923) 45, 49
Ironside, Michael (actor) 119

Jackson, Peter (director) *143*
Jaeckel, Richard (actor) 83, *84*, *125*
Jaws (1975) 132, 135–136, *136*
Jaws II (1978) 133
The Jazz Singer (1927) 39
Jeremiah Johnson (1972) 118
Jewison, Norman (director) 36
Johnson, Ben (actor) 62, 82–83, 86, *112*, *113*, 170
Johnson, Lyndon B. (U.S. president) 7
Johnson, Van (actor) 82
Jones, L.Q. (actor) 64, 76, 86–87, 91, 126
Jones, Quincy (composer) 120, 124
Judgment at Nuremberg (1961) 19
Junior Bonner (1972) 116, 118, 120, 123, *123*, 124
Jurassic World (2015) 133
Jurassic World: Fallen Kingdom (2018) 134
Justice League (2017) 134
J.W. Coop (1972) 123

198

Index

The Karate Kid II (1987) 133
Kdiry, Youssef (film programmer/reviewer) 169–172
Keith, Brian (actor) 30–31, *31*, 32, 82
Kennedy, Arthur (actor) 82
Kennedy, Burt (director) 3
Kennedy, John F. (U.S. president) 2; assassination 6; Vietnam 6–7
Kennedy, Robert F. (U.S. politician) 2, 83
Kill Bill Vols. 1 & 2 (2003, 2004) 119
The Killer (1989) 170
The Killer Elite (1975) 90, 120, 127–128
The Killers (1964) 74
The Killing of Sister George (1968) 21
Kilmer, Val (actor) *139*
King, Martin Luther (civil rights activist) 2
King Kong (movie monster) 23
Klute (1971) 135
Kristofferson, Kris (actor) 172
Kubrick, Stanley (director) *13*, 17, 41; work process 59–60, 71
Kurosawa, Akira (director) 24, 52, 65, 74
Kyser, Kay (band leader) 77

The Last Hurrah (1958) 146
The Last Picture Show (1971) 135
Law & Order (TV series) 120
Lawrence of Arabia (1962) 117, 132
Lean, David (director) 146, 148
Led Zeppelin (rock band) 1
Lee, Stan (comic book writer) 119
The Left-Handed Gun (1958) 52
Legends of the Fall (1994) 140
Lemmon, Jack (actor) 47
Lennon, Julian (singer) 129, 130
Leone, Sergio (director) 169, 171
Lethal Weapon (1987) 137, *138*
Lethal Weapon 2 (1989) 133
Levitin, Daniel (neurologist) 55
Levy-Gardner-Laven (production company) 29, 31, 37; Jules Levy 29
Lewis, Arthur (producer) 127
Lisa (1962) 19
Little Big Man (1970) 24
Logan (2017) 134
Logan, Joshua (director) 40
Lolita (1962) 41
Lombardo, Lou (editor) 75–77, 78, 82, 90, 92, 96, 170, 171–172
The Lone Ranger (2013) 140
Lonely Are the Brave (1962) 24, 50
The Long Riders (1980) 119
The Longest Day (1962) 132
The Lord of the Rings: The Fellowship of the Ring (2001) *143*
Love Story (1970) 132, 144
Lucas, George (director) 18, *137*
Ludlum, Robert (author) 129

Lumet, Sidney (director) 18, 30, 88
Lyons, Richard (producer) 32

Macbeth (play) 4
MacGraw, Ali (actress) *123*, 124, 172
Mackendrick, Alexander (director) 70
Mad Max (film series) 103, 140
Mad Men (TV series) 166
The Magic Christian (1969) 167
The Magnificent Seven (1960): *The Wild Bunch* parallels 52–54, 117, 150, 171
Major Dundee (1964) 34–36, *35*, 37, 51, 52, 55, 56–57, 58, 70, 81, 82, 86, 88, 90, 129, 131, 160
Malick, Terry (director) 124
The Maltese Falcon (1941) 3, 23
Maltin, Leonard (film critic) 72
The Man from Laramie (1955) 47
The Man in the Gray Flannel Suit (1956) 50
The Man in the Gray Flannel Suit (novel) 50
The Man Who Shot Liberty Valance (1962) 45, 49, 173
Man Without a Star (1955) 49
The Manchurian Candidate (1962) 18, 19
Mann, Anthony (director) 47
Mann, Michael (director) 170
Mannix (TV series) 78
Marks, Brian (film critic) 173–174
Martin, Strother (actor) 76, 86–87, 91, 100
Marty (1955) 84
Marvin, Lee (actor) 58, 69, 80–81
Marx, Groucho (game show host) 77
Marx Brothers (comedy group) 23
Mary Poppins (1964) 132
*M*A*S*H* (1970) 18, 20, 132
The Mask of Zorro (1998) 140
Maverick (1994) 140
Mayer, Louis (movie studio executive) 12, 40
McCabe & Mrs. Miller (1971) 118
McCall, C.W. (singer) 129
McCrea, Joel (actor) 33, *33*, 34, 72, 167
McHale's Navy (TV series) 78, 84
McQueen, Steve (actor) 20, 36, 53, 83, 123, *123*, 124
Mean Streets (1973) 135
Medium Cool (1969) 19
Melnick, Daniel (producer) 37–38
MGM (movie studio) 12, 14, 32, 40; merger with United Artists 14; *Pat Garrett & Billy the Kid* 125; *Ride the High Country* 34, 131
Midnight Cowboy (1969) 18, 20, 21, 132
Mildred Pierce (1945) 46
Milius, John (director) 119
Miller, Arthur (playwright) 50
Miller, George (director) 103
Miller, Roger (singer) 52
A Million Ways to Die in the West (2014) 140

Index

The Misfits (1961) 24, 41, 50
The Missing (2003) 140
Mission: Impossible (TV series) 78
Mission: Impossible—Fallout (2018) 134
Mission: Impossible—Rogue Nation (2015) 134
Mission: Impossible II (2000) 119
Mitchell, Elvis (film critic) 4, 7
Mitchum, Robert (actor) 21, 37, 47, 81
Monoghan, Dominic (actor) *143*
Morgan, Maribel (social conservative writer) 10
Morheim, Lou (producer) 52
My Darling Clementine (1946) 45, 49
My Fair Lady (1967) 40

Nabokov, Vladimir (author) 41
The Name of the Game Is Kill! (1968) 75
Nashawaty, Chris (film critic) 134
National Geographic (TV documentaries) 58
NBC Universal (media corporation) 14
Neider, Charles (author) 31
Nevada Smith (1966) 71
Newman, Paul (actor) 20, 36, 74, 117
Newman, Walter (screenwriter) 52
Night of the Living Dead (1968) *18*, 21–22
1968 Democratic Convention 10–11; "police riot" 11
Nixon, Richard (U.S. president) 2; Vietnam escalation 8; Watergate scandal 7
No Country for Old Men (2007) 146
Nolan, Christopher (director) 140
Noon Wine (TV movie, 1966) 37–38, 75, 78, 85
North by Northwest (1959) 59
NYPD Blue (TV series) 120

Oates, Warren (actor) 61, 86, 105, *112*, *113*, *126*, 127, 170, 172
O'Brien, Edmond (actor) 66, 85, 91, 170, 174
O'Brien, Pat (actor) *11*
O'Hara, Maureen (actress) *31*, 32
Once Before I Die (1965) 74
Once Upon a Time in the West (1968) 169
One-Eyed Jacks (1961) 31, 34, 57, 127
Open Range (2003) 140
The Osterman Weekend (1983) 106, 129
The Outlaw Josey Wales (1976) 140
The Outrage (1964) 24
The Ox-Bow Incident (1943) 46

Paar, Jack (talk show host) 77
Pacino, Al (actor) 64
Paint Your Wagon (1969) 80–81, 171
Pale Rider (1985) 140
The Parallax View (1974) 128
Paramount 37; ; acquired by Viacom 141; founder Adolph Zukor 40; Robert Evans as studio chief 17, 144
Pat Garrett & Billy the Kid (1973) 57, 124–126, *125*, 126, 129, 130, 131, 141, 145, 172
A Patch of Blue (1965) 19
Patterns (1956) 50, 146
Patterns (TV drama) 50
Patton (1970) 117, 132, 146
The Pawnbroker (1964) 19, 22, 88
Paxton, Bill (actor) *142*
Pearl Harbor (2001) 137
Peck, Gregory (actor) 21, 81
Peckinpah, David (nephew) 129
Peckinpah, Sam (director) 2, 3, 4, 5, 23, 25–26, *27*, 47, 52, 55–57, 58, 61, 68, 70, 98, 118, 131–132, 135, 139, 140, 141, *142*, 144, 145–146, 147, 148, 165, 167–168, 169–172, 174; approached by Ken Hyman/Warners 41, 42; *The Ballad of Cable Hogue* 121, 122, 131; blacklisted 37–38, 41; "Bloody Sam" image 124; *Bring Me the Head of Alfredo Garcia* *126*, 127, 145; career decline 127, 128, *128*, 131; casting *The Wild Bunch* 81–89; *Convoy* 128; *Cross of Iron* 128, *128*; *The Deadly Companions* 32, 56, 82, 87, 145; death 130; early life 26–27, 30, 55–56, 147; Ernest Borgnine conflicts 85; feud with Phil Feldman 64, 98, 121; filmography 183–185; fired from *The Cincinnati Kid* 36, 41; *The Getaway* 123, *123*, 124, 145; *The Glory Guys* 37; *Gunsmoke* *28*; improvising *Wild Bunch* Scenes 61–63, 91, 92; Jerry Fielding, composer 77–80, 120; *Junior Bonner* 118, 123; *The Killer Elite* 127–128; Lou Lombardo, editor 75–77, 78, 92, 96; Lucien Ballard collaboration 70–74, 78, 91, 92, 120; *Major Dundee* 34–36, 56, 86, 87, 88, 90, 129, 131, 160; military Service 73–74; *The Osterman Weekend* 129; *Pat Garrett & Billy the Kid* 57, 124–126, *125*, 129, 131, 145; research for *Villa Rides!* 37, 38, 57, 90; *Ride the High Country* 32–34, 52, 56, 57, 81, 86, 129, 131, 141, 167; *The Rifleman* 29–30, *29*; Robert Ryan conflicts 83; stock company 179–180; *Straw Dogs* 122, 145, 146; substance abuse 126, 127, 128, *128*, 131; TV career 19, 26, 37–38, 55, 82, 179, 181–183; 184; "Valotte" and "Too Late for Goodbyes" music videos 129, 185; violence 94–96, 119, 149, 166, 174, 177; *The Wild Bunch* 38, 52, 70, 89; *The Wild Bunch* revives his career 120, 124; *The Wild Bunch* screenplay 58–59, 65, 68,124; William Holden conflicts 81–82; work process 60–61, 126, 128; *see also The Wild Bunch*
Penn, Arthur (director) 18, 22, 30; *Bonnie and Clyde* climax 73, 74, 170
Peppard, George (actor) 83

200

Index

Persky, Bill (screenwriter/director/producer) 165
Picnic (1955) 81
Planet of the Apes (1968) 1, 18, 19
Point Blank (1967) 18, 21, 22, 23, 74
Polansky, Roman (director) 18, 22
Pollack, Sydney (director) 18, 118
The Pony Express (1953) 49
Porter, Edwin S. (director) 23, 44
Porter, Katherine Ann (author) 38
Preminger, Otto (director), breaking the blacklist 77–78
The President's Analyst (1967) 19
Pressure Point (1962) 19
The Producers (1967) 20, 22
The Professionals (1966) 24, 52, 69
Pulp Fiction (1994) 170
Pursued (1947) 47

The Quick and the Dead (1995) 140

Raft, George (actor) **11**
Raging Bull (1980) 172
Raiders of the Lost Ark (1981) 133
Rainer, Peter (film critic) 137
A Raisin in the Sun (1961) 19
Rambo: First Blood—Part II (1985) 133, 137, **139**
Ransohoff, Martin (producer) 36
Redford, Robert (actor) 117
Reflections in a Golden Eye (1967) 21
Requiem for a Heavyweight (1962) 146
Reservoir Dogs (1992) 170
Return of the Jedi (1983) 133
The Ride Back (1957) 52
Ride the High Country aka *Guns in the Afternoon* (1962) 27, 32–34, **33**, 37, 41, 52, 56, 57, 71, 72, 81, 86, 129, 131, 135, 141, 145, 147, 167
Ride with the Devil (1999) 140
The Rifleman (TV series) 27, 29–30, **29**, 31; Peckinpah quits 30
Rio Conchos (1964) 52
RKO (movie studio) 14, 83
Robards, Jason (actor) 85, 121
Robbins, David L. (author) 175–177
Robbins, Jerome (stage director) 88
Roberts, William (screenwriter) 52
Robinson, Edward G. **11**, 36, 39
Rocky IV (1985) 133
Rocky III (1982) 133
Rodriguez, Robert (director) 170
Rogers, Ginger (actress) 12
Rogue One: A Star Wars Story (2016) 133
Romeo and Juliet (stage play) 4
Romero, George (director) **18**, 21–22
Rosemary's Baby (1968) 18
Roshomon (1950) 24

Ross, Katharine (actress) **16-17**
Rossen, Robert (director) 36
Rowan & Martin's Laugh-In (TV variety) 1
RPM (1970) 19
Ryan, Robert (actor) 33, 66, **82**, 83, 91, 92, **114**, 167, 170, 174

Saboteur: Code Name Morituri (1965) 58
Sainte-Beuve, Charles Augstin (literary critic) 147, 150–151
Sanchez, Jaime (actor) 88
The Sand Pebbles (1966) 19, 175
Sapan, Josh (AMC Networks CEO) 166
Sarris, Andrew (film critic) 32
Saturday Night Fever (1977) 133
The Scalphunters (1968) 24
Schaffner, Franklin J. (director) 18
Schifrin, Lalo (composer) 78
Schlafly, Phyllis (social conservative writer) 10
Schlesinger, John (director) 18
Schoonmaker, Thelma (editor) 172
Schrader, Paul (director/film critic) 19; on edited *The Wild Bunch* 98
Schultz, Richard (prosecutor) 10–11
Scorsese, Martin (director) 18, 172; on *The Wild Bunch* 105
Scott, George C. (actor) 36
Scott, Randolph (actor) 33, **33**, 34, 47, 167, 171
The Searchers (1956) 45, 169, 173
Seconds (1966) 23
Sellers, Peter **13**
The Sergeant (1968) 21
Serling, Rod (screenwriter) 31, 50, 146
Seven Arts (production company) *see* Warner Bros.
Seven Days in May (1964) 19, 41, 85
Seven Samurai (1954) 52; slow motion 74
77 Sunset Strip (TV series) 78
Sevilla, Narciso Serradel (songwriter) 160
Seydor, Paul (author) 116
Shadow of a Doubt (1943) **60**
Shakespeare, William (playwright) 4
"Shall We Gather at the River" (hymn) 79, 89
Shampoo (1975) 135
Shane (1953) 49, 50, 170
Shane (TV series) 78
Sharp, Alan (screenwriter) 129
Shaw, Robert (actor) **136**
She Wore a Yellow Ribbon (1949) 45
The Shining (1980) 59–60
Ship of Fools (1965) 19
Sickner, Roy N. (stuntman/screenwriter) 57–58, 69, 80
The Siege of Trencher's Farm (novel) 122
Siegel, Don (director) 17, 26, **28**, 74

Index

Silke, Jim (Peckinpah associate) 56, 59
Silliphant, Stirling (screenwriter) 128
Silverado (1985) 140
Slotkin, Richard (historian) 54
Smokey and the Bandit (1977) 133, 172
The Smothers Brothers Comedy Hour (TV variety) 1
Solo: A Star Wars Story (2018) 134
The Sons of Katie Elder (1965) 24
Sontag, Susan (film critic) 19
Sony (media corporation) 14
The Sopranos (TV series) 166
Sorcerer (1977) 120
The Sound of Music (1965) 132
Spartacus (1960) 78
Spider-Man: Homecoming (2017) 134
Spielberg, Steven (director) 18, 124, 136
The Split (1968) 85
Stagecoach (1939) 45, 169, 173
Stalag 17 (1953) 81
Stallone, Sylvester (actor) *139*
Star Trek (1979) 133
Star Trek (TV series) 78
Star Trek IV: The Voyage Home (1986) 133
Star Wars (1977) 132, 136, ***136***, 140
Star Wars: The Force Awakens (2015) 133
Star Wars: The Last Jedi (2017) 133
Starship Troopers (1997) 119
Steinem, Gloria (feminist writer) 10
Stevens, George (director) 171
Stevens, Stella (actress) 121
Stewart, James (actor) 47
The Sting (1973) 133
Stone, Milburn (actor) 28
Stonewall riot 9
Straw Dogs (1971) 21, 122, ***122***, 124, 135, 145, 146, 168, 174
Sturges, John (director) 71, 171
The Sugarland Express (1974) 124, 136
Suicide Squad (2016) 134
Superman—The Movie (1979)
Support Your Local Sheriff (1969) 3, 24
Sweet Smell of Success (1957) 70

"Tales of Wells Fargo" (TV series) 26
The Tall T (1957) 47
Tarantino, Quentin (director) 119, 120, 140, 147, 170
Tarzan (TV series) 78
Taxi Driver (1976) 98, 135, 170
Taylor, Dub (actor) 79, 87–88, 89
television, increase in ownership 15; demographic changes 27; popularity of Westerns 27–28; programming 15
Tell Them Willie Boy Is Here (1969) 118
Texas Ranges (2000) 140
They Shoot Horses, Don't They? (1969) 18
Thief (1981) 170

Thieves Like Us (1974) 124
The Thomas Crown Affair (1968) 20, 22
Thompson, Jim (author) 124
Thomson, David (film critic) 19, 134, 135
Thor: Ragnarok (2017) 134
A Thousand Clowns (1965) 20
Three Days of the Condor (1975) 128
Three Stooges (comedy group) 23, 71
3:10 to Yuma (1957) 47
3:10 to Yuma (2007) 140
Thunderball (1970) 132, 175
To Kill a Mockingbird (1962) 19
Tolkein, J.R.R. (author) ***143***
Tombstone (1993) 140, 170
"Too Late for Goodbyes" (music video) 129
Top Gun (1986) 137, ***139***
Total Recall (1992) 119
Towne, Robert (screenwriter) 37
"Trackdown" (TV series) 26
Travers, Henry (actor) ***60***
True Grit (1969) 71, 87; box office 116–117, 119, 169
Trumbo, Dalton (screenwriter) 77–78
Tucker, Betty Jo (film writer, podcast host) 165
20th Century Fox (movie studio) 12; acquisition by Walt Disney Company 14, 141; Richard Zanuck as chief executive 17
The 25th Hour (1967) 19
Twister (1996) ***142***
2001: A Space Odyssey (1968) 22, 117, 132

The Undefeated (1969) 52
Unforgiven (1992) 140, 169–170
United Artists (movie studio) 14, 127; acquisition by MGM 14; collapse 140
Universal (movie studio) 40; monster stable 12; part of NBC Universal 13; release of *Jaws* 135

Valotte (album) 129
"Valotte" (music video) 129
Vega, Isela (actress) 127
Vera Cruz (1954) 52
Vietnam War 2, 8–9, 12, 18; allusions in movies 19, 21, 54, 167, 168, 170; anti-war demonstrations 8; Eisenhower Administration commitment 6; Johnson escalation 8; Kennedy commitment 7–8; 1968 Democratic convention 10; Nixon escalation 8; Tet Offensive 8; TV coverage 10
Villa Rides! (1968) 37, 38, 52, 57, 59, 90
The Virginian (novel) 47
Vogel, Joseph (studio executive) 34
Von Sternberg, Josef (director) 71

Wagon Train (TV series) 1
Wallach, Eli (actor) 53

202

Index

Walt Disney Company, acquisition of 20th Century Fox 14
The War Wagon (1967) 24
WarGames (1983) 120
Warlock (1959) 49
Warner, Jack 39; sells Warner Bros. 40
Warner Bros. (movie studio) 3, 116, 121, 131, 165, 170; Bahamas *The Wild Bunch* screening 117; crime dramas *11*; cuts to *The Wild Bunch* 98–99, 101, 105; founding 39; Harry Potter property 144; John Calley as chief executive 17; move into television 39; part of Warner Media/AT&T 13–14, 141; Warner Bros.-Seven Arts 38, 40–41, 64, 69, 78, 90, 96, 170; *see also* Warner, Jack
Warner Bros.-Seven Arts *see* Warner Bros.
Warner brothers (movie studio executives) 12, 39; *see also* Warner, Jack
Waterhole #3 (1967) 52
Watts riot 9
Wayne, John (actor; aka "The Duke") 12, 24, 45, 116, 118, 149, 167, 169, 171
Weales, Gerald (critic) 23
Weaver, Dennis (actor) 28
Welcome to Hard Times (1967) 24
Wellman, William (director) 46
Wells Fargo (1937) 49
West Side Story (1961) 41
West Side Story (stage play) 88
Western Union (1941) 49
The Westerner (TV series) 27, 30, *31*, 32, 47, 71, 82, 88; "Jeff" episode 27; "Line Camp" episode 47
Westlake, Donald E. (author) 147–148
Whatever Happened to Baby Jane? (1962) 41
White Heat (1949) 85
Whitty, Stephen (film critic) 167–168
The Who (rock band) 1
Who's Afraid of Virginia Woolf? (1966) 175
Wild Bill (1994) 140
The Wild Bunch (1969) 22, 25–26, 38, 41, 55, 56, 70, 89, 96–97, 118–119, 122, 129, 132, 135, 140, 144, 145–146, 147, 148, 149–150, 151, 169–172, 175–177; "The Battle of Bloody Porch" 92–94, *113*, *114*; box office 116–117; budget and schedule 89, 96; career impacts 120–121; casting 81–89, 167; critical standing 116, 117; cuts 64, 99–105, 106, 165–166; editing 96; filming in Mexico 90–91; "Gunman's Walk" sequence 62–63, 71–72, 80, 91, 92, *112*; historical period 2–3, 4, 5, 7, 9, 11, 43–44, 91; imitators 119–120, 172; improvised scenes 61–63, 92; Lou Lombardo, editor 75–77;

Lucien Ballard, cinematographer 70–74; *The Magnificent Seven* parallels 52–54, 117, 150; opening 2, 96, 99, 116; originates with Roy N. Sickner 57–58; Peckinpah's writing process 58–59; production credits 153–157; reviewers' remarks 163–166; revives Peckinpah's career 121, 141; *Ride the High Country* themes 33–34, 167; running time 96, 98, 106; scorpion sequence 61, 176, 177; screenplay structure 65–69; stock company 179–180; 25th anniversary re-release 98, 99, 104, 170; *Villa Rides!* historical research 37, 57, 59; village exit sequence 61–62, 92, 159–160; violence 94–96, 149, 164, 165, 166, 168, 170, 173, 174, 177; Walon Green 58, 120; Western tropes 43, 44–45, 140; *see also* Peckinpah, Sam
Wild in the Streets (1968) 19
Wild Seed (1965) 19
Wild Wild West (1999) 140
Will Penny (1967) 47, 71
Williams, Gordon (author) 122
Willis, Bruce (actor) 119
Wilson, Sloan (author) 50
Winner, Michael (director) 120
Wister, Owen (author) 44, 45, 47, 140, 148
The Wizard of Oz (1939) 12
Woman's World (1954) 50
Women in Love (1969) 21
women's movement 10
Wonacott, Edna May (actress) **60**
Wonder Woman (2017) 134
The Wonderful Country (1959) 52
Woo, John (director) 119, 170
Wood, Elijah (actor) ***143***
Wright, Teresa (actress) **60**
Wurlitzer, Rudy (screenwriter) 57, 126
WUSA (1970) 19
Wyatt Earp (1994) 140

You Bet Your Life (game show) 77
Young, Burt (actor) 128
Young Guns (1988) 140
You're a Big Boy Now (1966) 64

Zabriskie Point (1970) 18, 19
Zachariah (1971) 118
Zanuck, Darryl (movie studio executive) 12, 40, 135
Zanuck, Richard (movie studio executive/producer) 17, 135
Zinneman, Fred (director) 171